PEN PAL SUCCESS

THE ULTIMATE GUIDE TO GETTING & KEEPING PEN PALS

REVISED EDITION 2021

Josh Kruger

Special thanks to contributing author, Devin "Skylar" Mottley for the addition of our LGBTQ chapter in this revised edition 2021.

REVISED EDITION 2021
This publication has been revised to be in accordance with the Board Policy, 03.91, Uniform Offender Correspondence Rules and Regulations of the Texas Department of Criminal Justice.

FREEBIRD PUBLISHERS
www.FreebirdPublishers.com

Freebird Publishers

221 Pearl St., Ste 541, North Dighton, MA 02764

Info@FreebirdPublishers.com

www.FreebirdPublishers.com

All Freebird Publishers titles, imprints and distributed lines are available at special quantity discounts for bulk purchases for sales promotions, premiums, fund-raising, educational or institutional use.

ISBN: 978-0-9913591-2-7

Printed in the United States of America

Dedication

First to Emmanuel "Top Flight" Grant, who kept me in the pen pal game by making me use my talents. Because of him, I met several beautiful women who changed my life. And yes, I used the tactics in this book to find them. This book is dedicated to the all of them.

TABLE OF CONTENTS

Disclaimer

This book is designed to provide helpful and informative material on getting pen pals, building friendships and making connections. It contains the opinions and ideas of it's author. It is sold with the understanding that the author and publisher are not engaged in rendering professional services in the book. If the reader requires personal assistance or advice, a competent professional should be consulted.

It's not the purpose of this book to reprint every tip, tactic and/or strategy that is available to a prisoner for getting pen pals, but instead to complement, amplify, and supplement other books. You are urged to read all the available information and material, including the books listed throughout this book, learn as much as you can, and then develop your own strategies and work your own plan.

Getting pen pals is not some pie-in-the-sky happen overnight scheme. Anyone who wishes to have pen pal success must decide to invest a lot of time, and effort into it. Maybe a little money also? The advice and strategies contained in this book may not be suitable for every situation. The purpose of this book is to educate and entertain. Every effort has been made to make this book as complete, up-to-date, and error free as possible. However, there will be errors, both typographical and in content. Because of this, it should be used as a guide, and not the be-all, end-all book on pen pal success for prisoners.

The fact that a website, business, organization, and/or association is listed or referred to in this book as a citation and or a potential source of further information does not mean the author or publisher endorses the website, business, organization, and/or association, or what those entities may offer. It should be noted that the internet websites listed, and other entities referred to, may have, by the time you are reading this warning, changed, disappeared, closed and/or dissolved.

Some terms mentioned in this book are known to be or are suspected of being trade and service marks of different entities. Use of a term in this book should not be regarded as affecting the validity of any trademark or service mark.

The author and publisher specifically disclaim any responsibility for any liability, loss, or risk, personal or otherwise, which is incurred as a consequence, directly or indirectly, of the use and application of any of the contents of this book.

Introduction

I have written this book, my second, with a single objective in mind: to help you get pen pals and turn them into life-long friendships, maybe more? Are you tired of being alone? Do you wish they would call your name at mail call? Or that you could go on a visit or talk on the phone with someone outside of your family? Do you want to get married while in prison? Maybe you have different motives for wanting pen pals? No matter what your hopes or pen pal dreams are, you now hold in your hands the answer you've been looking for.

What You'll Find in This Book

In his great book, *How to Write & Sell Simple Information for Fun and Profit* (Quill Driver Books, 2010), author and copywriter Bob Bly says that there are three levels of How-To writing. These three levels are:

1. At the first level: it tells you what to do.

2. At the next level: it tells you how to do it.

3. At the highest level: it does it for you.

Let's look at these three levels in the sense of a how-to book for getting pen pals. A bad how-to book would only tell you what to do, i.e., "Go on a prison pen pal website to get pen pals." An okay how-to book would tell you *how to do it*, i.e., "Go on *www.writeaprisoner.com* and say you want to meet new friends." But the top of the line in how-to writing are those that show you how to do it, or as Bob Bly says, they *do it for you*. That is what I've tried to do in this book. Where it's possible, I've shown you how to do it, and have given you a template, or example to use. You can use these templates when doing your own ads and profiles. You can use the letter formats to help write your letters. Not only will this save you time and money, but it will get you the results that you want.

Who I am and My Role in Your Life

I am, by profession, a how-to writer of information that prisoners can use to make their life better. I am, by captivity, a prisoner serving a life-sentence for a felony murder conviction. I have over 18 years' experience in the prison pen pal game. And I have results, as I have had over 100 pen pals. At the height of my pen pal success I had 27 at one time. I have 6 solid, quality pen pals as I write this. I've been on numerous pen pal websites and I created the *How to Get Free Pen Pals* manual. O'Barnett Publishing and Superior Enterprises sold thousands of that manual to prisoners. The testimonials of people who followed my system, speak for themselves. I have had prisoners run across the exercise yard to tell me that they met their wife using one of my strategies. Even my free-world business partner had a woman falling in love with him. The truth is, I went from being a lonely lifer to being flooded with mail. So much mail that the guards would get mad. You'll read how I did it in a few minutes. I still use the strategies in this book and will continue to use them to meet new people. You can use them also. You now have the road map to find new friends, love, romance, or the answer to your business aspirations. If you have the desire to put these ideas to work then you can accomplish all of your pen pal dreams.

And that's the last part of the system. *They are your dreams*. If you want 50 pen pals, you can have them. If you want a wife or husband, you can have that also. If you don't believe that you can accomplish anything you desire while in prison then you should read my first book, *The Millionaire Prisoner: How To Turn Your Prison Into A Stepping-Stone To Succe$$*™. If you can believe, then this book is for you.

But not everything in this book may be for you. Some prisons do not let prisoners use online social networking sites? In some states, prisoners can't solicit new pen pals. I think these rules are draconian and unconstitutional, but if you're in one of those prisons, you'll find some strategies in *Pen Pal Success*™ that you can use. All of the tips and tactics in this book work. I've personally used them myself, or I've witnessed firsthand other prisoners using them to succeed.

This book is divided into four sections. In Section 1, you'll learn the proper mindset and outlook for pen pal success. In Section 2, you'll be given different ways to get pen pals. In Section 3, you'll learn how to keep your pen pals once you get them and turn them into fruitful friendships, maybe more? Finally, in Section 4, you'll find all the legitimate companies that can assist you in achieving your pen pals dreams. In all, I've spent almost a $1,000 researching the strategies in this book. I did this so you don't have to waste money finding out what does work. After reading this guide, not only will you know what works, but how to work it yourself so you get the results you want.

Before we get started on your pen pal journey, I need to make a few more valid points. First, this book is for both male and female prisoners. I've included strategies for both. Personally, I believe it would be much easier for a female prisoner to get pen pals than a male prisoner. Why? Because she will have less competition, and a woman who goes on the hunt, or who asks the man out, is bound to get results.

Second: I need to ask you a question. Why do so few prisoners have lots of pen pals? Because they sit around and do nothing. They expect someone to up and just write them out of the blue. But it doesn't work that way. To network you have to *work*. To be seen you have to stand out. I'll show you how to successfully do this in later chapters.

Third: Some of what is included throughout this book was also included in my first book, *The Millionaire Prisoner*. This is done on purpose. Mainly because those ABCs of success go hand in hand for any venture. Those strategies are the basic keystones to my success and I incorporate them into all areas of my life.

How To Get Your Money's Worth From This Book

In *The Millionaire Prisoner*, I shared a system of reading called "The Art of Reading Non-Fiction" (page 57-58, Chapter E: Education) that I learned from my mentor, Zig Ziglar. Here's how you can use the steps in that system to get the most from this book:

1. Read through this book quickly to get the gist of the message, underlining or highlighting the things that really "grab" you. Only stop to look up words you don't know, or write them down to look up later. This first reading allows you to become familiar with the book.

2. As you read this book the second time, keep a notebook of ideas generated by the book that you can personally use. The objective is not to see how quickly you can get out of the book, but what you can get out of the book.

3. In your third reading, invest time and patience in gleaning additional ideas you may be missing in your second reading. Carefully examine each chapter. Go over what you have highlighted or underlined. Put anything you missed in your notebook.

4. The fourth reading will enable the book to become an integral part of you, enhancing your effectiveness. After this reading, you can place the book in your collection, and it will be a treasure trove, ready and willing to supply you with any knowledge you may need.

5. Find other prisoners who have read this book, or share it with them, and then discuss it together to see what you got out of it. You may gain additional insights from their ideas and thoughts that you didn't see on your own.

I have used the above system of reading over the years and know that it works. Try it out yourself. You'll be amazed at the results. Lastly, all of the names of the people involved (except for mine of course), have been changed to protect their identities and not harm any relationships they are currently in. There are a few prisoners whose real identities are used because they either gave me permission or I felt they'd love the notoriety. But rest assured, what's in this book actually happened, and continues to happen in prisons all across the gulag archipelago. Okay, "Enough already", you're probably saying. You want to begin learning how to get pen pals. Well, you can begin with my pen pal story.

PEN PAL TIP

Always make note and acknowledge your pen pals special days (birthdays, holidays and any special events, etc)

Chapter 1

My Story...

"The author's character is read from title page to end." -Henry David Thoreau

It all started back in grade school when I began writing letters to girls in my class. I was a poor kid from the right side of the tracks (literally right next to the train tracks), who went to a middle school with all the rich girls. I didn't know it at the time, but these girls didn't want to be seen with me because I was poor, even though they would carry on secret conversations with me through notes and letters. Some of these girls would call my house and we would talk on the phone for hours. My love affair with pen pals and women started then and has carried on ever since. You see, I'm a "rake". I love writing letters to women, using words to get them to fall in love with me. I'm not ashamed of this fact and will not try and hide it. It's what I am and what I do. (So don't let me write your sister.)

After middle school, I went to high school and stopped writing love letters to girls because then it was all about face-to-face interactions and phone conversations. My success continued. At the age of 15, I ended up in juvenile prison and it was there that I really fell in love with writing letters to women. I started corresponding with a girl from my hometown-Mandy. She was a year ahead of me in school and had a boyfriend, but that didn't bother me, or her for that matter. We also occasionally talked on the phone. But she wasn't the only girl I was writing. There was Elizabeth, a fellow juvenile's sister from a suburb of Chicago. I was also trying to seduce a young prison nurse with my letters. She ended up succumbing to my youthful zeal and we began weekly phone conversations. Our secret relationship almost ended up costing me my parole and her the nurses' job, but I was smart enough (or scared enough) to curtail all communication. I signed up for the prison art class and began a secret correspondence with the hot college intern who volunteered to teach the class. I even wrote to some of the female teachers at our prisons' school, but was rebuffed. These rejections did nothing to dismay my ambition to write other women. It was during my two years in juvie that I really began to understand that I had a gift to write letters. Sure it was raw and unrefined, but it had an effect on the women I wrote and I liked their responses and the feeling it gave me.

After my parole, I went back to my hometown and began a few short-term relationships with a few girls. I ended up getting caught up when I tried to put two girls on the phone with each other. I thought I was a pimp or player, like *Too Short*. That didn't work out and both of them left me. Anyway, I eventually got nabbed after an armed robbery, and while in the county jail, I began writing my cellmate's sister. After she became smitten, he decided that he didn't like the idea of me writing his sister and picked a fight. When I beat him up, she decided she didn't like me anymore. Her loss, not mine I felt. I ended up pleading guilty for 6 years and off I went to adult prison. Not too long after I got to Shawnee Correctional Center, in Southern Illinois, I got a letter from Mandy, my hometown sweetheart and pen pal from juvie. Her boyfriend had left her and she needed someone to talk to. We began a 2 ½ year relationship through letters, phone calls, and visits. We ended up writing each other every day. I also started another correspondence with Amy, a Latino woman from the north side of Chicago, which a friend of mine hooked me up with. Some of the letters I was writing were epic, 32-page monstrosities, while others were just short notes or cards. I paroled out in February 1999 and went to live with Mandy at her apartment. Amy called my Mom's house and wanted to come down from Chicago to meet me, but I vetoed that idea and lost contact with her. Mandy and I had a passionate, if not explosive, relationship. She is the mother of my beautiful twin daughters. After I got locked up on this case we continued to write for another few years. I learned a lot from her. Not just about myself, but about women in general. She will always have a special place in my heart because she gave me my twins, Brittney and Jessica, but she's no longer in my life.

In 2001, I was in Menard Correctional Center and I happened to be reading my hometown newspaper, *The Commercial News*, and saw a girl's name that I knew. She had gotten arrested and I wrote her at the county jail. She wrote back and we began a great pen pal friendship. I also began a correspondence with an accountant from a small town in Illinois. I went back to my county jail in 2002-03 for a new trial and that's when I really started to get flooded with mail. I began corresponding with women prisoners from all over the country. I wrote a girl named Angie from my hometown that I had messed around with while on the lam. She's a sweet girl and wrote me every day for a couple of years. I had a couple of Christian pen pals that I wrote and a few other women that I found in the *Thrifty Nickel*, a free classified newspaper in my hometown. I got mail every day and the guards go so used to my volume of mail that they would make jokes to other prisoner's about it.

In the fall of 2003, I was sentenced to life in prison and was sent back to Menard Correctional Center. My brother's wife (whom he married while in the Pekin, Illinois federal prison), put me on two websites, *The Pampered Prisoner* and *Prison Talk Online*. I was again flooded with mail. I got over 50 cards and letters for Christmas from people wishing me well. I met a bunch of new friends and began corresponding with a few of them. I eventually devoted all of my time and attention to Allyssa. She was going to college in Georgia and was very appealing to me in personality and looks. We began writing every day and talking on the phone twice a week. But she wouldn't come and visit me. That was a major stumbling block for me so I decided to find someone who would come and visit with me at the prison.

One day a friend of mine let me read one of his newspapers and I saw they listed the addresses of people who got arrested, or ticketed for traffic violations. I began writing women who fit my age range and asking them to be my pen pal. It worked and I got responses. (I'll go more in-depth on this subject in the chapter: "How to Get FREE Pen Pals.") I met Kayla and she began writing to me every day and coming to visit every Tuesday. Because I had what I wanted: two solid pen pals and weekly visits, and a bunch of other friends that I wrote, I stopped seeking out new contacts.

Fast forward to 2006, I had lost the direct appeal of my case and began working on my post-conviction petition. Allyssa and Kayla left me because they didn't want a long-term relationship with a lifer. After I finished up the work on my post-conviction petition, I went on another website, Friends Beyond the Wall, and got 3 responses. Two of those were from homosexuals. I was very disappointed. So I went back to my system of writing women out of the newspaper and building up my list of contacts. I ran into another prisoner I knew and he showed me a pen pal publication from 3-G Company. I wrote a few of the women in that publication who said they would write prisoners and met Jennifer. She was a sweet secretary from the Midwest who had a lame husband. We wrote each other every week for a few years.

In 2007, I found out the power of writing churches. I got one pen pal, who is like my second mom, and I wrote one church and got 17 different responses. (You'll read more about this later in this book.) At the end of that year I began working on my first book, *The Millionaire Prisoner*, which took up most of my time. But I still wrote letters to my existing pen pals. After putting the finishing touches on that manuscript I decided to jump back down in the pen pal game. Because I knew that I wanted to write a pen pal book, I really wanted to use what I had learned in my studies and see what really worked and didn't work. As I write this rough draft I'm on 5 online pen pal websites and my ads are in numerous publications. The rest of this book will show you how you can get flooded with mail. All the secrets that I know are included in this guide. But there are two points that I want you to take away from my story.

The first point is that if you want pen pals you have to get out there and work the system. You have to write letters, place the ads, post your profiles, and let people know who you are and what you're looking for. Sure it's work, but it really won't be hard work for you. I've done all the hard stuff... and spent the money for you. Just follow some of the steps in this guide and you can be successful in filling up your little black book. I can't promise or guarantee you'll get the same results as me, but you should do better than the rest of your fellow prison comrades who don't have this book.

The second point I hope you got from my story is that there are many different people out there who'll write prisoners. They come from many different walks of life. For instance, Allyssa was a college student and Jennifer was a secretary. My Christian pen pal, is a retired hair-dresser who has her own salon. I've corresponded with a famous professional writer and editor. I've had stay-at-home moms and business people write me back. One lady owned her own bar. One was a farmer's wife. These people, and many more are out there. But you've got to get out there too. That's the main hurdle to getting mail. Sure, there are tips and tactics to make it easier for you and allow you to have better success, but the main thing is to get out there on the market. How do you do this? First, you have to form the right attitude. Turn the page to find out what the right attitude for pen pal success is and how to acquire it.

Chapter 2
The Right Attitude for Pen Pal Success™

"When you get your attitude right, you can handle anything the world throws at you. Even life in prison." -Bill Dallas

BECAUSE I CAN

Have No Fear

Personally, I've never had fear when it comes to approaching women. Rejection doesn't bother me because I know sooner or later, one of my targets will fall to my stratagems and say yes... And that "yes" will change my life just like all the other yesses have. But you'll never get your one "yes" if you allow the fear of rejection to stop you. Sure, there's a possibility that if you write a letter the other person will not answer it. Yeah, the first time you place an online profile you may only get three responses, like I did at first. Or you may get none like the other prisoners I know. Then again, you could get 10, 20 or even a hundred responses? You won't know what's possible until you try. The number one rule for *Pen Pal Success™* is *have no fear*!

This goes for women prisoners also. Get rid of the stigma that the man is supposed to ask you out or write you first. Its 2015! Have no fear and put yourself out there on the market. Plus, if you follow the guidelines in this book, you'll be too busy to worry about your fears anyway.

You can't let fear stand in your way. Only the person who has the courage to take risks can get the glory. Don't be scared to risk your neck in accomplishing your pen pal dreams. Yes, you may experience temporary defeat sometimes when a letter comes back "return to sender". But the only person who doesn't get these are those that never write letters. Besides, a "return to sender" letter isn't a rejection that should be taken personal. It's reflective of other factors that have nothing to do with you. If you want to become a *Pen Pal Success™* you can't live a life where you never try.

>*"Winning isn't everything, but trying to is."* -Vince Lombardi

Prisoners who won't stake everything on their dreams are living a life based on fear. Some prisoners worry their money will be lost if they invest in an online pen pal website. That may be the case if they were to use a bogus site, but by using this book, you can put yourself in a better position to get the results you want. It still takes the courage to try. If not, your pen pal dreams will die. Just remember that fears are only a limitation of the mind.

>*"Courage is resistance to fear, mastery of fear-not absence of fear."* -Mark Twain

When you have fear in your pen pal life you expect bad things to happen. You may start thinking, "What if I don't get any hits?" "What if she doesn't write back?" "What if it doesn't work?" When these things happen you act as if they were supposed to happen. But they weren't. Instead of thinking about the what ifs of the world, become a prisoner who thinks "I can and I will".

I'm sure there's something in your past that you once feared but now you don't? It's the same with pen pals. Guess what? I lost all those pen pals. But a funny thing happened, I realized it wasn't that bad. I didn't have anything to fear. Now I sit here writing this book with way more pen pals than I've ever had and get mail every day they pass it out. Always remember that you have nothing to lose, but everything to gain. You won't be any worse off than you are now if you fail. I love 50 Cent and Robert Greene's book *The 50th Law*. It gives you many strategies and tips based on the philosophy: Fear Nothing!

>*"Life is either a daring adventure or nothing."* -Helen Keller

A lot of you hope that you could find a special friend? Or many special friends? But who will hear your request if you don't have the courage to speak up or write the letter? Or post the ad? There will come a time when you're done reading this book and you have to decide what to do? Do what the unsuccessful prisoner won't do. Dare to go after you pen pal dreams. I did it, and you can do it also. The prisoners in this book also did it.

They were once where you are, but they went after their dreams. No fear is the motto of the prisoners going after *Pen Pal Success™.*

> *"That which we call 'genius' has a great deal to do with nerve."* -Nathan Branden

Knowing That You Are a Salesperson!

The second step is to know that you're a salesperson. Because you are, you're marketing a product called *you*! That's why they are called "personal *ads*." Ads is short for *advertisements*, and an advertisement is the attempt to call attention or promote a product. With an ad you're trying to induce someone to take action. For a personal ad, the action you want the other person to take is to contact you in some way. This goes for all your initial marketing efforts to get pen pals.

Once you understand that you're selling a product, i.e. marketing yourself, then you can learn the successful marketing techniques that help sell products. I'll share some strategies with you throughout this book that can assist you in your goal to get pen pals. You can use those tips to help sell yourself better. Some of you will naturally sell yourself well, others won't. The good news is that everyone can learn how to do it.

Here are a few basic marketing success tips and tactics that you should learn now:

- First, you must know who you are marketing to. In the pen pal game, you need to find out what you want. Who are you looking for? Once you decide that, and are honest about it, then you can tailor your profile ad to speak directly to that person. You should always write your ads like you're speaking to one specific person. My friend *Player*, wrote an ad with the headline "Big Girls Turn Me On!" Of course the only people who responded to his ad were plus-size women, but that is what he was looking for. He knew what he wanted and tailored his message for it.

- Second, you must know your "USP" or Unique Selling Proposition. You must put your best foot forward to make the best impression... And you must transform your features into benefits. I'll discuss this more in depth later, but for right now, just ask yourself: What makes me different from every other prisoner? Because possible pen pals will ask themselves: Why should I write him instead of any other prisoner? Find that answer out and turn it into a benefit for your possible pen pals.

- Third, great marketing materials are specific, not general. Because specifics stand out. Once I learned this, I started getting better results and responses to my ads. I used to say things like: "I like cowboy flicks, football and reading books." Now I might say: "I like Clint Eastwood spaghetti westerns, Baylor College football, and non-fiction How-To books". See the difference? Don't worry about trying to be general so you speak to the broadest possible market of pen pals. Go back and read the first point. You are trying to stand out and you can't do that by being a general, run-of-the-mill prisoner. I knew I was on the right track when the people who started responding to my ads said, "You write a great profile. It stood out from all the others." And I thought it was all because of my great looks.

- Next, you need to know if the medium is right to reach your chosen pen pal type. In the advertising world you must know what magazines your market reads? What TV shows do they watch? What radio stations do they listen to? Why? So you can place your marketing messages on or in these mediums to reach them. So if your goal is a freaky pen pal that you can write sex letters, you need to find out what website or magazine you can place your ad in to reach that person. Some prisoners know what they want, but they don't consider how to best reach their goals. There are many different online venues available today that will allow you to reach a specific demographic of people. I'll discuss lots of them throughout this book. It will be up to you to pick the best one you can. That way you can have a better chance of success.

- Finally, you aren't using a headline or great opening sentence. Why are headlines in ads so important? Because you're trying to get someone to stop and read your ad. It goes back to the "standing out" principle again. When people look for pen pals or dates online they scan photos first, then headlines next. If you don't have a great first sentence, they'll move on to the next profile. It's a little different for us prisoners because we read every ad and every word in a magazine. Especially a pen pal magazine. But in the free world, people have a limited amount of time to spend on your ads... And they are bombarded with ads from all kinds of media. So how are you standing out? With a great headline or first sentence you can put yourself in a better position for *Pen Pal Success™*.

These are just a few tips to remember. I'll discuss marketing and selling yourself throughout the rest of this book, because it's so important.

Resource Box

George Foreman once said that if you know how to sell you'll never go hungry. So allow me to recommend two great books on selling. First, *No B.S. Sales Success in the New Economy* by Dan S. Kennedy (www.NoBSBooks.com). Second, *Uncensored Sales Strategies* by Sydney Biddle-Barrows (www.EntrepreneurPress.com/UncensoredSales.html). That way you'll never go hungry again.

Believing That You're the #1 Product on the Market!

Once you get it down that you're a salesperson, then you must believe in your product. That product is you... And you must believe that you're the number one product on the pen pal market. Not arrogantly so, but confidently. To the opposite sex, confidence is sexy. This belief will help you get out there and seek pen pals. You must begin to see yourself as a rare commodity. There are over 300 million people in the United States, but only 2.3 million prisoners. That means 297 million people can't do what you can. They don't have the time available to them like you do. Your time is your greatest asset. Like the rich, you must learn how to invest your time so that it benefits you in your future. There are millions of people out there in the free world who might be willing to write a prisoner. But they don't know who you are. They will never find out who you are unless you believe in yourself and take the steps in this book to announce it to the world. I wrote this book to help you do just that.

Here are some tips to help you gain that belief in yourself:

- Examine the competition. I love the saying *"get better or get beaten"*. A lot of prisoners say, "You are not better than me" when they see someone having success. Maybe not as a human, but when it comes to pen pal success, yes I am. Why? Because I'm willing to put in the hours of research on my competition so that I can outsell them. I hate being compared to the lame's from Des Plaines that surround me. But I pay attention. I read their ads and profiles if I can. I look to see what media they are using. I ask other people about them and their results if I can. Then I compare myself to what they are doing. If I can learn from them I do. If not, I move on. I do this so that I can have more to offer and know how to position myself better than them. Therein lies the rub. I'm not better than my fellow prisoners, but I can do stuff BETTER than them. You can be the judge on what that means. In this book, you'll learn how to get these results and believe in yourself. By learning about the competition you can position yourself to outsell them. If you can't outsell them, you better transform yourself so you can. Remember, *"Get better or get beaten!"*

- Examine your past successes. This is really an easy way to get confidence. No matter how small it is you can use it to boost your morale. Getting one poem published in an anthology was the catalyst that started my writing career. One pen pal success can propel you also. Get a notebook and brainstorm over your accomplishments. Then write them down no matter how small. Reread them over and over. Every time you achieve something, write it down in your notebook. Prison tends to break someone down. Other prisoners are jealous and will envy your success. Then they will hate and try to downgrade it. Don't pay attention to them or any other critics for that matter. Read your success notebook for confidence and encouragement. This will help you gain the belief that you're number one!

You're ahead of the game because you have this book. There are over 2400 prisoners on *LostVault.com* alone. If you place an ad on that site, you'll be in competition with them. But guess what? As much as I'd like them to, not all of them will buy this book. Their loss. (And mine financially). But because you now have in your hands a resource to help you become the best prison pen pal you can be, you can run circles around them if you apply yourself to using this book. Let me put it another way. If you and I were in a fight and I had a knife and you had an AK-47, wouldn't you feel more confident in the outcome? This book is your assault weapon that can help you mow down the competition. Once you get the belief that you're number one, then you just need to follow two more tips to succeed in the pen pal game.

Be Ready to Work the System

Someone once said that the dictionary is the only place where success comes before work. None of the tips and tactics contained in this book will do anything for you unless you put them to use. Yes, it will take a little work, but in the end, you'll achieve your pen pal objectives.

To become a *Pen Pal Success*™, you must put in the time and effort to utilize the tools that you have available to you. A tool is anything you can use to assist you in achieving your goals. Your bed and pillow are tools that help you sleep better. An *iPod* is a tool that allows you to listen to music. Your clothes are tools that you use to present the best possible appearance and provide some protection from the weather when needed. My typewriter was a tool I used to assist me in my writing until ILDOC took them from us. What tools do you have available to you?

Whether it's a mental tool like imagination or concentration, or a physical tool like a typewriter or a paintbrush, a tool is a tool. They were created to be used. Don't neglect the tools you have available to you. Only through use can they become stronger. In this book, there are tips and strategies to aid you in getting and keeping pen pals. If you fail to use them, you'll find things tougher. Disuse is misuse. Your mind is the key to the future you desire. Begin to tap into the power that you mind holds. Use this book as the tool that it is, and stop surviving and start thriving.

> *"My brain is the key that sets me free."* -Harry Houdini

One of the secrets of successful people is using systems to get the results they seek. It's no different in the pen pal game. Whether you use someone else's system (like this book), or start your own system from ideas that you have, you have to work them to get pen pals. You can't sit around and wait for someone to contact you. You have to put in the work. The good news is that you don't have to reinvent the wheel because it's already been done for you. Maybe new technologies or new websites will pop up, but the basic principles have been the same since settlers in the American West started advertising for love in the 1800s. I'll share with you the reliable systems others have used to gain pen pal success. I will also share with you some ways to build your own systems. These systems will be the tools you use to get the results you seek.

Another way to look at copying successful systems is to call it the ability to "stand on the shoulders of giants". By doing this, you can reach heights you never thought possible. So many prisoners jump down in the pen pal game without first doing a little research. All they have to do is look at those few who have successfully traveled before them to see how to do it, or not do it.

"Imitation is part of the creative process for anyone learning an art or craft. Bach and Picasso didn't spring full-blown and Bach and Picasso; they needed models." -William Zinsser

Two hours spent in the library may give you enough educational life experiences to allow you to leapfrog your fellow prisoners in the pen pal game. Read non-fiction books, poetry books, sales and marketing books. Read the biographies of great leaders from history. These are people you can learn from. I have the habit of looking for people who've successfully done what I'm trying to do. Once I find these people I'll try to read everything I can about them. That way I can profit by their experience. Earlier I mention that I'm a "rake". Well, one of the most famous "rakes" in history is the poet, Lord Byron. So I sought out anything I could find on him to read, copy, and better accentuate my own seductive powers. So should you!

Take a cue from the people you find in your research and learn how to act on your own rise to pen pal success. Extract their winning strategies for your own life. Try and get some of (if not all) the books listed in the bibliography. Step your game up.

It's a form of folly to try things on your own without looking to the examples of others to see how you could first save time, money, and face. Their mistakes and initial blunders are an early warning system for what you should watch out for. Experience is the wisest teacher, but it takes way too long to learn that way. That's why it's called the school for fools. But you are not a fool because you have this book in your hands. Use the combined experience of the examples in these pages and get what you want.

"The trouble with experience is that by the time you have it you are too old to take advantage of it." -Jimmy Connors

This doesn't mean you should blindly copy someone. For one, that's illegal. Plus, you don't want to be a clone, just another rip-off artist. Don't imitate, create. Put your own spin on things. When you find someone who has done something that you want to do, ask them some questions. Here are a few you can use:

- How did you do it?

- What did you learn along the way?

- What would you do different?

- How can I do it better and easier?

You want to copy their successful systems and use them in your own life. Copy the how-to part!

"By observing the traits of successful people, you can create your own system for success." -Ryan Blair (*www.nothingtolose.com*)

When Sam Walton, the founder of *Wal-Mart*, first decided he was going to open up his retail store, he became a spy. He got a little notepad and pencil, and went around to all the successful department stores and took notes. He wrote down what they were doing, how they were doing it, and anything else he could use. Then *Walton* went back to his little store in Arkansas and implemented what he had in his notebook. He used their successful strategies, but put his own spin on things. Walton stood on the shoulders of giants and now his store is the giant, with more department stores than any other company is the world.

Do the same in your life. Whatever you choose as your pen pal goal, there are those who have gone before you. They supply the keys to success. Find these people. Study them and copy their moves. But don't forget to put your own spin on things, and use new technology to make your moves faster.

"If I have seen further, it is by standing on ye shoulders of giants." -Sir Isaac Newton

The Prince

In 1512, Niccoló Machiavelli was sent to prison for a conspiracy plot. While there, he was tortured, but refused to talk to his interrogators. After he was released from prison, Machiavelli secluded himself on his family farm and began to write. Prisoners are familiar with his books, *The Prince*, *The Art of War*, and *The Discourses*. Many of our prison systems outlaw these books because of the power they contain. There are several strategies that he used to perfect his philosophy and books. I'll share two of them here that can help you achieve your pen pal goals.

First, he secluded himself so he could think and work. This way he would be free from outside influences that may corrupt his thoughts. We are already secluded inside prison, but can be easily influenced by our fellow prisoners. You must learn to tune out the daily prison noise. Using earplugs or headphones works. Staying up at night when its quiet works. You must learn to tune out the jibber-jabber of prison if you want to become a *Pen Pal Success*™.

Second, Machiavelli would hold imaginary conversations in his mind with great people from history. He did this to try and learn from them. In conducting research for my first book, *The Millionaire Prisoner*, I found that Napoleon Hill (*Think and Grow Rich*) would do the same thing. He would hold roundtable discussions with great people in his mind and learn from them. You can do the same in your own life. Here's how:

Before you retire at night, close your eyes and imagine yourself at a roundtable with Cupid, Casanova, Lord Byron, Cleopatra, Neil Straus, Mystery, Mehow and many other seducers. Ask them questions in your mind and allow them to answer. As you begin doing this each night, continue to read more about the lives of the great seducers you have chosen for your roundtable. As you do this your subconscious mind will influence your imaginary roundtable discussions, and they will bear more fruit. You can learn from the great ones who went before us, and Machiavelli is certainly one who can teach us a lot.

> *"Men almost always walk in paths beaten by others and act by imitation. Though he cannot hold strictly to the ways of others or match the ability of those he imitates, a prudent man must always tread the path of great men and imitate those who have excelled, so that even if his ability does not match theirs, at least he will achieve some semblance of it."* - Niccoló Machiavelli

You can become a *Pen Pal Success*™ by standing on the shoulders of giants and using their successful systems in your own life.

Practice Persistence Until You Find What You're Looking For!

The prison hierarchy considers must prisoners lost causes. They don't think we can change. A lot of them are passing laws to stop prisoners from using pen pal websites and social media. I don't agree with them. It's your duty to stick to it and shine like the diamond that you are. The key is persistence. Without it, you'll have a hard time getting the pen pals you want. Let me share with you a story about the power of persistence.

In 1977, at the age of 18, Dewey Bozella was arrested for a New York murder. But the grand jury returned a no bill because there was no evidence linking Bozella to the murder. Six years later, Bozella was in college when he was rearrested after two convicted felons implicated him. They were released from prison after their testimony helped convict Bozella and he was sentenced to life in prison. While inside, he joined the prison boxing program and became the undefeated champ. In 1990, his conviction was overturned because prosecutors excused every juror who wasn't white. He was offered a plea deal for manslaughter where he would be released if he would sign a paper saying what happened, but Bozella refused because he was innocent. The case went to the jury and they found him guilty. Bozella went back to Sing Sing, where he worked on getting his education. He met Trena Boone in the prison visiting room when she was visiting her brother and they married in 1996. He was denied parole four times because he wouldn't confess to a crime he didn't commit. Eventually his conviction was overturned when lawyers found new testimony that his original lawyers never saw, and the state declined to retry him because he was innocent.

After his release, Bozella started The Dewey Bozella Foundation, which aims to help at risk kids, find a place to box and train. In 2011, he was given the *Arthur Ashe Award* for courage at the *ESPY*'s. His dream was to have one fight professionally and Oscar De La Hoya and Golden Boy Productions stepped up to give him that fight. But first he had to pass the examination to get a license to box in California and no one had ever gotten approval at the age of 52 like Dewey was. He was denied, but given 30 days to train and try again. Bozella trained at *Bernard Hopkins* gym in Philadelphia and passed the examination. On October 25, 2011 he won his first and only professional fight. ESPN Films produced a movie, *26 Years: The Dewey Bozella Story*, about his life. In that film you can see Dewey's determination to achieve his dream to have one fight professionally. Bozella's motto is one we can all use: "Never give up".

That's what it's all about: *never giving up*. Go after your pen pal dreams. Don't let anyone tell you that you can't get married while in prison. Or that you can't become a pen pal with a celebrity. Don't allow the haters and critics to steer you off track. Don't allow the naysayers to force you to quit.

"When going through hell, keep going. Never, never give in." -Winston Churchill

I believe that it's possible to learn how to be persistent. It's pretty simple. Just take a step here, a step there. Do a little every day. The best way to eat the elephant standing in your path is to cut it up into little pieces. Prison is the elephant standing in your path. By cutting it up into little pieces, your path will be clear. The same for getting pen pals. I've tried to break the process down into little steps so it's easier. But you can't be idle. All day watching TV will not cultivate pen pals. All day "kicking the bobos" with the homies will not get you pen pals. There will be some days that you do not want to read or write. That's when you have to keep going. Your reward is just around the corner. Move forward one step at a time until it becomes habit. I'll give you steps to take in later chapters that can help you move forward, just make up your mind that you won't quit.

"Life is like riding a bicycle; you don't fall off unless you stop pedaling." -Claude Pepper

The pen pal game is a game of numbers... And in games of numbers, the law of averages is in effect. The more you sell the more chances you have that someone will buy. Persistence is the key to success in this game. Some things may not work the way you want them to. Or the timing might not be right? But if you keep going, keep writing letters, and keep placing ads, you'll eventually get what you want. I can't guarantee you that the first ad you place, or the first letter your write will get you responses. I can tell you that if used, the tips in this book will give you a better chance of getting responses. But you have to be willing to keep going until you get what you want. If you prepare yourself now for that, then you can achieve everything you want. You can't quit at the first sign of rejection. I've tried to make it easier for you to experience success with this book, but in the end, it's up to you to put in the work to get what you want.

Here are six steps that will help you on your pen pal journey.

Step 1: Decide on the pen pal objective that you want. Do you want a wife? A husband? Just a friend? A business partner? A mentor? Be honest with yourself about what you really want and need.

Step 2: Using the tips in the next chapter, recreate your pen pal life into what you want it to be. By using self-control direct the thoughts that reach your subconscious mind. Watch out for any negative influences that keep you from accomplishing your goal.

Step 3: Be ruthless with your time and those you associate with. If possible, surround yourself with people who encourage and inspire you. Especially others who are knee-deep in the pen pal game.

Step 4: Prepare when others are playing so that you'll have more time to play in the future. (I work late at night and into the early morning when everyone else is asleep. Find your time to get ahead.)

Step 5: Do not stop until you reach your goal. If you fall down, get back up and try again. If your plan doesn't work, make a new one. Keep doing that until you find one that works.

Step 6: Develop necessity in your life. Put your back against the wall and succeed in getting all the pen pals you could ever need.

By utilizing the above steps, along with the strategies throughout the rest of this book, you can achieve your pen pal dreams.

"The difference between a successful person and others is not the lack of strength, not a lack of knowledge, but rather a lack of will." -Vince Lombardi

A Final Parting Thought

The steps in this chapter will enable you to have the right attitude for pen pal success. Always remember that it's a game. Never take it seriously. Your life doesn't end or begin with pen pals. But they can be a part of your life... And they can make your life more enjoyable. Even if you are looking for your soulmate, it's still a game. Because it's a game, you can laugh at your mistakes. You can laugh at any problems that arise. You're not going to die if a pen pal leaves you and stops writing. The world is not going to end. Since it's all a game, in the next chapter I'll show you how to come up with your own game plan.

PEN PAL TIP

Never stop growing your learning potential. Constantly read non-fiction, self-help and relationship books.

Chapter 3

Millionaire Prisoner Pen Pal Growth Plan

"Growth is one of the few areas in which the more you use, the more you get back."
-John C. Maxwell

Before I move onto the actual steps of how you can get pen pals I'm going to list a few more preparation techniques that will assist you on your quest. The name of this book is called *Pen pal Success*™, but what does this mean? The answer depends on what you are looking for. This chapter will help you decide what type of pen pal success you're after. Some of you already know what you want to accomplish with this book. That's fine. But don't neglect reading this chapter because you can still get some tips that will help you.

First, I want to tell you a story that will illustrate why this part is so important for pen pal success. In 2003 when I went back to Menard Correctional Center to begin serving my life sentence, I felt I needed a woman to hold me down and help ease the burden of prison. Why? Because that was what every other prisoner was doing. They were playing the pen pal game trying to get a woman to take care of them. So that's what I did. The problem was that I didn't really want a pen pal relationship, I wanted (needed) legal help and money for commissary. (FYI: I'll be honest, I didn't get this truth back then in my early 20s, but I do now at 36 years old.) So I did what they were doing because I thought that was how it was done. I found a college girl that started holding me down. But I had become a professional pen pal. I literally wrote every day, talked on the phone twice a week, and spent most of my time doting on her. She loved it, but I didn't. I loved getting money for commissary, but to me, my time is more valuable than that. It wasn't until years later that I realized that I needed to spend my time more wisely. And I needed quality pen pals. So I sought out a business pen pal, mentors, and other free-world successful people. I started raising my net worth by improving the quality of the friends I had in my network. That's when it hit me. To have true success in the pen pal game, you have to go after what's really important to you. You can't settle for someone else's dream. There's nothing wrong with writing pen pals all day if that's what you want. Just make sure that's what you want. Then decide what type of pen pals you want. Only then will you be able to have your version of pen pal success. This chapter will help you answer these questions.

Because prison is such a negative place, it's useful to read stories of success and inspiration. One of my favorite magazines is *Success*. It helps me keep *The Millionaire Prisoner*™ mindset and attitude. It also supplies a lot of "aha" moments. I had one of those moments while reading John Maxwell's column on leadership. He wrote that we should stop working on our weaknesses because that's where we're weak at, and that we should grow our strengths to maximum potential with a "grown plan". That was my moment. I had a "Growth" Chapter in my manuscript for *The Millionaire Prisoner*™, but I had no growth plan. So I went through all the books in my personal library and put together a "Millionaire Prisoner Growth Plan™". You can do the same for getting pen pals. Make sure you write your plan down on paper and keep it handy so you can review it. Here's how to formulate it:

1. Identify 3 areas of your pen pal life that you want to experience growth in. For example: Relationship/ Friendships; Spiritual; and business. To help you decide this, here are some questions you can ask yourself:

    *   Do I want one pen pal or many pen pals?
    *   Do I want sexual friendships and freaky letters?
    *   Do I want long-term friendships or am I just trying to pass the time?
    *   Do I want to learn more about my religion or other spiritual matters?
    *   Do I have business goals and need a partner or mentor?

    You may not honestly know the answers yet? Your motives may change like mine did over the years. That's okay. It's just better to have these answers ahead of time.

2. Break each one down further. If you put down "Relationship", decide what type you want? Casual? Marriage? Sexual? Then describe your ideal partner. Write it down, and try to be as specific as you can. Think about your ideal pen pal's looks, weight, height, age, interests, career, character, health, personality and spirituality. Brainstorm. Write down anything that comes to mind. After you're done, go back over what you wrote and delete stuff that means the same thing or is irrelevant. Make sure

you have stuff that you won't compromise on, like "Non-smoker" or "Must be a Christian". Remember, this is your ideal pen pal. Do one for each category.

3. Set goals with timelines for reaching them for each pen pal category that you listed. When you reach your goal, set a new one and go after it.

4. Reach out to people and ask for their help. If they can't, ask them to connect you with others who can. Don't take "no" for an answer, keep asking others. (I'll go more into this later on in this book.)

5. Never stop learning and growing your potential. Constantly read non-fiction, self-help, and relationship books. Always look to gain at least one tip to use in your life, and in your correspondence.

Pen pal growth doesn't have to be a long drawn out process. If you work on your strengths, talents, and passion, you'll reach new heights in no time. And you'll be so busy writing letters that you'll forget about your weaknesses. Successful people never stop seeking new ways to experience growth. They understand that life is a never-ending journey, and you always have room to get better on every level. But I've found that the funniest thing to do is to get new free-world friends. It can be the most rewarding thing you do.

"Success has to incorporate the personal as well as the professional. And it must be about character rather than property and possessions." -Rabbi Shmuley Boteach

Using Imagination to Aid You on Your Pen Pal Journey

Now that you have your pen pal growth plan I want to give you a few tips about how you can tap into your powers of creativity. This will aid you in becoming more resourceful and help you get more pen pals. Your imagination will enable you to overcome the prison walls that confine you.

"What is now proved was once only imagined." - William Blake

Napoleon Hill (author of *Think and Grow Rich*) called imagination the workshop of the mind. Picasso said that everything you can imagine is real. Imagination will deliver ideas and thoughts that can assist you in becoming a *Pen Pal Success*™. But if you can't see it in your mind first, you'll never see it in your future. Your success first begins in the form of a thought or idea. Then you must put ideas to work if you're going to be able to achieve your pen pal plan. How do you do this?

First, realize that all new ideas sound foolish in the beginning. Sometimes you'll have an idea and then think "that won't work" or "nobody will like it". You have to learn to override those thoughts and believe in your idea or dream. When I first came up with the idea for some of my pen pal strategies, I don't normally like them. They sound too easy sometimes. I even go so far as to change them. But after writing them down and thinking them through, my original ideas and strategies make sense. Without these original ideas in this book you wouldn't be holding it in your hands today.

Did you catch that last little bit? "After writing them down…" That is the key. You have to capture your ideas so that you can act on them. The main way is to write them down. Bestselling author, Stephen King, gets a lot of his book and short story ideas from his own dreams. He writes them down immediately upon waking up so he doesn't forget them. Pay attention to your thoughts when you first wake up in the morning. You might find something valuable.

Pick-up artist *Mehow* (http://www.mehow.tv/htt2hw), author of *How to Talk to Hot Women: The 9 Secrets to Getting and Keeping the Woman (Women) of Your Dreams*, said that he got a lot of his ideas while in the shower and would jump out, write them down, then rehearse them, and practice them in the clubs at night. All it takes is one good idea to cement your name in the hall of fame. It would be a shame if you had that idea and then forgot it. Always remember the maxim: *A short pencil is better than a long memory.*

"The presence of an idea is like that of a loved one. We imagine that we shall never forget it and that the beloved can never become indifferent to us; but out of sight, out of mind! The finest thought runs the risk of being irretrievably forgotten if it's not written down and the beloved of being take from us unless she has been wedded." - Arthur Schopenhauer

Everyone is different and you may come up with your own way of keeping track of your ideas, but you must secure them somehow. When you're out of your cell, carry a pen or pencil and some paper with you at all times. When something comes to mind, write it down. Of course, when you're in the cell it will be much easier. Keep a pen or pencil and some paper next to your bed, or by your desk if you have one. You must get in the habit of capturing your ideas. You never know which one will be profitable for you in the future.

"A man would do well to carry a pencil in his pocket and write down his thoughts of the moment. Those that come unsought are commonly the most valuable and should be secured because they seldom return." - Sir Francis Baron

After you write your ideas down, you have to keep them in something. Eminem keeps his rhyme notes in shoeboxes. In *How to Get Girls While You are in Prison, Freedom Jones* advises that you keep a notebook. I keep my ideas and notes in file folders. Whether it's a notebook, folder, box, or bag, it doesn't matter as long as you're keeping them. Review them periodically, and you'll find many golden nuggets that you can use in your pen pal letters and relationships. Most of the strategies in this book started as ideas and thoughts on scraps of paper in my idea folder. As I worked my way deeper into the pen pal game, I found a wealth of information and ideas in my notes. All I had to do was organize them and put them to work for me. You can do the same when writing letters to pen pals. All it takes is one good idea.

"One good idea can enable a man to live like a King the rest of his life." - Ross Perot

The Art of Visualization

Your imagination also encompasses your ability to dream. Lots of prisoners have dreams of having a flock of pen pals writing them. But for some reason they don't allow imagination to lead them in achieving those dreams. The reason this is so is because they are being led by their experience instead of their imagination. Your experience is the failure of prison and drive-bys at mail call. So your frame of mind is negative about getting mail. Since the pen pals you want reside outside the walls of your prison, here's how you can allow your imagination to lead you over those walls.

If you can dream it you can do it. Using simple meditation tactics, you can learn to visualize your new pen pal life.

Step 1: Select a soothing piece of music that calms you. Classical or instrumental music works best. This allows your brain to focus on something while all the small noise of the prison is negated.

Step 2: Place a "Do Not Disturb" sign on your cell door. Then sit in a chair or lie down on your bunk. You don't have to sit cross-legged unless you want to. Just find a position that is comfortable.

Step 3: Close your eyes and relax. Slow your breathing with deep slow breaths. Imagine being surrounded by nothingness.

Step 4: Once you are calm, imagine getting a letter from your pen pal. Imagine reading it. Then writing a response. Imagine your pen pal reading it and writing you back. Imagine talking on the phone with your pen pal, or going on a visit with them. When you do this, try to feel what it would be like when you actually experiencing these things in real life.

Step 5: Remain in this visualization state as long as you like. To come back to reality, just become aware of your body and open your eyes.

Practice this process daily. Play out your pen pal dreams. See yourself accomplishing your pen pal objectives. Imagine yourself writing the hot girl or guy and getting mail every day. Pretend you're watching a movie about your pen pal life and everything goes right for you in that movie. Believe that it can happen and you'll make it happen.

"The empires of the future are the empires of the mind." -Winston Churchill

But you can't just visualize it and think it will happen. You have to use this tactic along with *action*. This means spending your time wisely in using the rest of this book. You can't waste time. Now is the time to act. Now is the time to go after pen pals. Now is the time to build your network.

How to Make the Most of Your Time

If you're watching TV, do tasks during the commercials. The ads are unimportant to you anyways. You're in prison and can't order a pizza, go to a restaurant, or buy a Mercedes right now. This stuff just makes you daydream about what you're going to do once you get out. Instead, write down your thoughts or ideas. Read a few lines in your favorite or seduction book. Work on a poem or a letter. Listen to an audio book. Do anything except pay attention to the commercials.

If you have read my first book, *The Millionaire Prisoner™*, then you know I really don't like television that much except for sports and movies. But here's a way to watch it that can help your pen pal game. Every time you hear or see something that sounds good or looks good, and you think you can use it in your letters, write it down. Especially if you are watching relationship shows or documentaries. Make your TV viewing profitable. And I will have more to say about TV later.

Another way to gain time is in those moments when you're waiting. Take a pocketbook with you to the hospital. While you're waiting for the doctor or dentist to call you, read a chapter or two. Or take a pen and some paper and work on a poem or rough draft of a letter you've been meaning to write. There are so many moments in prison when you're just waiting. Learn how to turn these moments into profit by using them to your benefit. Take control of your time so it becomes your greatest asset.

"Things may come to those who wait, but only the things left by those who hustle." -Abraham Lincoln

You must also watch out for prison time's vultures. You know the type of prisoner I'm talking about. They ask you a question and they want to debate the answer with you for an hour. Or they want to tell you stories about their past. What you must do is politely excuse yourself and get back to work on your pen pal dreams. Remember, it's your time, so value it. Time *is* money! In this book's sense, its pen pal money. Use your prison time wisely so you can turn your sentence into a benefit.

"As every thread of gold is valuable, so is every moment of time." -John Mason

---

Resource Box

For more on using your time wisely, check out the following books: *168 Hours* by Laura Vanderkam; and *No B.S. Time Management for Entrepreneurs, Second Edition* by Dan S. Kennedy.

Pen Pal Success™ **Case Studies**

One of the most profitable aspects of writing my first book, The Millionaire Prisoner, was learning about all the other prisoners who became successful. There was a lesson in each prisoner's story. That's why there are so many prisoner-examples in my book.

One of those prisoners is Billy Wayne Sinclair. He ended up on Louisiana's death row after a robbery went bad. While he was in prison he met a reporter from a local television station and they hit it off. Sinclair and the reporter, Jodie Bell, began corresponding through letters and talking on the phone. They wanted to get married, but the prison system didn't allow it at the time, so they did it by proxy. When Jodie's employer found out about her relationship with Sinclair they threatened to fire her if she didn't stop seeing him. So she quit her job. Their story can be found in the book they wrote together, A Life in the Balance: The Billy Wayne Sinclair Story. He got off death row and was eventually paroled in 2006. They also wrote another book together called Capital Punishment. Getting her as his pen pal and wife, was a major support system for Sinclair. Maybe you'll find yours?

Another great example of using a pen pal relationship to help with your goals can be found in the story of Stanley "Tookie" Williams. Tookie was one of the co-founders of the Crips street gang in California. He was sent to death row for his role in four murders. During his time on the row, Tookie began to write. He wrote an eight book series aimed at preventing youth violence in 5 to 10 year old students. That series, Tookie Speaks Out Against Gang Violence, was co-authored with Barbara Cottman-Becnel. He would call Cottman-Becnel collect and dictate to her what he had wrote. She would then type it into her computer and edit it. One of his other books, Life in Prison, won two national book honors. Some of you may remember the made for TV movie, Redemption, starring Jamie Foxx as Tookie Williams. The state of California executed Tookie, but his legacy lives online at www.tookie.com.

These are just two of many prisoners who have achieved pen pal success. You'll learn about others in the rest of this book. In this chapter you learned simple techniques that will help you as you embark on the pen pal journey. How do I know? Because these are the same tactics that I, and other prisoners, have used to get pen pals. Do not neglect them once you start the process of making connections. Keep coming back to them and adding to them. Reformulate them, rehearse them, and apply them to your life. They will help you immensely, and before you know it, you'll be living and breathing pen pals. Since that's the whole goal of this book, let's get right down to the how-to in How to Get and Keep Pen Pals.

Chapter 4
Your Pen Pal Network

"A good general cultivates resources." -Sun Tzu

Have you ever had an idea that you wished you could put into practice, but couldn't because you didn't have the right person in your address book? Have you ever sat in your cell and wished you had a reliable pen pal? Or wished someone would accept your collect call? Maybe you needed money to hire a good appellate lawyer? If you had any of these wishes, then you can understand the need for a reliable network, i.e., pen pals and friends.

To get where you want to go, whether relationship or business-wise, you're going to need help. With the right people in your life you can turn your dreams into a reality. After reading this book you should have enough information to enable you to begin building a reliable network.

> *"If I had to name the single characteristic shared by all the truly successful people I've met over a lifetime, I'd say it is the ability to create and nurture a network of contacts."* -Harvey Mackay

What is a Network?

Simply defined, a network is a group of contacts and their own contacts. A network will allow you to go from prison to the penthouse by the shortest route in the least amount of time. In the prison complex, it could be explained by getting something done without having to file a grievance, or go on a hunger strike.

Some experts believe that a network is not a team. I agree with them in part. We are not trying to build the New York Yankees. But you do need some designated hitters that you can call on and get some home runs hit out of the ballpark. In that essence, you do need some team players. You need people who can step outside their normal comfort zone and come through in the clutch. This will allow you to live in a world without boundaries.

A reliable network can get rid of the limitations of your incarceration. The people in your network can give you positive advice, where your fellow prisoners mostly offer negative advice. Through your contacts, you can get access to information that you couldn't get by yourself. You may also get to meet people you never had the chance otherwise. Access is the greatest gift we can offer each other, and a network allows this. It can be a source of new ideas, experiences, and knowledge. You may have great ideas and plans, but without the right people to help you put them into play, they will die. Prison is where people go to rot away. Unless you take it upon yourself to stay connected you will never achieve your dreams. The good news? You're only one person away from achieving those dreams.

> *"People are bridges you must cross to get where you want to go."* -Bob Beaudine

How to Get FREE Pen Pals

I previously wrote about these strategies in my booklet, *How to Get FREE Pen Pals*, which has been sold by *O'Barnett Publishing* and *Superior Enterprises* for a few years now. This tactic is not novel to me and prisoners have been using it for years to meet new friends. I was just the first prisoner that I know of to put it into salable form and market it. Let me give you the back story about this stratagem so you can fully understand the process better.

> *"The arrow shot by the archer may or may not kill a single person. But stratagems devised by a wise man can kill even babies in the womb."* -Kautilya, 3rd Century B.C. Philosopher

In the winter of 2003-2004, I was transferred to Menard in Southern Illinois, to begin serving my life sentence. The mother of my twin girls no longer wanted anything to do with me, and most of the pen pals that were writing when I was in county jail, no longer wanted anything to do with me, since now I had life. Besides my mom and sister, I really had no one else in the free world to count on. Lucky for me, my twin brother Joe, who was doing 17 years in the federal system for bank robbery, had met a young woman who he married. For a Christmas present she put me on P*rison Talk Online* (www.prisontalk.com) and the now defunct website, *The Pampered Prisoner*. I got lots of replies and came up with a young woman named Allyssa off Prison Talk Online. She was in college in Georgia, and we wrote each other every day and talked on the phone twice weekly. But I still didn't get the kind of response I was looking for. So I tried another site for my birthday, *Friends Beyond the Wall* (www.friendsbeyondthewall.com). I received some replies, met a few women, but after a few months on that site, I no longer go any replies. My attitude went to an all-time low. In the free world I had no problem getting women, but there I was, an outcast, who couldn't even get a quality pen pal.

My next step was to try buying a few pen pal lists. I wrote every woman on the lists and I got a lot of return letters. The few women who did write me back said they didn't even want pen pals, and wondered how I got their info? I did get two pen pals, but they only wanted to be friends, and were married. I was looking for a little more than "Just Friends".

In 2005, I was at the law library and happened to run into a prisoner name G. We knew each other from juvie and started telling each other war stories. Eventually, we got around to pen pals and started talking about who we were writing. I told him about Allyssa and my other two pen pals. When it was his turn he told me about Lisa, Jennifer, Kristy, Amanda, Janelle, Elizabeth, and Samantha. Those were just his main girls. He had 29 other pen pals. So I asked him what website he was on and he laughed. He said none, and that he had never been on one and never would go on one because there was no need to.

That statement caught me off guard because every prisoner I knew, said that if you wanted to get pen pals, you had to go on a website. But G told me that a true pick-up artist does what everyone else isn't doing. He told me that he didn't want to fish in the same pond as every other prisoner, but wanted a pond all to himself. What was my next question? The logical one of course,

"So G, how do you get your pen pals?"

"Man, I get them out of the newspaper or wherever I see an address!"

I laughed a little at that and said: "So you just write any woman's address that you see?"

"Yep, that's how I get my pen pals. It's that easy, try it."

If any other prisoner would have told me that, I would've let it go in one ear and out the other. But I know G, and I trust him. So I went looking for a newspaper. I found a prisoner who had a subscription to *The Southern Illinoisan*, and I stated looking through it with a fine toothed comb. I didn't think I was going to find any addresses, but they were there. I found seven addresses in the arrest reports. That's when I realized that G's strategy just might work. I immediately went to work and started writing. I sent out a letter to all seven women that I found. Then I waited. The results? One week later, I had received no return to senders and two replies. The first woman wanted to know how did I get her info?... And the second woman, Judy, was willing to be my pen pal.

Now I'm not stupid, if you show me something that works, I'm going to work the hell out of it. So I kept writing addresses down, and every time I got extra envelopes, I wrote more women. The results? I came up with two lesbian chicks who lived together in Du Quoin, Illinois got another pen pal from Salem, Illinois who worked at a factory as a 3rd shift security guard, and who spent her shift writing to

me, every night! I now had multiple pen pals and got mail every day. Plus, I never missed commissary. But something was missing. I wanted a woman to come visit every week.

At about that time, I started ending my letters with a line where I gave them an option to pass my letter on to someone else if they were not interested. I didn't know if it would work, but I figured it couldn't hurt. I wrote a woman from Carbondale, Illinois, which is 30 minutes from Menard, and waited. A few weeks later I got a letter from Carla, someone I didn't know or write. She said the woman I wrote was married, but she had read my letter and decided to write. She had just went through a divorce and was lonely. One month later we had our first visit, and every Tuesday after that, I was in the visiting room eating and playing cards with Carla. Life is good when you have free world friends to help you out.

I must be honest with you. I was not running game. I was telling the truth in my search for pen pals and friendships. I never lied to any of the women who wrote me back and told them I had life in prison. That's the key. If you're not honest and seek to build real friendships, you'll come up. Now back to our story.

At the time Carla and I started having our weekly visits together, I slowed down in writing new people because I had too much on my plate. I had Allyssa in Georgia, who wrote every day. I had Carla, who wrote every day. Plus, I had other pen pals who wrote once a week. On top of that, I was beginning to research my post-conviction petition. Anymore work and I wouldn't be able to keep up, so I cut back on writing new people.

A few years later, I had lost contact with a few of my pen pals and was about to go back on a writing campaign when I happened to see a televised church service for a church in St. Louis. The pastor was unlike any other I had seen. So I started watching his service every week. After a few months, I wrote him and told him that I enjoyed his service and really liked him. Thanking him for his work, I asked him for a pen pal from his church. He read my letter to the congregation and the following week I received letters and cards from 17 different women, all wanting to be my pen pal. I had hit the jackpot! I had found the golden goose, churches. So I started writing churches, asking for pen pals and I started getting them.

I happened to run into G once again in the law library and he asked me how it was going and started discussing the pen pal game. He was impressed with how I was doing and then I floored him with my 17 women response story. As is true, when two or more people come together to discuss things without any animosity between them, they'll form a third mind, and fresh ideas will flow forth. It happened with me and G. We came up with the idea to put ads up on college campuses saying we needed pen pals. I was game if he had someone who would post our ads for us. One of his girls strategically placed the ads around the University of Illinois, and we waited. Within a few weeks we were swamped with pen pals wanting to write. I can't remember the exact ad we used, but here's how I would do it now with my current address and email;

Josh Kruger

HELP WANTED – PART TIME

Pen pal needed. Position available for a dependable, mature woman. No experience required. Rewarding position with lots of bonuses. If a quality friendship with a unique, honest, SWM, published poet and author is what you'd like, apply soon! Interested parties submit letter to:

Full Name
Complete Mailing Address
Email Address

If you choose to use this strategy have your assistant post the ad on the college student boards, unions, laundromats and inside women's bathrooms. Guerrilla marketing at its finest. I know one prisoner named Black, who took this idea, and said in his ad that he was willing to be a "subject" for their class requirements. That was brilliant because a lot of "criminal justice" and "criminology" students have a prison and parole class. So if your family and friends live by a college they can post your ads all over. You're bound to get some hits. In his book, *How to Get Girls While You are in Prison, Freedom Jones* advises writing the criminal justice department of colleges to get pen pals. I've seen it work with my own eyes, so I know it works.

Are you a published author of a book dealing with prison-related theme or topic? Then you have a guaranteed opening with any college or university that deals with prison and you may be able to make a little money also. This is how Michael Santos, author of *Inside: Life Behind Bars in America and About Prison*, made over $200,000 in royalties off his book. He also developed mentorships with numerous university professors. On the next page is a sample email/letter that you could send to the professor leading the class: If they accept your book, you'll make money off the royalties when the students purchase your book as "required reading." And you're bound to get some pen pals off your book, as long as your contact info is listed prominently throughout the book!

The Easiest Way to Get Pen Pals

Network with your comrades. Ask the prisoners you know who have pen pals. Especially the ones that go on visits and get big mail. Ask them if their pen pal, girlfriend, wife, or sister could find you someone to write or has a friend? Most will say no, but every once in a while, you'll find someone who has someone you can write. I met a wonderful girl named Amy from Chicago this way. We corresponded for about two years before we lost contact due to my being paroled. My brother got a pen pal/visitor this way when one of his friends' girl didn't want to ride to the prison by herself. And she didn't want her girlfriend to sit alone in the car for a few hours while she visited. So my brother got put in the car with the friend and now he's writing, emailing, and going on visits with the girl. Sometimes it's not what you know, but *who you know*.

Sample Letter for Professor:

Greetings (Professor or Mr./Ms./Dr.) _____,

My name is _____ and I'm a prison-based author of _____
. I'm contacting you to explore the possibility of your school (or
institution) considering my book for an adoption or supplemental text in
your graduate criminal justice programs, or wherever you feel it would
best fit?

The book is not theoretical. It's based on my specific real-life prison
experiences and trying to achieve success from prison. Books from
incarcerated authors, such as _____ can nicely rout out
a graduate curriculum injecting a needed insiders perspective.

I invite you to visit my website/blog _____ for more info on
the title including sample chapters, table of contents, testimonials and
more.
Shall I send you a desk copy? If so, to what address? Thank you in advance
for your consideration, and I look forward to discussing this further.

Sincerely,

__(Your Name Here)___

__(Your Address Here)___

_____

P.S. If you feel this proposal would be best directed to another faculty
member or department in addition to or instead of you, I'd be sincerely
grateful if you'd either pass it on or steer me in the appropriate direction.
Thank again.

Your family and friends are a great source of potential contacts. They bring their own list of contacts with them in these people. Ask yourself: how could they benefit me? Can I help them? May I need them in the long run? If you graduated from a college or university, you already have a ready-made network in the alumni club. Be active in it as much as you can from prison. Facebook allows you to connect by the school you went to. If you were in the military before you came to prison, build on that network. If you have a paralegal certificate, you can join the network of paralegal and legal assistant. If you paint, network with other painter, or join an art class or club. If you write poetry, join the creative writing class. Begin with the things you know and the people that are already in your life.

Most of us prisoners limit our contacts to a tiny social demographic. We keep company with those who are from the same hood as us, who are the same race as us. It's even worse when we factor in gang ties. We don't step out of our boundaries. A lot of this has to do with the prison microcosm of gang life, past history, and personal bias. But prison is not where we're trying to stay, so don't allow your mind to stay in prison.

Successful prisoners think outside the cell. Just remember to ask, seek, and knock. Then ye shall find. You have to ask first, or else you will never know!

An Untapped Goldmine

You can look in your local newspapers. This is the main strategy that I first wrote about in my booklet, *How to Get FREE Pen Pals*. There are numerous places to find addresses in a newspaper, but you should concentrate on four sections;

- Arrest reports or court roundup section;
- Classifieds for legal notices and real estate deals;
- Obituaries; and
- Religious sections.

I will deal with each of these sections separately so that you can see where to look, and which addresses are good or bad.

Arrest Reports

Every local newspaper lists the names of people who have been arrested. But not all newspapers list addresses. It may say: "Jane Doe, of the 1200 block of Walnut, was arrested…" in that example, they've put the block number and not the actual house or apartment number. These kinds of newspapers are no good for the arrest reports. But they still may be good for the classifieds and/or the religious sections? What you need are actual house numbers. If they say: "Jane Doe, 1218 N. Walnut, was arrested…" then you can write them knowing that your letter will be delivered to the address. (That doesn't mean you'll get a response though.)

The key to looking for addresses in the arrest reports is twofold:

- What were they arrested for?
- Is the address a house or apartment?

Here's why. If they were arrested for something major, like murder; then they are most likely still in jail and will probably never get your letter. But if they were arrested for something minor, like a traffic violation, retail theft and/or disorderly conduct, then they are probably back on the street and may get your letter. The other thing about what they are locked up for is that you can get a sense of what type of person they are. Someone arrested for drugs most likely won't write you back. After they are released, they'll go back to their drug of choice, and that's not you. My best successes have come from people arrested for traffic violations. But I have got many pen pals from other people as well.

If you're allowed to write prisoners, consider writing some of the people who are locked up in the county jail. I've had great pen pals who were locked up. Because we developed a great friendship while they were inside, they continued to write once they got out. Remember that you're locked up also. You share a common bond and can use that to build a friendship.

Now the second point, house number or apartment number? In my experience, it's better to write people in a house rather than apartments! Why? Because people tend to move more often when they live in apartments instead of a house. And in a lot of apartment buildings they have a bunch of mailboxes on the first floor. If they name on the mailbox doesn't match the name on the letter it could be returned to sender. With a house, the mail normally is just put in the mailbox or pushed through the mail slot in the door. That's been my experience as I have got more "return to sender" letters when writing apartments than houses.

There are a couple more things you can tell by the addresses themselves. First, if you are from the town of that newspaper, you can tell by the street and block numbers in the addresses what type of neighborhood it is. Even if you aren't from that town or area, someone in your prison is and can tell you about the area or street. Sometimes it's good to find out this information and then tailor your letter accordingly.

Second, a lot of newspapers will list different cities or towns in these addresses because the newspaper covers an area, not just one city. Most of the time they don't publish zip codes in the arrest reports. So you'll have to find them on your own. If they town is over 5000 people, you can find the zip code in *The World Almanac and Book of Facts*. If you can't find it in the almanac, most prison libraries have a directory where you can find zip codes for different cities in your state. Or you can have someone in the free-world look them up at: www.usps. com, under "Mail & Ship", you can select "Look up a Zip Code". You can find some zip codes for different towns in the newspaper itself. Look at the advertisements. Some companies list their full contact information. Write the city and zip code down. That will save you a lot of research later on when you start finding addresses.

One last thing about these addresses. When you look up a town in the almanac, you'll get the population. This is important. You should have more success writing people in smaller towns instead of large cities. Why? Because there is nothing to do in a small town. People are bored and you are something new to them and they have time to write.

Newspaper Classifieds

This is where you can find the personals and legal notices. But you will not find too many personal ads anymore. Most of the personal ads are now online with *Craigslist* or *Backpage.com*. Every once in a while you'll find something there. The main reason to look in the classifieds, is the legal notices. When someone opens a new business their name and address of their business is placed in a legal notice in the classified section. A lot of these will be women who work from home. Find them and write them down. Some newspapers will also have a listing of the real estate deals in the legal notices. People who are selling houses are not good addresses because they are moving or have moved. People who have bought the house are good prospect. If you see an address like that, write it down.

Another listing that I've seen is those who have filed for bankruptcy. In the *Chicago Daily Law Bulletin* they list these and in a few months I had compiled addresses from hundreds of Chicago area women. But for some of you who use pen pals for your hustle, these may not be profitable. I just wanted to give you another place to look. You could write them and ask them to help you with your business ideas. Maybe because they need money they'll help? I didn't spend my time writing these women, but I did sell these lists for $10 per 100. That was my success.

Religious Sections & Obituaries

"The church is among the more desirable sources through which one may meet and cultivate people, because it brings people together under circumstance which inspire the spirit of fellowship among people." -Andrew Carnegie

It was after reading the above quote from one of the richest men ever, that I started writing churches requesting pen pals. In every newspaper you can find the addresses of churches. Sometimes they are listed in a religious section, while other times you have to look in the obituaries for the service notices to get them. In my hometown paper, *The News-Gazette*, the religious section is printed once a week. As you find these addresses, write them down. Most prison systems get free-church channels via satellite and if you pay attention during the broadcast they will give out mail and email addresses. When you see them, write them down. You can also have someone search online for you. A good website is www.churchangel.com. On *Church Angel* you can search for church addresses by city, state, and zip code. Your prison chaplain can also supply you with a list of addresses of churches and religious organizations. As you get these addresses write one church a day asking for pen pals, prayer partners and or to place your letter and address on the prayer list or bulletin board. There's a sample letter you can steal from the next following pages.

There are many people of your faith who would be willing to help you and become members of your network. There are even websites devoted to getting single religious people together: ChristianMingle.com; BigChurch.com, and JDate.com (Jewish). If you're a Jewish prisoner, then have your family and friends check out www.lasurim.org for you. Three free websites are: ChristiaNet.com; ChristianPenPals.com; and ChristianConnectionNetwork.com. But you have to find these pen pals. Don't try and run game in your letters. You can't build a network that way.

President Obama's former church has a pen pal program. Write them and tell them you would like a pen pal. Be forewarned, you may get a male pen pal. And you write through the church. But it's still a way to get a possible pen pal. Here's the address:

Trinity United Church of Christ

Attn: Gayle – Pen Pal Program

400 W. 95th St.

Chicago, IL 60628

In the next two pages, there are twp sample letters that you can copy and send in with three FCS or Forever stamps and you may get a pen pal? I did it and they sent me three possible pen pal addresses of females in my requested age group. One was from Hawaii, one from Nebraska, and the other was a married woman in Michigan who wanted to write dirty letters and sex-texts!

I found that last one crazy because these are names and addresses were taken off the computer by Christian people who go to *Joel Osteen's Lakewood Church*. They probably aren't paying attention to what the prospective pen pals are saying online? Instead they are just printing off three or four pen pal bios in the age group you requested. There's no guarantee what you'll get, but you will get some pen pal addresses for a few stamps. It's certainly worth a try.

Letter Requesting Pen pals from Churches

> Central Christian Church
>
> Address
>
> City, State, Zip Code
>
> USA

Dear Central Christian:

I wonder if you could help me out of a little difficulty.

I am in search of a Christian who would be willing to correspond with me as a pen pal. Ever mindful of the Scriptures: "to have no fellowship with the works of darkness," my quest is imperative because all those around me want to lie, cheat, gossip, and practice many other forms of evil in this den of iniquity. My present incarceration causes me a limitation in access to those I can have inspirational, uplifting conversations with. So my search is in essence, for someone who will accept me as their brother and friend.

I understand that there will be times when I will need the value of a friend. There will also be times when I could offer kind words and prayer for others. I would love to share with others. I have tried numerous websites for prisoners to obtain pen pals, but I have been discouraged because the replies I have received have not been from the type of people I'm looking for.

If your church has a bulletin or prayer request board, would you please post my letter and photo on it? Anyone wishing to contact me may do so by writing to me at the below address.

Thank you for taking the time to consider this letter of request. May God bless you and peace be unto you.

Respectfully requested,

> S/_____

> Correctional Center
>
> Address
>
> City, State, Zip Code

Inspirational Pen pal Club

Hi,

To receive a pen pal fill in this form...

Circle your preference:

Sex: Male   Age Group: 19-22
                    Female   23-30
    31-40
    41-50
    51+

Inmates Name: _____

Inmates Number (#) _____

Mailing Address: _____

_____

_____

_____

Send $20 and this form to:

        I. P. P. C.

        P.O. Box 141696

        Austin, TX 78714

Please make copies and give to your associates, who would also like a pen pal.

Thank you,

_____

Pen Pal Success™ Story

Emmanuel "Top Flight" Grant is one of my old cellmates who was knee-deep in the pen pal game, and one of his accomplishments is legendary in Illinois prison pen pal lore. While he was in segregation, an outside volunteer, who happened to be a minister, came to speak to the guys in the prison. Emmanuel talked to him, but at the end of the talk he told the minister that he was going to forget about him just like every other volunteer that came in. The minister promised him he wouldn't. A short time later, Emmanuel received a letter from the minister and their friendship began. Our prison rules dictate that this minister would lose his "volunteer" status once he came to visit other prisoners, but the minister and his wife began visiting him regularly at the prison. They even set up a donation box in their church just for him and every once in a while they would empty the box and send him the money. The minister also has other people from the church writing him and sending him books and magazines. Now, some years later, he has a full support system in place for when he goes home. His story is proof that church going people can help prisoners. You just have to be open-minded about such things.

> "Don't wait for extraordinary opportunities. Seize common occasions and make them great. Weak men wait for opportunities; Strong men make them." -Orison Swett Marden

Becoming a Sleuth

You do not have to limit your search for addresses in the newspapers. I've used magazines where I just wrote the person "in care of" the magazine. And they got the letter and replied! One of those responses is still my pen pal today and she is a famous west coast writer and editor. I'm not telling you this to brag, but to illustrate that people are willing to write prisoners and help out. You just got to reach out and don't take no for an answer. You have to keep asking and keep writing. Never say no for the other person. Anyone can become your pen pal.

My three best (and long-term) pen pals all came from this strategy. Not off a pen pal list and not off a website. One pen pal sends me books off Amazon.com all the time. One sends me money on my birthday and Christmas. The other is my business partner and we have made thousands of dollars together. I've been writing all three for years now. Don't neglect this strategy in your quest for pen pals. When you just write someone out of the blue you are basically "cold calling" them with your letter. Back to the "sales" thing again. Let's look at this more in-depth.

Direct Mail Sales Secrets for *Pen Pal Success™*

When I first started writing people out of the newspaper that I didn't know, I couldn't understand why I had better results than any ad I placed. But as I read more about direct mail business tactics, I realized that you are marketing yourself to the possible pen pal. They either buy or sell what you have to say.

Here are 10 things to remember when writing a pen pal on your own and out of the blue:

1. You are your own master. You don't have to wait on a pen pal company to place your ad, the prison to send out the check, or anything else. Your letter goes out when and how you want it to!

2. You select the type of communication that your prospective pen pal receives. You can send an email, card, letter, gift, painting, or whatever floats your boat. It's your choice.

3. You determine who gets your letter or email. When you place an ad you have no idea who is going to see it, if anyone sees it at all. But when you write people on your own, you select who sees your missive. You're in control of the process.

4. The prospective pen pal gets what you send exactly as you give it to them. This is an extension of the last point and is key. I hate when nincompoops at online pen pal companies change my ad from the format I sent. Don't they understand that I set up the ad specifically the way I wanted it for a reason? When you're in control of the process you don't have to worry about someone else changing your ad or letter.

5. You determine the timing. You can tailor your mailing so that your prospect receives it on Valentine's Day or around Christmas. But if you're at the mercy of others, your plan for timing may go awry. I planned an online blog for my pen pal page with the headline of "FREE Christmas Gift." Needless to say, it didn't get put on till January and my headline didn't carry as much weight. You don't have to worry about this when you control the process.

6. Your prospective pen pal focuses only on your letter. Unlike a pen pal or dating website, where there are so many things going on, your letter can hold their attention. If your letter is focused on them (which it rightly should be), then they will love getting a personal letter devoted just to them. This is better than having to compete with other people for their attention.

7. You can motivate your prospective pen pal to act now! You should also do this in all of your online ads. But in a letter where you're not on a word count, you have more space to do it. Make it easy for them. If you have e-mail, tell them they can get at you that way.

8. You can send mass e-mails to many different possible pen pals. Although I don't like this approach because I detest form letters, this can help you out if your budget is low. Plus, with e-mail technology, you can make the e-mail sound personal by putting their name in the e-mail.

9. Small towns are better than large towns. Remember this when writing people out of the blue. People are bored in small towns because there isn't much to do. They need excitement and you can provide that excitement. When I say small towns, I mean under 5,000 people.

10. Give your prospective pen pal the benefits of why they should write to you. Try to give at least six of them. Make sure they are benefits and not features. Features for me are: "I'm 6'5", a lifer, poet, writer, and have blue eyes." Benefits are about the other person. They are: "You'll get a man solely devoted to sharing with you." Write your letter with this in mind. Use "You" more than "I". Just like there isn't an "I" in team, there isn't one in network or success. Always remember: benefits are more important than features.

Do these tips work? Yes. Think of how most pen pal and dating websites work. The person looking for a possible pen pal logs on to the site, then scans each entry until they find what they're looking for. Are they really focusing on what you have to say? No, they're just scanning photos and headlines for something that catches their eye. Your profile is in effect competing with everyone else on the site for one person's attention. I've always had more success by putting myself in situations where I had no competition. Writing someone on your own does this. They are reading your letter only, not looking through a bunch of ads.

One last thing. You may think that if you just write someone out of the blue they won't write back. A lot of times these people will because they've never considered writing a prisoner before. The truth is that there are a lot of lonely people out there. If you can turn your letter into a benefit-laden marketing letter selling them on what they'll get when they do write you back, you'll get responses. It's worked for me and it just might be the answer you've been searching for?

> *"I would rather sit on a pumpkin and have it all to myself than be crowded on a velvet cushion."*
> -Henry David Thoreau

Advance Direct Mail Pen Pal Strategy

To take my strategy further I did more research on direct-mail marketing. After reading numerous books on marketing by direct mail I happened to purchase Freedom Jones' book *How to Get Girls While You are in Prison*. In that great book he says that direct mail can be a strategy, albeit a "tricky one". He writes about using list brokers to compile lists of people (women) and gives an example. That's when the light bulb went off in my head. Here's my direct mail pen pal strategy based on my own research:

- Find out who your ideal pen pal is? For me, it might be "small town, mid-western women who are single and bored".

  Use a list broker (www.infousa.com or www.srds.com) to compile a list of addresses of your ideal pen pal.

- Compose an opening letter (i.e. sales letter) that you send to your prospective pen pals. For more about how to write a sales letter, get *The Ultimate Sales Letter, 4th Edition* by Dan S. Kennedy.

- Send your letter out then forget about it. You're not going to get flooded with mail by doing this. But if you know "who" your ideal pen pal is, you just might be able to target them using direct mail.

- Have a system in place for when you do get a response from this. That means capturing the pen pals imagination and showing them the benefits of corresponding with you.

If this is something you're interested in and would like to explore more, I highly recommend *The Direct Mail Solution* by Craig Simpson & Dan S. Kennedy. It's not a pen pal book, but you can utilize the strategies for getting pen pals.

Okay, that's how you can get free pen pals basically on your own with little or no outside help at first. In the next chapter, I'll show you how to write pen pal letters than get responses. Just remember this chapter, it could be worth more to you than any other tactic in this book. It has been for me.

Chapter 5
Power Through Correspondence

"There's no problem for which a great sales letter can't be the solution!" -Gary Halbert

America was started based on the Committee of Correspondence. The original thirteen colonies used letters to organize and solve the problems they faced against the British. It was through letters that the First Continental Congress was convened. These are facts that you may find in any adequate history book.

Mumia Abu-Jamal corresponded with many jailhouse lawyers across the country when he was conducting research for his book, *Jailhouse Lawyers: Prisoners Defending Prisoners V. The U.S.A.* He does not allow his confinement to stop him or his journalism and continues to network through letters.

The road to freedom for Rubin "Hurricane" Carter started with his book, *The Sixteenth Round*. Lesra Martin bought the book at a book sale for 25¢ and read it. Eventually he sent Carter a letter, which led to a friendship that birth the Hurricane's release. It all started with one letter.

Michael G. Santos, author of *About Prison*, and other books on prison, built a large support group through letters. He said he would write hundreds of letters with the hope of getting one reply. It worked. He was mentored by university professors and leading penologists all because he took the time to write letters.

I'm the same way. I try to write someone new every day the mail goes out. I have gotten lots of responses so I know that if you take the time to sit down and write letters, you'll get some responses. Not everyone will answer, but some will. All of the above examples illustrate that you can build a great network from inside the prison your currently in. Are you writing letters?

Letter Writing 101

> *"Letter writing is the only device for combining solitude with good company."* -Lord Byron

Because so much of your communication will be done through the written word, it's imperative that you learn the art of good letter writing. It is an art that can be learned by practice. Study the letters that you get in the mail already. Are they good? Bad? This chapter will help you perfect the art. As you write more letters your overall writing will get better.

Remember that you are a salesman and selling a product. You are trying to get your reader to do something, i.e. your trying to get them to buy you as a friend and pen pal. You want your letters to make the best impression possible. One way that you can do this is to use effective marketing principles to aid you in making your letters the best they can be. Advertising gurus have used the acronym AIDA for years when creating successful sales letters. AIDA stands for Attention, Interest, Desire, and Action. Here's AIDA applied to a winning pen pal letter.

1. Get the reader's Attention
2. Interest them in you or what you can do for them
3. Create a Desire for the benefits of them writing back.
4. Demand Action from them.

As you read this chapter keep in mind these four steps above and the AIDA acronym.

> *"A letter is a secretive communication; one is master of the situation, feels no pressure from anyone's actual presence, and I do believe a young girl would prefer to be alone with her ideal."* - Soren Kierkegaard, *The Seducer's Diary*

How to Write an Effective Cold Letter

When I say "cold letter" I mean a letter to someone who is not expecting it and who doesn't know you. These tips and tactics can be used when writing people you find in the *How to Get FREE Pen Pals* subsection, and when writing to people you get off pen pal lists. Responding to a pen pals letter is a little different, but you can still use the strategies throughout this book in all your other letter writing. Let's dive right in to developing an effective cold letter.

First, pay attention to how you package your envelope. Package design has become a trillion dollar industry. The reason is because companies have figured out that package designs sells products, plain and simple. So make your envelope stand out! You don't have to go overboard with some elaborate artwork, but do make it memorable in some little way. I usually put a colorful border around my envelopes and use the same color markers in a neat script to address my envelopes. A lot of my new pen pals have said they responded because they were impressed that I took the time to do that for them. Make your envelope stand out from the stack of junk mail. (Some direct mail/mail order professionals believe that a plain white envelope with handwritten addresses will pull responses. I can see the validity in that because that alone will stand out in this day's barrage of colorful junk mail. Test different strategies to see what works for you.) Here are some more tips for your envelopes:

- If enclosing a photo, always write: "Photo Enclosed! Please Do Not Bend!" on the outside of the envelope.

- Stamp it with a nice saying if your prison allows it? Younger females enjoy the "S.W.A.K." on the back flap, with means "sealed with a kiss." I've also seen "Dear Postman: If this letter is unable to be delivered as addressed, please send it to heaven because it's fit for an angel." Remember, these things should be used with younger females. (18-24 years old)

- Try to use crisp, brand new envelopes even though they may still get beat up or ripped in the mail. Save your crappy envelopes for your existing friends and family who only care about the letter or note inside.

- If you can typeset your return address and recipients address with a typewriter, try it. You need to test out different envelope tricks to see which get the best responses.

These are just a few things to remember when contemplating the envelope (package) of your outgoing letter.

Selecting the Tools of the Trade

Before you get into the actual contents of what you put into your letter, you first have to choose what tools you're going to use to craft this masterpiece. I'm speaking about the writing tool, the paper, your handwriting, and/or a typewriter. Let's look at each one of these tools.

You should use a good ink pen or thin art marker to write with. If you only have one of those crappy 4-inch flex pens that a lot of prisons sell, then take your time and make sure your letter is error free. (FYI: I'm writing this chapter with one of those "security" pens, so don't let it stop you!) No crossed out words, or ink blotches. Put your best effort into your letters and you'll be rewarded. I have seen pen pals use pencil when writing letters. To me this is kindergarten-ish! Maybe that's all you have? If it is, don't let it stop you. I just prefer a pen. I am 35 years old now.

Now, to the paper you select. Never use yellow, legal paper unless you absolutely have to. If you have to, then try and use a red ink pen, or blue pen. It will contrast nicely on the yellow paper. Instead of yellow legal paper, try and order stationary if you can. If you can't, get the best paper from the commissary that you can afford. For guys, black or dark blue ink on white, light blue, or gray paper is traditional. For women, you have a larger selection to choose from, but cream and pink paper are common. For those of you who can't get good paper, here is something you can do. Use good, heavy typing paper. Take a sheet of notebook paper and tape it to the back of the typing paper. The lines should show through. This will allow you to write straight sentences. After your done writing the letter, carefully separate the notebook paper form the typing paper. You should have a perfectly straight letter. And your possible new friend will be amazed at how you did it. Never tell them how you do it, just say you take your time.

As far as handwriting versus typewritten. I prefer handwritten letters mostly. It shows the letter writers personality and is more close to the heart and soul. A typewriter should be used for business and legal letters. But I have received letters from tech savoy college coeds that were computer generated and were aesthetic masterpieces. These young people said they were used to typing on their computer and could do it faster than a handwritten letter. So I do understand the points for both sides. Yet I still prefer a handwritten letter. With that being said, some of you just have bad handwriting. In that case, you can use some language like this in your opening letter:

> "Please excuse this letter being typed, but my handwriting is bad, and I wanted you to at least be able to read my letter."

Just remember that typed letters seem less personal and in my experience, you'll get better response from the letters your write out in longhand! Now that we have discussed the tools of the trade we can examine the "what" and "how" to writing an effective cold letter.

The Sales Pitch, i.e. Your Letters Contents

Remember that you're writing a cold letter, and it's your one chance to make your pitch. An effective cold letter does four things:

- It shares commonality;
- It stirs interest and desire;
- It develops rapport and promise benefits;
- It give the contact a choice to act.

Remember these four principles as we go along, because they are the key to getting responses. (Think about the AIDA acronym I wrote about earlier: Attention, Interest, Desire, and Action. Same thing)

First you have to know how to write a proper letter. A good letter consists of seven parts. They are:

- The Heading (name and address)
- Date
- The Salutation
- The Opening
- The Body
- The Closing
- Your Signature & P.S. (Post Script)

I will discuss each in turn as I go through our effective cold letter.

The Heading: Always put the name and address of the person you are writing at the top of the letter. This does two things. First, in case the envelope is damaged, it would still be possible for the letter to be delivered.

Second, people reading the letter know who it's supposed to go to. This is good in cases where you are writing to people who live in college dormitories, or people who live with a lot of relatives.

The Date: People want to know what day you wrote them. Show them that you are writing them the same week they're reading your letter. (Overseas will be more like two weeks.)

The Salutation: Always start your letter, "Dear [*insert their name*]". This is the universally accepted proper way to begin a letter. If you ever get the urge to try other openings like: "Dear Sweetheart" or "Hello Friend". Don't! For one, this person you're writing cold is not your friend yet, and they're definitely not your sweetheart. If the person is older, you could use: "Dear Mrs. [*insert their name*]", if you wanted to because it shows respect. Stick to those two until you get to know your contact better. If they have a specific title: "Professor", "Doctor", "Lt.", or "Colonel", make sure you use that in your salutation. For instance, "Dear Dr. [*insert their name*]," or "Dear Professor [*insert their name*]".

The Opening: What is the most used prison pen pal opening? "I hope this letter finds you in the best of health and spirits." It seems every prisoner uses this opening first line. I'm even guilty of it because I advocated using it in my *How to Get FREE Pen Pals* booklet that I sold through O'Barnett Publishing and Superior Enterprises. But during my O'Barnett days, I received so many letters from prisoners with that opening line that I have since change my thoughts on using that line. Your goal is to show that you're different from the crowd. And you can't do that when you write what every other prisoner is writing. So I don't use that line anymore.

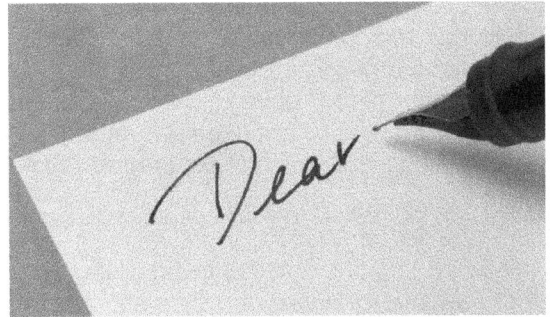

Because your opening is one of the most important parts of your letter, you want your first few lines to make people read on, lest they throw your letter away. Your opening must *compel* them to read on. Since I think we prisoners need fresh opening lines, here are some that you can adapt to fit your own letters. (These openings are taken from some of the best sales letters of all-time. Remember, you're a salesperson now.)

- "Will you do me a favor? I promise not to ask too much…"
- "Will you help me out with a little difficulty?"
- "Congratulations, you have won a …"
- "Imagine, for a moment, that it's 6 months from today…"
- "I'd like to tell you about…"
- "This letter is not like any you have ever received, or one that I have ever written…"
- "This may be the luckiest day of your life! You are the only person to receive this letter…"
- "Please excuse my audacity, but I'm willing to bet that your life can be more exciting than it is right now…"
- "If you are satisfied with your life, or have it all, then you need not go further into this letter…"
- "I'm excited about something very important that I want to share with you immediately. Please take a few minutes to read it now."
"Allow me to introduce myself. My name is _____. Chances are you haven't heard of me before, but when you finish reading this, you'll be glad you did."

- "I've got to get this off my chest before I explode..."

- "You've got enough people trying to waste your time with things you don't really want or need. I'm not one of those people..."

- "First, there are brief questions – If I may?"

Maybe some of these openers will spark your creativity and allow you to challenge the status quo of "I hope this letter finds you in the best of health and spirits..."

After the opening line or paragraph, I like to use the following:

"I know it may come as a shock to receive a letter out of the blue from someone you don't know, but I hope you will allow me to take up a few minutes of your time so that I can explain who I am and why I'm writing you."

This sentence does a couple of things. It gets the reader to agree with you because it is a shock for someone to receive a letter from a prisoner they don't know. Then it states a time frame, "a few minutes." People value their time and don't want to read a 12-page cold letter. Depending on where you got the address from, your prospect may be getting a lot of mail. Plus, you are probably in competition with all their other free world activities and responsibilities. So keep your initial cold letter short and to the point. (If you got their name off a pen pal list or you're responding to an ad they placed, you should not use the above line. Why? Because they are expecting mail from people they don't know!)

After you've mastered your opening you can move onto the next part.

The Body: This is where you begin to show commonality. There are several factors to this. People like those that they share a bond with. It may be that they share friends, experiences, problems or where they live. (Think about the popularity of Facebook and other social networking sites.) But as a prisoner, you're invading someone else's home when you write them a cold letter. To get over the bias that humans have about unsolicited mail, you have to show commonality. How you do this depends on where and how you got your prospective pen pal's address. If you got their address from a fellow prisoner then you could use the paragraph that I've used for years when writing people out-of-the-blue. It works for both:

"My name is _____, and I received your name and address from _____. He thought you would be open to corresponding with me?"

You introduced yourself and told them how you got their information. Of course if you got their info out of a newspaper or magazine, then you didn't get it from another prisoner. In that case use "John". Why John? Because almost everyone knows a John! Would you rather tell them that you got their name out of a newspaper? Using this line has gotten me responses like, "who is John, what's his last name, and how did he say he knew me?" Curiosity killed the cat. I'll simply tell them that John lives in another cell house, but when I see him I'll get his last name and ask how he got the info? Then I never mention John again. You can certainly tell the truth, but then you may sound like a creep. Not good. Stick to the John line or a variation of it, and you'll be surprised at how many responses you get.

Next, you should write a line or two to explain what you're after. I've used the following:

"I'm in search of a pen pal who would not mind writing and develop a friendship."

It's always best to assume a harmless front, and you've just explained your angle. Of course they already knew you had one, but "writing and developing a friendship" is a lot better than "develop a long-term relationship", or getting "a cougar". It's easier to move from friendship to matters of love in the future. But if you come across aiming for something more than friendship, you'll not get as many response as you would like. Sometimes, the specific ad that you are answering may dictate that you say you're open to a relationship, but most of the time, just say you're looking for friendship. You can always write this:

"I'm looking for friendship, maybe something more if the stars align?"

Some people will stop reading your letter right there and throw it away. That's ok, because the pen pal game is a numbers game. The more people you write and the more ads you answer, the better chance you have of getting replies. I normally write a letter to someone new and then forget about it (or try to) after I send it out. I've already moved on to the next prospect in my mind, or I'm back to working on one of my book projects. If they write back then it's a blessing. If not, who were they?

Back to my opening letter. I like to continue on with the friendship theme with the next line:

"I also believe that true friendships should be built on trust, respect, honesty, appreciation, sincerity, and attention."

Here you have just written numerous principles that should be in every friendship. Not only do you tell them these things, but if they write back, make these principles a part of your friendship. The goal is not to see how many responses you get, but to build real and lasting friendships. Since you wrote the word "honesty" in the above line, you can throw in this line:

"Because I believe in being honest up front, feel free to ask any questions you may have for me, okay? No topic is taboo either!"

You have just given them permission to ask you anything. This is key, because it removes all barriers, and opens up your side of the correspondence. It expressed that you have nothing to hide, and that is good.

Then you can transition to your photo (you have one, right?) with something like:

"I have enclosed a photo of myself so that you can see the face behind my words. You can keep it, and hopefully I'll have some better pictures available for you in the future."

There will be more about photos later, but it will help you get responses if you have a good one to send.

After the photo line, I normally use a few short sentences to explain my interest. There is no need to go in-depth about yourself in this letter. Should you get a response, there will be plenty of time to discuss your interests. There is no perfect way to express your interests. Everyone has different likes. Here are some guidelines to remember when talking about your interests:

1. Be Specific: Don't say, "I like to paint, watch sports, and listen to music." Say you like to "paint watercolors, watch college football, and listen to classic rock-n-roll." Don't use general, stale words.

2. Be Brief: Your first opening letter should be used to get a response. The more you say about yourself, the more risk there is that you won't get a response. The only reason why you are putting in your interest is to humanize yourself.

3. Never Complain: Do not say what you dislike or make any negative comments. Be positive and you'll get responses. Remember that people in the free world have a myriad of problems and responsibilities, they really don't need or want to hear about yours. Especially not in the first letter.

After stating my interests, I wrap the paragraph up with something like the following:

"I love to write letters and meet new people, and I really hope we can connect and become great friends. I don't think we can have too many of those, do you?"

Once again you are reiterating your aim and asking a question. We hope that they answer in the affirmative again.

So far your letter has stirred interest, maybe desire, and you have developed rapport with your reader by strategically placed questions that get a "yes" answer. Now, with a letter to someone you don't know who didn't place a pen pal ad, you have to promise benefits. Some prisoners try and run game about money or their lavish lifestyle on the streets, but that is a superficial way of seducing. If you're a man writing a woman, remember that they are ruled by their emotions, more so than fancy toys or what the eyes can see. Men are the exact opposite. Knowing this, I use a paragraph that promises emotional benefits and safety for any reader. Here is what I say:

> "[*insert their name*], nothing in life is guaranteed, but should you consider becoming my pen friend, here are some things I promise to be for you: someone you can come to for comfort, eyes you can look into and trust; a heart that understands and doesn't judge; a supporting shoulder to cry on; a prompt reply to all your letters and time devoted to you and you alone. If this sounds like something you'd be interested in, then don't hesitate to write back."

You start the paragraph off with their name, because it's the launching pad into your spiel. Everyone loves hearing their name called. It's reassuring and calming. Then you go into the benefits of a friendship with you. All of them are what a woman desires in a relationship and should produce a desired effect on her. If she is not getting these from her current friendships and relationships, she will want to have them. And you can be the answer to her problems. Understand: if they don't have needs or problems you won't reach them anyway. You are in the problem solving business. Your letters are an escape. Always remember that.

For someone's ad that you are answering you want to comment on what they put in their ad. They put it in there because it's important to them. Show that you have some common interest. Ask them questions about their likes. Ask them what they are looking for in their life or from their pen pals? They placed an ad so they are looking for something specific. Find out what it is so you can decide if you are that person.

The Closing: Now is the time to end your letter and give them a choice. First, clear up any possibility that your letter has been misconstrued with the following line:

> "If I have offended you in any way by writing this letter, or by something I've said, that was not my intention and I offer my most sincere apology. My only intention was, and is, to gain a friend."

I have actually had my new friends say that they were not offended by my letter and they wouldn't mind having me as a friend. Next, close your letter with the following:

> "Thank you in advance for taking the time to consider my letter and photo. I look forward to hearing from you soon. If you are not interested in corresponding with me, but know someone who might be, please pass my letter and photo on to them. No matter what you choose, I hope that you and your loved ones are blessed this year."

Here you thank them for taking the time out of their day to read your letter and tell them that you look forward to hearing from them. Then you give them a choice: they can write you or give your letter and photo to someone else. Not everyone you write will have the time to write you back. Others will be in a relationship or married, and not want to write a prisoner. But because you have been respectful and given them a choice, they may pass your letter on to a friend. I have gotten quite a few replies because of my request that they pass my letter on to someone else.

Your Signature and Post-Script (P.S.): There are two that work for the opening letter. I use "Your new friend," then I sign my name and print my correct mailing address underneath my signature. You can also use "Sincerely." Stick to these simple sign-offs until you get to know the new friend better. For those of you who would like to see some more closings here are some:

- Peace
- Cordially
- Best Wishes
- Yours Truly
- Forever
- Warmly
- Waiting for Your Answer
- Best Regards
- Your Personal Casanova
- Faithfully Yours
- Respectfully Yours
- Love Ya
- Thanks
- Write Back Soon

Here are some more last lines you can use in your letters:

- Please don't let silence be your response,

- To find out more about me, please put pen to paper,

- Be sure to check out my (blog, profile, and/or website) at _____,

- I'll write more later, as always,

- You're a true friend and I'm grateful to have you in my life,

- I just want you to know that you're special,

- Thanks for everything you do that makes you such a special friend,

- If there's anything I can do, just let me know,

- In the meantime, take care _____ ,

- Keep your head up,

- Always & Forever,

- For now, as always, I remain,

- Amor,

- I'll be thinking of you,

You don't have to use a post-script (P.S.), but I like to. It gives me one last opportunity to show my personality. What I use is:

"P.S. I love quotes, and here is one from my favorite poet, Lord Byron – "Woman are the rainbows in the storms of life." Unfortunately for me, I haven't found my rainbow yet."

If you decide to use "P.S." for quotes or something else, make sure it's memorable and fits your personality. It's the last thing they'll read. Here is how my formula cold letter might look in its completed form:

Letter to a Possible Pen Pal

Dear (*insert their name*):

I hope this letter finds you in the best of health and spirits. I know it may come as a shock to you to receive a letter from someone you don't know, but I hope you will allow me to take up a few minutes of your time so that I can explain who I am and why I'm writing you.

My name is _____ and I received your name and address from John. He thought you might be open to corresponding with me? I'm in search of a pen pal who would not mind writing and developing a friendship. Someone once said that a stranger is just a friend you have not met yet. I believe that is true, do you? I also believe that true friendships should be built on trust, respect, honesty, appreciation, sincerity, and attention. Because I believe in honesty up front, feel free to ask any questions you may have for me, okay? No topic is taboo either!

I have enclosed a photo of myself so that you can see the face behind my words. You can keep it, and hopefully I will have some better pictures available for you in the future.

(*Put your interests here*)

I love to write letters and meet new people, and I really hope we can connect and become great friends. I don't think we can have too many of those, do you?

(put their name), nothing in life is guaranteed, but should you consider becoming my pen-friend, here are some things I can promise to be for you: Someone you can come to for comfort; eyes you can look into and trust; a heart that understands and doesn't judge; a supporting shoulder to cry on; a door that is always open; and time devoted to you alone. If this sounds like something you'd be interested in then don't hesitate to write back. If I have offended you in anyway by writing this letter, or by something I've said, that was not my intention, and I offer my most sincere apology. MY only intention was, and is, to gain a friend.

Thank you in advance for taking the time to consider my letter and photo. I look forward to hearing from you soon. If you are not interested in corresponding with me, but know someone who might be, please pass my letter and photo on to them. No matter what you choose, I hope that you are blessed this year.

Your new friend,

S/_____

(*Your address*)

P.S. I love quotes. Here's one from my favorite poet, Lord Byron:

"Women are the rainbows in the storms of life."

30 Tips for Successful Letter Writing

Most of you have grand visions of writing letters and getting your named called every day when they pass out mail. But not many can say that you have accomplished it. While the free world has embraced technology to communicate, most of us must still use snail mail. With this in mind, here are some guidelines to remember when writing your letters. I've learned there's rules over my 15 plus years behind bars writing pen pals and networking through snail mail. (Even if you have access to email, these tips will help you in your communication.)

1. Never write a one-page personal letter. At least make it go to the next page. This means using the front and back of two pieces of paper. Business letters and most emails can be only one page. As your friendship increases you can expand the number of pages in your letters. Ask you pen pal if they like long or short letters? In their special report, "How to Write Letters to Women," Moonlite Productions (P.O. Box 1304, Miami, FL 33265) said that you should keep your letters about the same length as hers, or a half-page more than hers. I like that idea because it shows her that you're putting in an effort to build something with her. Just remember, one page is not enough unless you are intentionally using it as a stratagem. (More on that in future chapters.)

2. Write legibly and neat. I had a friend who wrote long letters and had practiced his handwriting so much that it looked like fancy script or calligraphy. The problem? You had to strain to read his letters. He asked me why he didn't get that many responses and I looked at his letters and determined it was his handwriting. It was too fancy. Your handwriting shows your personality, but it must be able to be read. Practice making it neat.

3. Try to end your pages in the middle of the sentence. This makes the reader turn the page to keep reading. I learned this from direct mail sales letters. It's a psychological trick that helps keep your reader into the actual physical aspect of reading.

4. Use language that invokes emotions. Not cold, dead, stale words. Be personable and friendly, not business or legal. Here are some examples:

Unfriendly	Personable
Your letter at hand	I have your letter
I shall advice you	I'll let you know
As per your letter	According to your letter
And oblige	Thank you
Owing to the fact that	Because
At an early date	Soon
At the present writing	Now
In re matter of	Regarding

5. Know the meaning of the words you use. Look them up in your dictionary to make sure they are the right ones. But don't try and use big, convoluted words. Write like you talk so you'll be understood.

   "The difference between the right word and the almost right word is the difference between lightening and the lightening bug." -Mark Twain

6. Always check grammar and punctuation. Get it right. This is where your dictionary comes in again. A good one explains these two important topics. I use Merriam-Webster's Collegiate Dictionary.

7. Remember to use the correct color paper, ink and envelopes for your age and gender. If you are a 30-year old male, you should not use "Hello Kitty" stickers on your envelopes!

8. Be positive, funny and entertaining in your letters. Make it a joy to read your letters. Just be careful with humor and jokes because some people will take them the wrong way.

9. Try and keep your letters to one main theme, two at the most. Most people will be able to process only one central idea in a reading anyway. So if you spend most of your letter answering questions your pen pal has asked, leave it at that. If you have more to talk about, write another letter. They love getting two letters in the mail on the same day!

10. Give your pen pal tips that add value to their life. It should be something they can use immediately to improve their life or situation.

11. Send newspaper and magazine articles that may be of interest to your readers. You can also use these as sources when trying to make a point to your reader.

12. Poke fun at yourself by using self-deprecating humor. Try to do it by using stories and don't make it seem like you got low self-esteem. Like any humor, don't overdo it.

13. Never forget to send cards on birthdays and holidays. Preferably homemade ones because they mean more. (I'll have more to say about this later.)

14. Avoid using abbreviations and slang because they can be misunderstood. Unless you are 100% sure your pen pal will understand. To be safe, don't do it.

15. Never write or send a form letter. Make your letters unique. Tailor it to the person you're writing. My "formula cold letter" should only be used as a guideline, not copied word for word.

16. Ask open-ended questions that encourage your reader to answer with more than just a "yes" or "no". (See "Getting to Know Your Pen Pal" in Part 3 of this book.)

17. Do not write about your extra or other pen pals unless you are asked about them. It's common that pen pals are writing more than one person, but no one needs to hear about your other conquests. (Unless you're writing a book like this.)

18. Use stories and analogies to make a point. The more you tell the more you sell. And stories are the key to getting pen pals to see your point of view.

19. Don't discuss all of your problems, your pen pal is not your psychiatrist. They want you to help them with their problems. Once you do that, then they'll hear and help you with yours.

20. Never send a letter written in anger. Wait until the next day to reread it. You'll be glad you never sent it.

21. Don't talk about sex, unless your pen pal brings it up or asks. The one exception is if you answer a Hedonistic or Swingers personal ad. Hey, whatever floats your boat? (See "Matters of Sex" later in this book for more.)

22. Avoid excessive talk about religion, unless you're writing your pastor or religious leader. The one exception is if you got your pen pal from a religious website or pen pal list. Then it's natural to write about it. Just don't do it excessively. Religion isn't everything!

23. Don't sound narcissistic when writing about your looks or body. It's better to just send a photo and let it do the talking.

24. Be accurate in what you say. Make certain that what you write is absolutely true. Try and be fair

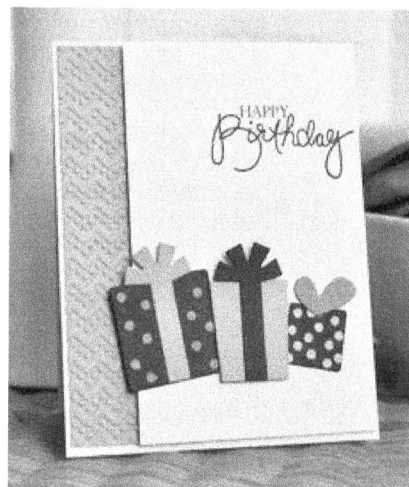

and not biased. It's better to be known for telling the truth than embellishing.

25. Don't douse your letters and envelopes with cologne or perfume. Less is more. If you already wear it, then it will naturally come off on your letter when you write. That's enough.

26. Don't gossip about the other people in your life. I wrote about this in my first book, The Millionaire Prisoner, but it applies to your letters as well. We don't trust gossips! So don't gossip.

27. Never end your letter with bad news. Begin with the negative and always end on a positive note.

28. Keep your P.S. short if you use one. Three lines at the most, preferably less. Anything more than that and you probably should have wrote it in the body of your letter.

29. To spice your letter up, end it with a quote from a famous person that fits the theme of your letter. (See my "formula cold letter" for an example.)

30. Lastly, don't rush things. Take your time and your pen pal friendships will develop naturally.

Hopefully these tips will help you out with the letters you write to your pen pals. You can also learn from others by reading their letters looking for not only what they say, but also *how* they say things. What little tricks do they use? Find them and use them for yourself in your own letters. One last very important tip. In his classic book, *Writing to Communicate*, Carl Gueller said it best: "Never put down in a letter to one person something you wouldn't want shown to plenty of other people as well." Remember that.

Envelope Tips

Here are some things that the United States Postal Service wishes you knew!

Mail is delivered to the address appearing on the line immediately above the city and state. And the zip code must match that address.

- Apartment numbers go on the same line as the address, or on the line above the address, like this:

  1218 N. Walnut, Apt. 3B *or* Apt. 3B, 1218 N. Walnut

- USPS uses automated optical character readers (OCRs) i.e. "computers" and prefers that you use BLOCK LETTERS when addressing the envelope.

Just remember these three envelope tips should help you cut down on the return to sender letters that you may receive.

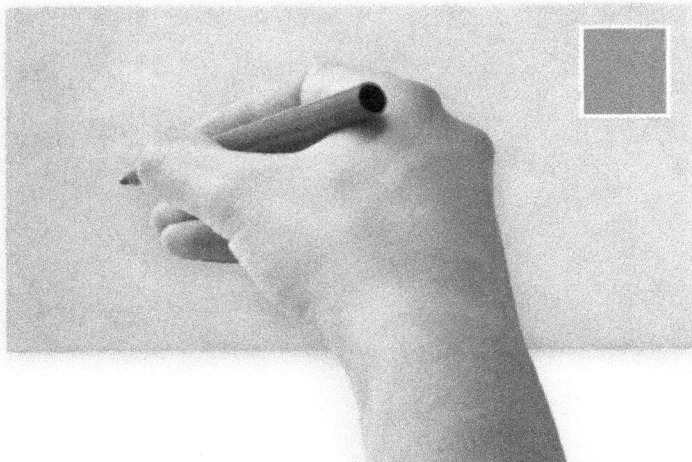

Resource Box

In case you feel that I have not given you enough ammo to become an effective letter writer, here are some more books that can help you out:

- *The Art of the Personal Letter: A Guide to Connecting Through the Written Word* by Margaret Shepherd;

- *500 Letters for Difficult Situations: Easy-to-Use Templates for Challenging Communications* by C. Sandler and J. Keefe;

- *How to Write First-Class Letters* by L. Sue Baugh;

- *Everyday Letters for Busy People* by Debra Hart May

- *The Art and Power of Letter Writing for Prisoners* by Mike Enemigo

---

A Few Final Words

Begin to develop your network from your cell. The rest of this book can supply the information needed to cultivate and maintain your pen pals. The prison walls and fences are not permanent obstacles. You can, and you will, get over them by the power of corresponding with your network.

One last gem. Who is the greatest networking prisoner of all time? I submit that Saint Paul is. In a time with no modern post office or email, he built a network using only his epistles (or letters). His network still stands to this day. Don't neglect the power of a personal letter. Successful prisoners work on their network every day.

"The richest people in the world look for and build networks; everyone else looks for work." -Robert T. Kiyosaki

Chapter 6
Writing Your Profile and Ads

"Advertising doesn't automatically work. There's a lot of competition out there."
-Ted Nicholas

To achieve pen pal success you have to use multiple ways of getting pen pals. You have already learned a few avenues in the previous chapter, but another strategy is to place your own ads and answer other people's ads. This chapter will teach you how to do both. First, let me teach you how to decipher the personal ad codes. Doing so will help you immensely on your journey.

Speaking the Lingo

In many classified and pen pal ads, you'll find confusing letters and codes. They are used because space is at a premium. The less words used, the better. If you're a beginner to the personal ad, pen pal game then it can be hard to decipher the meaning behind these abbreviations. This chapter will help you out.

Normally, the first letter used is always used to signify marital status: S = Single. The second letter is used for race: SB=Single, Black. The third letter is used for gender: SBF = Single, Black, Female. Sometimes the advertiser will list their religion? If they do, its listed second and race and gender go after that: SCBF = Single, Christian, Black, Female. With these basic rules in mind, here's what all the abbreviations mean.

21+: Legal Age Adult

BB: Body Builder

BBFN: Bye-Bye For Now

BBW: Big Beautiful Women

BD: Bondage/Domination

BF: Boyfriend

BL: Blue

BLD: Blond

BRD: Beard

BRN: Brown

CHUB: Overweight

CLN: Clean

Closet: Hiding Ones Sexual Pref.

CPL: Couple

CUT: Circumcised

D & S: Dominance & Submission

D/DF: Disease/Drug Free

DAD: Daddy

DD: Dildos

DF: Drug Free

Dis: Discreet

DK: Dark

DOB: Date of Birth

Docile: Submissive

Dom: Dominate Male

DOMME: Dominate Female

DSB: Disabled

EDUC: Educated

EMS: Email Soon

EX: Exhibitionist

FA: Fat Acceptance

FB: Friendship Book

FCS: First Class Stamp

FEM: Feminine

FR: French Passive

FS: Financially Secure

G/P: Greek Passive

GC: Gay Couple

GL: Good Looking

GR: Greek

GS: Golden Showers

GSOH: Good Sense of Humor

HE: Holiday Exchange

HWP: Height Weight Proportional

IPT: Is Partial To

IRC: International Reply Coupon

IRL: In Real Life

ISO: In Search Of

JO: Jack Off

Jock: Athlete

LD: Light Drinker

LDR: Long Distance Relationship

LKG: Looking

LL: Long Letter or Levi Leather

LLO: Long Letter Only

LLP: Long Letter Pals

LOL: Laugh Out Loud

LS: Light Smoker

LSASE: Large Self-Address Stamped Envelope

LTR: Long Term Relationship

M/S: Master/Slave

Masl: Masculine

MC: Married Couple

MM: Marriage Minded

MMA: Mixed Martial Arts

Musl: Muscular

NND: No Drugs

ND: Non-Drinker

NK: No Kids

NNPP: No New Pen Pals

No Chains: No Chain Letters

NPW: New Pals Wanted

NS: Non-Smoker

ORL: Oral

P: Professional

PC: Post Card

ROFL: Rolling on the Floor Laughing

ROMAN: Group Activities

S/ACT: Straight Acting

SD: Social Drinker

SI: Similar Interest

SKS: Seeks

SLV: Slave

SM: Sadomasochism

SNNP: Sorry No New Pals

SOH: Sense of Humor

SUB: Submissive

SWA: Swaps with All

T/C: Take Care

TOP: Greek Active

TTYL: Talk To You Later

UC: Uncut

V: Voyeur

VGL: Very Good Looking

VID: Video

VP: View Card (Postcard)

W/B: Write Back

W/O: With Out

W/W: Worldwide

W4W: Women for Women

WAA: Will Answer All

WBS: Write Back Soon

WBSP: Write Back Soon Please

WS: Water Sports

X: Extreme

XXX: Adult-X-Rated

Y: You/Your

YNG: Young

YO: Years Old

Typically, the person writing the ad lists their bio first: SWM, 34, 6'5", 185, BRN, BLUE, writer, likes WS, movies… Hair color is always first, then eye color next. After the writer's bio, the advertiser usually lists what they are looking for: ISO SWF, 21+, w/SI. So his ad might say:

SWM, 34, 6'5", 185, BRN, BLU, WRITER, Likes WS, movies, LKG 4 SWF, 21+, w/SI. Write to me at: P.O. Box XXX, Catlin, IL. 61817.

This ad means that a single white male, age 34, 6 feet 5 inches tall, 185 pounds, brown hair, blue eyes, who is a writer and likes water sports, and movies, is in search of a single, white female, of good legal age with similar interests. Now that you know how to decode the ads, let's get you up to speed on how to write an effective ad.

Writing Your Own Ad and Profile

Now that you know how to read a personal ad, it's time to start writing your own. But just because everyone else writes their ads the way I described earlier, doesn't mean you have to or even should do so. The goal is to write a successful ad or profile (one that generates responses). Everyone's successful profile should consist of four parts:

- A killer headline or opening sentence that stops them in their tracks

- A description of the advertiser

- What/Who you're looking for

- How to contact you

Let's look at each one of these parts more in-depth.

A Killer Headline or Opening Sentence

Why is this so important? Because you're in competition with everyone else seeking pen pals. If your using an online pen pal site, that means hundreds (if not thousands) of people and ads. If your using a magazine or newspaper, that means hundreds of other ads, articles, and visual distractions. To get your ad or profile to stand out you must use a killer headline *targeted for your ideal prospective pen pal in combination with a nice photo*. I'll deal with photos later, but you must have an eye-stopping headline or opening sentence.

The key to a killer headline or opening sentence is that it's about *them*, not you. Did you do the Pen Pal Growth Plan™ in chapter 3? If so, then you know *who* your ideal "them" are. Write a headline for them. Is your ideal pen pal a Christian? Then write a headline with a Christian theme. Is your ideal pen pal a business woman? Then write a headline with a business theme. As you can see, you must first know who your ideal pen pal is before you can write for them. This is marketing 101. You have to tailor your ad/profile to fit your ideal pen pal's hopes, dreams, wants, and needs. By tailoring your headline or opening sentence to you ideal pen pal, you'll get them to read on. Here's what you're trying to accomplish:

You want your prospect to stop at your ad/profile,

You want your prospect to read your ad/profile,

You want your prospect to contact you after reading your ad/profile

So you can see why getting them to stop at your ad/profile is the first and most important thing on the above steps. If they don't stop at your ad/profile, they can't read it. Some of you may be thinking that you are going to write and ad/profile that reaches "everyone". But there is no such ad. If you try and write for everyone, you'll target no one. Let me share a fishing analogy that illustrates what I'm talking about.

As a kid I used to go fishing a lot. Mostly in rivers, ponds and lakes around my small hometown. There were many types of fish in these waterways and I had to use different types of bait for each fish. For instance, if I was at the dam fishing for catfish, I would use cut up shad with a stink bat coating. I'd throw that out into the river at the bottom of the dam. But that wouldn't work for bass. For them, I'd use a shiny lure or fake frog and have to keep tossing it out and slowly reeling it in. For bluegill or crappy, I could use a regular worm and bobber and just wait on them to bite. I could go on and on about different types of bait for the different types of fish. But it's the same in the pen pal game. You are "fishing" for pen pals and your ad/profile (or letter) is the "bait." You have to ask yourself if your bait is the right one for your fish? (Ideal pen pal) To be successful you must tailor your bait to your target's preference!

There are different types of headlines, but my favorite is the question. I like these types of headlines because if used right you can get the prospective pen pal involved and saying "yes" before they even read your ad/profile. For years I have used this question as my opening sentence:

> "Are you tired of the same old personal ads and lies? Or guys who are lacking honesty, sincerity and respect?"

It's really two questions and I'm going to start experimenting by changing it up. Maybe switch it around?

> "Are you tired of guys who lack honesty, sincerity and respect? Or the same old personal ads and lies?"

Or just go with one question not two? To become really successful you have to test different headlines to see what really works. Here are some other question-type headlines to help you:

> Are you still single?

> Wish you had a faithful man?

I like questions, but here is another way to use the question/headline. Direct response marketers have been using this technique for years. It's the tactic of getting permission to sell by asking a question. I learned this from the great marketing guru *Dan S. Kennedy*. In our pen pal context it could be something like this:

> "If I could show you how to get more pen pals than you ever had in your entire life, would you be interested in knowing more about it?"

If you use this strategy then you have to follow up and show them what you're saying you can do or you'll lose them.

There are other types of headlines. I used a direct one like "Tall, Rich and Lonely." It worked, I just got gold diggers who were broke and thought I could help them. That wasn't what I was looking for. Another headline I like is the "warning" one. It might be:

> "Warning for Single Mothers" or "Warning for Divorced Baby Boomers"

See how it's targeted to a specific group of people. All your headlines or opening sentences should be targeted as well. Before I leave the topic of headlines I want to give you some questions you can ask yourself about the opening sentence you've wrote:

> Does my headline motivate them to read further?

> Is my headline interesting and action-orientated?

> Am I talking specifically to my ideal pen pal?

> Is it speaking about a benefit my ideal pen pal wants? Needs?

Try to write out as many different headlines as you can. Study the ads you see in magazines and newspapers. Write down the headlines you like. Try and use them. Use other peoples opening sentences. For instance, here's one I'll use after I reworded it to fit myself:

> "Tall, Skinny, White Guy Seeks Big Gal!"

Maybe I'll run that on BigBeautifulWomen.com? Or run this next one on BlackPlanet.com?

> "Tall, Skinny, White Guy Seeks Big Black Gal!"

That's why you come up with multiple ideas for headlines that you can tailor to your ideal pen pal. After you come up with your headline or opening line, you must tie it all together by writing the description of yourself.

The Description of the Advertiser

This is the main part of your ad/profile. The key to a winning profile is to have a positive upbeat ad that is tied into the headline. To start out, just write down all the words that describe you and your interests. To help you out in doing this you can use the word bank I've included. In this first draft do not worry about word count. Just use as many of the words that describe you. This word bank is not an exhaustive list. If you want more words you can use, check out *Roget's Super Thesaurus* by Marc McCutcheon or *Words That Sell* by Richard Bayan.

Word Bank – A Few to Steal

Appearance

Adorable	Agile	Angelic
Athletic	Attractive	Appealing
A spare tire	Average build	Average looks
Bearded	Beautiful	Big and beautiful
Balding	Brawny	Better-than-average
Big, beautiful woman	Busty	Buxom
Curvaceous	Chubby and cute	Comely
Classy	Casual	Colossal
Clean-cut	Chiseled	Cowboy
Debonair	Dandy	Exquisite
Elfin	Full-figured	Fit
Firm	Folically-challenged	Fashionable
Full-length	Full-bodied	Fancy
Good-looking	Gorgeous	Glamorous
Husky	Healthy	Handsome
Honey-eyed	Immaculate	Impeccable
In blue jeans	In tuxedo	In lace
In sequins	Juicy	Knight in shining armor
Knight in rusted armor	Knightmare	Lanky
Lustrous	Luscious	Luxurious
Medium build	Muscular	Mustached
Matronly	Motherly	Militaristic
Nice-looking	Neat	Petite
Properly proportioned	Pretty	Preppie
Rugged	Rubenesque	Sexy
Slim	Slender	Skinny
Solid	Stocky	Shapely
Statuesque	Southern-belle	Six pack short of a keg
Stylish	Tiny	Tall
Trim	Teddy bear type	Tomboy
Tweedy	Voluptuous	Visual delight
Weight-proportional	Well-groomed	Yuppie

Attitudes

Adaptable	Aristocratic	Avant-garde
Apollonian	Balanced	Business owner
Conservative	Children oaky	Career oriented

Considerate	Compassionate	Capitalistic
Cautious	Church-going	College educated
Cultured	Dependable	Environmentalist
Eastern philosophy	Entrepreneur	Ethical
Friends	Family-oriented	Faithful
Folksy	Generous	Growth-oriented
Heath conscious	Heathen	High-class
Independent	Liberal	Moral
New aged	Non-judgmental	Non-religious
Open-minded	Old-fashionable	Philosophical
Politically aware	Responsible	Traditional
Well-read		

Character

Adventurous	Assertive	Abrasive
Aggressive	Amorous	Animated
Attentive	Bashful	Barbaric
Brazen	Bubbly	Carefree
Cocky	Confident	Candid
Comical	Classical	Cheeky
Cantankerous	Creative	Dreamer
Daring	Down-to-earth	Easy going
Extraverted	Energetic	Enthusiastic
Extreme	Explicit	Expressive
Exuberant	Fun-loving	Fun to be with
Fearless	Funny	Finicky
Fresh	Frank	Good listener
Good-natured	Gregarious	Habitual
High-spirited	Hot-blooded	Humble
Happy	Humorous	Introverted
Joker	Jolly	Kind
Kind-hearted	Lighthearted	Loco
Liberated	Mischievous	Mover and shaker
Normal	Nutty	Over-achiever
Outrages	Outgoing	Optimistic
Playful	Perky	Passionate
Romantic	Rogue	Rascal
Rake	Smile easily	Silly
Sensuous	Successful	Spontaneous
Unique	Unusual	Warmhearted

Interests

Animals	Anarchy	Arts & crafts
Amusement parks	Antiques	Art galleries
Auctions	Astrology	Baseball
Bicycling	Beaches	Boating
Bowling	Baking	Ballet

Camping	Cars	Country western
Comic books	Children	Community service
Cooking	Computers	Concerts
Church	Collecting stamps/coins	Country drives
Dancing	Dog races	DVDs
Friends	Favorite team	Flea markets
Festivals	Family	Fishing
Graphic novels	Gardening	Golf
History	Hip-hop	Hiking
Jogging	Jazz	Marathons
Museums	Musicals	Movies
Mythology	Numerology	Night clubs
Nature	Nascar	New age
Networking	Oldies opera	Outdoors
Parks	Picnics	P90X
Politics	Philosophy	Painting
Paranormal	Poetry	Racquetball
Running	Rap	Rock-N-Roll
Reading	Roller coasters	Rodeos
R&B music	Skinny-dipping	Softball
Symphony	Sports	Spectator sports
Snow skiing	Swimming	Sailing
Tennis	Travel	Triathlons
Top 40's	Time alone	TV
Theatre	UFOs	Video games
Volleyball	Walking	Water sports
Working out	Wine lover	

After you've written down as many words that best describe you, get out your dictionary and see which words mean the same thing or are synonyms. I have been called slim, skinny, slender, thin and gaunt. But they all have different meanings and sound different. "Tall and slim" sounds better than "Tall and skinny" or "Tall and gaunt".

They also have different connotations. Go through your word list and get rid of similar words and choose the words that best describe you. But *do not lie* about your looks, characteristics or interests.

Once you have your key words that describe you then you can begin to form sentences that describe you. The easiest way to do this is write "I am a _____, _____, _____, _____, _____ and _____ guy." Then fill in the blanks with some of your keywords. Pay particular attention to how the words sound and how you group them together. You want them to flow and roll off your tongue when you say them out loud.

You also want to write about your interest. You can use the following sentence:

"I like to _____, _____ and _____." or "I spend my time _____, _____, _____ and _____."

Remember to be specific and not use general statements. If you wrote down "watching TV" then list what your favorite TV shows are. One of my pen pals responded because I said my favorite TV show was ESPN SportsCenter. It was hers also! Those are the types of responses you get when you are specific about your interests. Next, you can work on the description of what you're looking for.

What You're Looking For?

This is a little easier than everything else so far. If you did your own Pen Pal Growth Plan™ then you know who your idea pen pal is. You can now tailor your closing to fit this. Here are some words to help you do this:

Affection	Attention	Adventure
Appreciation	Back rubs	Best friends
Business partnership	Companionship	Co-eds
Correspondence	Cohabitant	Children
Eroticism	Escapades	Email pals
Family life	Fantasy	Friendship first
Friends w/ benefits	Fun	Harmonious relationship
Hugs	Kinky sex	Kisses
Laughter	Love	Long-term relationship
Meaningful relationship	Marriage	Necking
Pen pals	Patrimony	Quiet-time together
Quality time	Romance	Share life's finest
Smooching	Swingers	Soulmates
Tickling	Tryst	Whatever's clever
Wine and dining		

A couple of sentences at most is best for this part. Just do not be too discriminatory when doing this part of your ad/profile. And don't be negative unless there is no compromise in your standards. "No smokers please…" "No inmates please…" are some of the two most popular qualifications I see in women's ads. Just remember to tie this part of your ad into the whole concept of your ad/profile…and of course, tailored to fit your ideal pen pal.

How to Contact You

This mainly depends on what medium or website you're using to advertise. Online? Then use something like this:

> "If this sounds like something you're interested in, then send me an email so we can connect."

Offline in a magazine or newsletter? Try something like this:

> "If you'd like to get to know me better, please send me an email at: _____@_____.com or drop me a note to: (*name*) _____ (*address*) _____, (*city, state, zip code*) _____, USA."

On a lot of prison pen pal websites they list the options of how to contact you right on your page. If the site does this you can say this:

> "If you'd like to get to know me better then don't hesitate to use one of the options below to send me a note."

Always have a call to action in your ad to get the person moving in the direction you want: contacting you.

A Final Thought on Writing Ads

Most pen pal websites or pen pal newsletters have a word count limit that you can use. If you go over that word limit you have to pay extra. I have always stayed under the word limit because I want to spend the least amount of money I have to. So if the website has a 100 word limit, I try and use the "40-40-20" rule. Forty words for the headline and opening paragraph. Forty words for what I'm looking for and twenty words for the call to action. If the websites word limit is 250 words, then its 40% (100 words) for headline/opening paragraph, 40% (100 words) for what you're looking for, and 20% (50 words) for the closing call to action. That is my school of thought, but there are others.

A Latino prisoner named Conflict, has about 1000 words on his WriteAPrisoner.com profile. And he's getting hits. So there might be something to that? I haven't tested that out, but there is a saying in marketing literature: the more you tell the more you sell. The more words you use the better story you can print. That might be better? Then again, it might not. The key to everything in this book is to test it out for yourself. Test, test, test. When you find something that works, use it. Change things up at times. Keep your profiles fresh and upbeat. Spend time working on your ad/profile pages and know that you can write a successful one using the tips in this chapter.

Answering Other Peoples Ads

A lot of you like to write people who advertise in pen pal magazines and on pen pal lists. There's nothing wrong with this and I used to do it a lot. But as a prisoner who has bought, sold, and traded pen pal lists, I think it time to discuss if they're really worth the money or not? First, there are four kinds of pen pal lists. They are:

- Compiled lists: There's are lists of names and addresses that are taken from printed sources like telephone books, newspapers and magazine subscriptions. My "100 Chicagoland Women" and "100 Wealthy Women" lists were examples of compiled lists. These types of lists have the least value because you don't know if these people will respond to your letters.

- Pen Pals: These are lists of names and addresses of people who requested pen pals. A lot of companies comb the internet pen pal websites and compile lists of women who did not say "no prisoners" in their ads. Then they sell these addresses to prisoners. Yes, there are real people who want pen pals, but you just don't know if they'll write a prisoner until you write them. (I'll have more to say about this type of list in a moment.)

- Pen Pals Who Will Write Prisoners: These are people who requested to write prisoners. This is the rarest list of all and the most valuable of all the lists. But I've only seen two such lists in the last five years.

- Prison Pen Pals: If you just want mail and can write prisoners this list can be your goldmine. In 2002, while in the county jail, I bought such a list and every prisoner but one responded. If you can't write prisoners then this list has no value to you. (FYI: *Outlaw Biker* has female prisoners looking for pen pals and love in almost every issue!)

Now that you know the different types of lists in the prison pen pal game, you must examine the problems with these lists... And the main problem with all of the above lists is that you don't know how old they are. It would be nice to write the company selling the lists and get answers to the following questions:

- How did they compile the list?

- Where did the names and addresses come from?

- How old are the lists?

- Do they replace "return to sender" letters (called nixies) with new ones? New address?

- Do they sell the same list to different prisoners?

Most companies won't give you the answers so you just won't know until you buy a list and start writing letters. I don't like those odds and neither should you.

My verdict is that pen pal lists are more fool's gold than anything else. I've spent hundreds of dollars on such lists over the years and haven't had more than a few successes, except for the prison pen pal list that I ordered while in the county jail. There are better options available to get pen pals, so save your money and don't buy pen pal lists anymore. You've been forewarned.

But remember the companies that go online to get addresses then sell them to you? Why not do it on your own? If you have someone who can do research for you online then here are some great websites you can search for your ideal pen pals on.

- *Pen Pals Now* (www.penpalsnow.com)

  You are allowed to search by age, gender, country, and by snail-mail pen pals. *Pen Pals Now* has thousands of American women looking for pen pals.

  Sassociations (www.sassociations.net)

  You're allowed to search by these age groups: 18-24, 25-39, and over 40. You can also search by sex and country. The thing I like about this site is that they list the ads that have either been submitted or updated in the last nine months. Using this site could be the answer to your pen pal dreams.

These are only two of the websites I've used. But there are many more. Thousands if you count online dating sites also. If you don't have anyone to help you out with this then you may want to order the pen pal lists sold by the following company:

  Girls and Mags

  PO Box 319

  Rehoboth, MA 02769

They sell lists of 200 pen pals for $19.98. Some have photos, some are American women and some are overseas. Just remember what I've said earlier about these types of lists.

Worldwide Private Pen Pal Magazine

I like 3-G Company's pen pal magazine. I advertised in their worldwide booklet and didn't get any replies. However, I did write all of the women that interested me and three wrote me back. One was a sweet secretary from Kansas, who became a long-term pen pal. So yes, the women in 3-G's publications are legit. But remember that if you got their pen pal magazine, many other prisoners have it also. So you're opening letter and photo, (which you better have) is in competition with possibility thousands of other letters from prisoners. Here's a tip when using the 3-G worldwide pen pal booklet:

- Do not respond to ads that say "No Prisoners Please". It's a waste of your time and stamp. Stick to the ones that don't say that, or better yet, find the ones that say "Prisoners Welcome" or "Inmates Welcome". My secretary's ad said "Lifer's Welcomed". Since I was a lifer, I wrote her and we began a fruitful friendship. Pay attention to what the ads say!

Below is a sample form letter that you can use when answering ads. Yes it is short, but your first response doesn't have to be long. You're trying to establish contact not interrogate them.

Dear _____,

I saw your ad in (or on) _____ and it caught my eye. I knew I had to respond to find out more about you.

My name is _____, I'm _____ years old. I'm ____tall and weigh _____. You said in your ad that you like to_____. We have that in common because I love to _____.

I have enclosed a photo so that you may see the face behind my words. If you would like to begin a pen pal friendship, you can write to me at the below address, or you can email me at: _____

Whatever you do, please don't allow silence to be your response. May you be blessed in all that you do.

        Sincerely,

        S/ _____

Name

Address

City, State, Zip Code

USA

You're not restricted to the same pen pal ad as all the others included in the publication. Here's how prisoner Norm Harms did his ad in 3-G Company's *Worldwide Private Pen Pal Magazine*:

LOST:

If you happen to be a Male or Female

21+ from anywhere in the USA or around

the world. Write today! I MISS YOU!

100% Reply (Sorry no inmates)

Norm Harns # 305391 - Cedar Hall A10

P. O. Box 900 - Shelton, WA 98584   USA

His ad certainly stood out among the other typical mundane ads. Yes, he had to pay more but I bet he got better results. Try to find ways you can make your ad in 3-G's publication stand out if you use them.

Answer all personal ads that interest you, but just don't expect a lot of responses. I answered 50 ads and got 3 replies. Not good odds, although one of those responses became a long-term pen pal.

The whole key to answering someone else's ad is to write about what they wrote in it. If they put it in there it's important to them. So write about that. Show them that you are paying attention. In his book *Love by Mail*, Richard Coté had a panel of four single women evaluate 351 letters from men who responded to an ad. The most important thing he found out was that the men who made the best impression were the ones who responded by mentioning what the woman wrote about in her ad. So remember that. Your response should be about them and their interests. Especially what they wrote in their ad!

Your Secret to Pen Pal Success – Photographs

What's the first thing people look at when viewing your pen pal ad? Your photograph. Yes, some mediums don't allow you to post a photo, but most online websites do. *Playboy* (Oct 2014) reported that a study conducted by the journal *Psychology of Popular Media Culture* found that people make judgements based on the photos people have on their social media pages. Makes sense given that most people are scanning photos as they search for people online. In the *Guide to Ad Success* pamphlet, *Friends Beyond The Wall* lists the #1 tip for your ad photo to be a "smiling teeth showing photo." I agree, but would go a step further. The best photo to use is one of you smiling, doing something you love to do, which is clear and up-to-date. Of course I understand that a lot of prisoners don't have these types of photos. You'll have to use what you got. Even if all you got is your DOC photo, there are companies that can help you fix that one up. Hollywood stars are using digital technology to Photoshop their pictures now-a-days, so why not you? Just don't alter your photos too much. Keep it real. One of my friends, Flaco, had another prisoner draw a portrait of his DOC photo and posted that. It looked a whole lot better too. Here are some more photo tips:

- Never send one of you with another woman. Unless she's your mom, grandma, or sister. If you do that, you must explain who she is in your profile.

- Try not to use the typical prisoner thug photos where you're posing in a three-point gangsta-stance unless all you want are thug girls in response.

- Photo of you with your favorite pet are great. But you will turn people off who don't like animals or that type of pet. So you might not want to post that if you're worried about turning people off.

- Photos of you as a kid are good ones to use also. I've got a lot of responses because of my kid photos.

- Try to use photos of you in different clothes with different backgrounds. Even if it's one of you in the prison visiting room and one of you in sweats on the yard, it's still better than two of the same.

- Never use only one photo if you can use two. Three is even better. More is always best.

- When writing letters never send your only photo. Use a photo duplication service to get extra copies made.

If you are writing letters and emails and don't have any photos available to send, but have some online at another site you can do what I do. I use a postscript (P.S.) at the end of my letter (email) saying:

> "P.S. I have more photos posted at: www.prisoninmates.com/JoshuaKruger50216. If you go there and click on my albums, you'll see photos of me and my family."

Always do this in all your first letters (emails) if you have other photos posted online somewhere.

In Neil Strauss' book, *The Game*, he discussed the tactics pick-up artists use to pick-up women. Some of these are called "routines". They are elaborate actions that create a desired effect on the woman (target). One of these is called the "photo-routine". This routine is demonstrated by having a group of photos available as if they were just developed. But each photo is in fact preselected to convey something in the pick-up artist's personality. I share this so that you can be mindful of what photos you're posting and what they portray. You can't go wrong with family photos, action photos, photos with you and kids, and animal photos. Whatever you do, DO NOT post a photo of someone else saying it is you. No catfishing allowed!

Now, let's say you are one of the lucky ones who took a lot of pictures when you were free. What do you do and how do you decide which ones to use? Here's what. Get all your photos together and ask a female guard or teacher, which ones are best to use, in their opinion. Tell them why you are asking and what you're trying to do. They'll be glad to help out. (FYI: I've used this tactic for letters, my ads, and artwork. I've also made some great friends (yes, with female guards) this way also!)

In my experience you'll get more hits to your ads if you use photos and follow the tips in this section. They can be your secret weapon that sets you apart from every other prisoner searching for pen pals.

Resource Box

For more help to Photoshop your DOC picture, you might want to check out one of these services:

Anna Sperber
Photo Service For Inmates
Sturmstrasse 10
90478 Nuernberg
GERMANY
(send for brochure)

IPP Company
P.O. Box 2451
Forrest City, AR 72336

Now that you know how to write an ad and answer ads, let's examine some more avenues to get pen pals.

Chapter 7
The World is Now Flat

"The internet is becoming the town square for the global village of tomorrow." -Bill Gates

Technology has leveled the playing field and there are now NO boundaries anymore thanks to the internet. A good book to read about this is *The World is Flat* by Thomas Friedman. But for those of you who do not have access to the internet, you can get over this hurdle by having someone in your network who is web-savvy. This "personal assistant" can help with research online, send emails, post profiles on FREE pen pal websites, publish your blog, and anything else under the sun that you can think of. The possibilities are endless if you have this person in your corner... or on your payroll.

Your Outside Connection – Email

Some of you now have access to email at your prison through companies like JPay or Corrlinks. Utilize it when building your pen pal network. It's just a fact of life in our technology driven world that email and texting are the main forms of communicating. Yesterday I was talking to a younger prisoner in his 20's and he said his friends don't email anymore, they only use text messaging on their cell phones. As much as dislike hearing that, it is what it is. Knowing this is half the battle, doing something about it on your end of things is the important half. In my experience there are two reasons why a prisoner needs access to their own email account:

It's faster than snail-mail. A lot faster!

It allows you to connect with people who don't have time to write letters by snail-mail.

Getting my own email account was the catalyst that opened the door for me to build my business connections. I started ending my letters with a line that said:

"If it's more convenient, you may respond by sending me an email at: millionaireprisoner@gmail.com."

Most business people did use that option to reply. Another good thing that email is good for, is soliciting quotes on projects that you're working on. It's quick and easy for the person to just type out a quick response and hit send. Trust me, this convenience will help you build your network.

But don't be fooled by prisoner email companies that charge you high monthly fees to run your email account. MSN Hotmail, Googles Gmail, and Yahoo.com are all free email services. The only time you should pay for email service is if you don't have anyone else in your network to help you out. If you do use a paid email service then you need one that types your emails into the computer and doesn't scan them in. Other questions that you need to ask are:

- Do they send your emails weekly or biweekly?

- Is there a limit of emails sent for the week or month?

- Does postage cost extra?

I used TIF Services, LLC as my email provider in the past. If you have to use a paid service, try to find someone who'll do it for you for free as soon as you can. Here are some tips to remember when setting up your email account:

1. Have a great email address. Most people use their name or something catchy that's is significant for them. Don't use goofy email addresses like thugpassion@gmail.com or golddigger@hotmail.com. Put up a professional front.

2. Set up an email auto response that says something like this: "Sorry, but I'm away from the computer at this time and will get back to you as soon as possible. If you need a faster response, please send me a

letter, note, or postcard by snail mail to the address below. Thank you, hope you have a great day!"

3. Be cautious of what you write in your subject line. This line is what people see first and it helps them decide whether to open your email or not. Most email service providers use 25-character lines. So create catchy, short, subject lines that make someone want to open your email.

4. If you're using email to market your service or products then here are some tips that I learned from marketing expert Marcia Yudkin (www.yudkin.com):

   a) Highlight why your email is important;

   b) Don't repeat who you are in the subject box because the "From" box already says that;

   c) Use the word FREE if you're offering something valuable;

   d) Try to create temptation in your 25 characters.

   For more about email marketing you might want to check out *The Rebels Guide to Email Marketing* by Jason Falls.

Having an email account will open the door for you. It will increase the mail you get and allow you to contact mentors, businesses' and other people who toss out mail from prisoners, but always check their email inbox.

Resource Box

Two of the better known prisoner assistant companies are:

Help From Outside
2620 Bellevue Way NE#200
Bellevue, WA 98004
www.helpfromoutside.com
(206)486-6042

Fast-N-Friendly
Inmate Services
P.O. Box 10064
Springfield, MO 65808

Both require you to set up accounts and pay monthly fees, but if you have the income, I advise you to start your account today. (FYI: I had an ccount with HFO and reccomend them first.) You can also get a personal assistant by advertising on Craigslist.com. Other sites to find online help is with the International Virtual Assistants Association (ivaa.org); OnDemandVA (www.ondemandva.com; Worldwide101.com (for global VA's); and elance-odesk.com. To get reviews and rates of VA's check out VirtualAssistants.com. whatever you do, get connected!

Do You Have an Email Signature?

If you have your own email account, then you need an email signature (.sig). An email signature is the line of type at the end of your email message. If you have anything to sell, run a business, or offer some type of service, you need a .sig. people must know who you are, what you do, what you have to offer, and how to contact or find you. Here are a few reasons why you should have a .sig:

- Its free to setup

- Every time you send an email it will be attached to it.

- You don't have to retype it over and over

- It's another easy way to market your product or services

Here's something I learned from Peter Bowerman's book, *The Well-Fed Self-Publisher*. A lot of people just list who they are and their accomplishments. Better for you would be to make you .sig a call to action. You want someone to do something if you have a website or blog. So move them to action through your .sig. Here's what an email .sig could look like for me:

> Do you know anyone that has a loved one in prison? Send them to www.millionaireprisoner.com for a FREE report: "How to Help Turn Prisoner into a Stepping-stone to Success" by Josh Kruger, author of the bestselling book, *The Millionaire Prisoner*. www.carceralwealth.com

Have your internet savvy person setup your own .sig today. Just have them go to your email account provider, (Gmail, Yahoo, Hotmail, etc.) click on Help, and type in Signature. Then they would just have to follow the instructions provided to setup your .sig. If you're using Gmail, it's easier to use the Tools key. Or you can have a company like Airtime (airtimehq.com) turn your email .sig into a branded message. They have some plans that are free.

Resource Box

For more about all the different apps that Google offers, check out *How to Do Everything with Google Tools* by Donna L. Baker

---

Here are a few more things to remember about emails. You can't read body language or handwriting so it's easier to be, and to, misread what the other party is saying sometimes.

- Do not type in all capital LETTERS! It means SHOUTING ONLINE!

- Always type "www" prefix before any website (craiglist.com vs www.craiglist.com) so that the person reading your email can link directly to the website from your email from a simple click of the mouse. Your email program should automatically make it into a link.

- If it's a business email, do not use jargon or acronyms, unless the person will really understand it.

- Less is more in emails (250 words or less). Longer than that, send a snail-mail letter.

- When you could email someone you need to quickly tell them who you are, why you are emailing, and a link to where they can find more or contact you if possible.

- Lastly, try and keep your emails to one thought, or one theme only. As they say, get it and get out. (a good example is my email to writing expert *Peter Bowerman* on the next page.)

It's imperative that you setup your own email account so you can take advantage of the next avenue for getting pen pals.

Free Pen Pal Websites

A lot of companies are marketing to prisoners, offering online services like setting up pages on *Facebook*®, *Google*®, and *LinkedIn*®. Some of them say they will put you on many pen pal websites for a fee. I don't blame them. A billion dollars is spent online for dating services each year in America. Who doesn't want a piece of that pie? But you may not know that websites like PlentyofFish.com, Zoosk.com, DateHookup.com, and BlackPlanet.com are all free to post a profile on. So are the above social networking sites.

More important for our discussion in this chapter are the numerous FREE pen pal websites that you can post your profile on. Here are some of the better known FREE online pen pal sites:

www.PenPalworld.com
www.PenPalParty.com
www.SignalPenPals.net
www.PenPalsPlanet.com
www.PalsForFree.com
www.aPenPals.com
www.PenPalsAnywhere.com
www.BrownPride.com
www.PenPalsOnline.net
ThePlaceForPenPals.tumblr.com
worldofpenpals.narod.ru

www.InterPals.com
www.PenPalsNow.com
www.MyLanguageExchange.com
www.WorldNation.net
www.Marriage88.com
www.BlackandPink.org
www.HolyTitClamps.com
www.PenPalGarden.com
www.penpalscommunity.com
www.Sassociations.net

G⊠ail

Joshua Kruger

The Well-Fed Self-Publisher

2 messages

Joshua Kruger <millionaireprisoner@gmail.com>   Wed, Aug 29, 2012 at 2:12 PM
To: peter@wellfedwriter.com

Dear Peter:

I just finished The Well-Fed Self-Publisher for the second time. I want to thank you for writing it. It is funny, a great read, and inspiring. I'm currently in the process of trying to self-publish my first book, The Millionaire Prisoner: How To Turn Your Prison into a Stepping-Stone to Success, and your book makes me feel like it's possible.

Please sign me up for your E-zine, The Well-Fed E-Pub, if you don't mind. I would do it myself, but I'm in prison and do not actually have access to a computer. I want to be notified when you develop new content and products.

Once again, thanks for the great book, and helping me formulate my compass, and get rid of my map. May all your publishing endeavors turn into gold.

Respectfully,

Josh

Peter Bowerman <peter@wellfedwriter.com>   Fri, Aug 31, 2012 at 8:31 AM
To: Joshua Kruger <millionaireprisoner@gmail.com>

Thanks Josh.

Good to hear from you, and thanks for taking the time to write such a great note.

Glad you found the book so useful, and hats off to you for (if you'll forgive the cliche) turning adversity into opportunity. That takes some strong stuff!

I'll sign you up for the ezine with this address, though, you DO understand that the ezine is focused on commercial writing, not self-publishing. That said, it IS the best way to stay in the loop on anything new I come out with.

I wish you the best as you move forward, and thanks again for reaching out!

PB

If you find a website that you think should be in the next edition of this book, please let me know at millionaireprisoner@gmail.com

The thing to remember about theses websites is that they are not "prison pen pal" websites. The ones listed about are free world pen pal sites mostly used by free world people. But that doesn't mean you can't utilize them for your own success. You just have to be mindful that most of these people are not looking for prisoners to write. And a lot of the above sites make you put on your profile page that you're in prison. So don't hide this fact, but instead, play it up. You'll be surprised at how many people contact you. Most of them allow you to post photos and a small bio. But the key to using these websites is having an email connection and I'll get into that next when I tell you about some of my experiences on a few of these sites.

InterPals.net

I first heard about *InterPals* from a friend of mine who came off death row. He was on the site and met a young, beautiful, blonde German girl. I always wanted to go on it, just never got around to it. Finally, after taking advantage of *Inmate Shopper's* 2014 FREE Pen pal offer (no longer available) of catalog plus placement on three FREE pen pal websites, I went on *InterPals*. (My Profile is on the next page.) Let me tell you a little more about *InterPals*.

InterPals is not a prison pen pal website, but instead a pen pal site for anyone. It started in 1998 as International Pen pal Page and was later shortened to *InterPals* (www.interpals.net). *InterPals* has thousands of pen pals on their website. It's also a good site for people wanting to learn new languages. And this is now one of my favorite pen pal websites.

After placing my profile on *InterPals*, I realized there was a whole lot more that I could do with my page. (In *Inmate Shopper's* brief description it said only 100 words and 1 photo.) But I quickly learned I could add photos, posted to my "wall" (like *Facebook*), list my hobbies, interests, favorite music, TV shows, books and quotes. I realized that to take advantage of this website, I would have to be interactive with it and other people. But as you can see, my profile was very basic and guess how many hits I got? I received 22 emails from pen pals wanting to write. These were people from all over the world. And that was in the first week alone. Imagine what would happen if you did a full profile and stayed active on *InterPals*? I will do that and update my progress in the next edition of this book. But I recommend that you get on this website and start building your list of contacts.

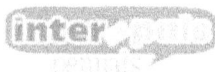

Hi, Penpalsuccess!
Not you? Sign out

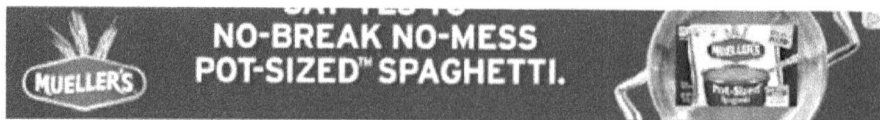

My Home   My Profile   Messages   Friends   Wall   Photos   Notes   Bookmarks   Settings

interpals   search   forums   online (12209)   language exchange   chat

Josh-Kruger   Josh, 36 y.o.

Pontiac, United States

Online 8 months ago

Speaks   English

Looking for   Email Pen Pals
Snail Mail Pen Pals
Friendship
Romance / Flirting
A Relationship

Joined 9 months ago, profile updated 9 months ago.

Message · Bookmark · Add Friend · Comments · Block · Report

About

Hi there! I'm hoping to meet some new friends from all over and learn about as many different cultures, lifestyles, and perspectives as possible, including yours, that's why I've posted this profile. I'm a poet and author. My hobbies are: reading, watching football, and writing letters.

I'm searching for a meaningful and lasting friendship. Inner warmth is more important than anything else, because I want to get to know you from the inside out. If this sounds like something you're interested in, don't hesitate to email me: jkruger216@gmail.com or write me anytime at my snail mail address:

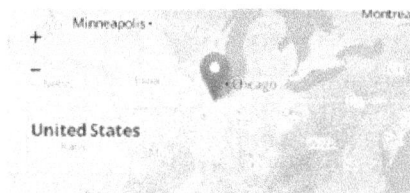

You must activate your account in order to post messages.

No comments yet!

http://www.interpals.net/Josh-Kruger

Minneapolis · Montreal
Chicago
United States
Enlarge map
Josh-Kruger lives **0 miles** away from you.
It's **10:10 am** (CDT) in Josh-Kruger's time zone.

Also online now

VESTA_BEL 41   MICKYBRICKS 44   CYCLE_FINN 15
KRAKOW   DURHAM   BAD BRAMSTEDT

CHRIS2015 25   MANAL7024 25   YUMMYLICIOUS 25
BEIJING   BERLIN   KIEV

You are currently logged in from 24.34.236.25.   View account activity.

About	Help	Language Practice	Make New Friends	Your Profile
About InterPals	Frequently Asked Questions	Learn Spanish	Who's Online Now?	Account Home
Advertising	Help Forum	Learn Chinese	Live Global Updates	Edit Profile
Blog	Forgot Password	Learn French	Search & Meet people	Your Messages
Donate	Contact Us	Learn German	Forums & Topics	Upload Photos
Feedback		Learn Japanese	Language Exchange	Your Friends
Jobs		Learn Russian	Invite Friends	Your Bookmarks
		Learn other languages		Your Settings

© 2015 InterPals Terms of Service | Privacy Policy
0.090s

PenPalsNow.com

I also went on PenPalsNow.com and posted my profile. (See below). I got seven replies to my ad that first week. This is another website that I recommend you post your profile on. It's another great site to search for pen pals on!

Craigslist

I also posted my personal ad on CraigsList.com and wanted you to see how it looks (See below). You should also post your ad on *BackPage.com*, another great free classified listing place. I'll keep updating you in future edition of this book about how these personal ads have done.

CL > bloomington, IL > all personals > strictly platonic   [account]

reply   prohibited [2]   Posted: seconds ago

★ Josh Kruger - m4w - 36 (Bloomington)

age : **36**   body : **athletic**
height : 6'4" (193cm)   status : **single**

Hi there! I'm hoping to meet some new friends from all over and learn about as many different cultures, lifestyles, and perspectives as possible, including yours, that's why I've posted this profile. I'm a poet and author. My hobbies are: reading, watching football, and writing letters.

I'm searching for a meaningful and lasting friendship. Inner warmth is more important than anything else, because i want to get to know you from the inside out. If this sounds like something you're interested in, don't hesitate to email me by replying or write me anytime at my snail mail address:

• do NOT contact me with unsolicited services or offers

How to Win Friends & Influence Pen Pals

Using these FREE pen pal websites can boost your pen pals by the hundreds. But to make real and lasting connections you have to get interested in the other person. This is that whole precept behind Dale Carnegie's masterpiece *How to Win Friends & Influence People*. (A great book that you should read.) Here's how to do it using online profiles when others contact you first:

- When a prospective pen pal emails you or writes you at the prison, have your personal assistant (or family member of friend) go online and print out their profile. (Or do a Google and Facebook search on them.)

- Upon receiving their profile pages, read it to learn their likes, wants, favorites, etc. use that information in your response.

- You should also actively use the search options on each pen pal or dating website. This allows you to tailor the pen pals that come up in your search. For instance, say you want to find a female pen pal in the USA, who is between 31-40 years old, and wants to use snail-mail. You could put those parameters into the search option on the site, and only the matches would come up. Have your personal assistant print out the profiles of the prospects and then go through them and see which ones you have common interests with and want to write. When composing your letters and responses you need to use items from their profiles in your notes. Here are some response templates to use:

- An acknowledgement or compliment about something they wrote:

   "I see that you _____. I never could do that no matter how many times I tried. How do you do it?"

- Their job or career is worth writing about:

   "You mentioned that you're a _____. My dad was a _____, and had _____ years in before he retired."

- Asking questions in my main strategy in the beginning, here are some you could use:

   "Hi, I see that you have a photo in your email .sig. My personal assistant said that they couldn't get it to work. Can I get you to tell me your trick?"

   "Your profile says that you like to _____. Does that mean you're good at it? I like to _____, but I haven't been able to _____."

   "Hi there _____, I see you're deeply involved with _____. Can you tell me more about how you got involved?"

These are just a few templates you can use. All you have to do is fill in the blanks with your prospective pen pal's likes or interests. Anything they reply with to the above is great because all answers except silence are winners!

A Final Parting Thought

Online pen pal websites do two things you can't do yourself:

- They introduce you to a large population of people who are visiting the website for one reason: looking for someone to write.

- They give you access to millions of possible pen pals, twenty-four hours a day.

Online pen pal strategies should be the focal point of your pen pal success. In this chapter, I've dealt with FREE online pen pal websites. In the next chapter I'll deal with paid prison pen pal websites. Don't forget this chapter if you want to build a stable of pen pals.

LOOKING *for* NEW *and exciting* CONNECTIONS?

Penacon is owned and operated by Freebird Publishers, your trusted inmate service provider.

Penacon.com dedicated to assisting the imprisoned community find connections of friendship and romance around the world. Your profile will be listed on our user-friendly website. We make sure your profile is seen at the highest visibility rate available by driving traffic to our site by consistent advertising and networking. We know how important it is to have your ad seen by as many people as possible in order to bring you the best service possible. Pen pals can email their first message through penacon.com! We print and send these messages with return addresses if you get one. We value your business and process profiles promptly.

Get your Profile noticed!

Get noticed faster and more often with some of our featured profile additions. At Penacon we are constantly looking for more opptortunites to help your pen pal journey flourish. Try out our Prmier sections to boost your exposure. We'll place your profile on our front pages in sections like Featured Members, Looking for Love, Friendships Wanted, White Collar, Girl/Boy Next door and more.

Penacon.com
Text: 774-406-8682
diane@freebirdpublishers.com

To receive your informational package and application send SASE with two stamps to:

PENACON

221 Pearl St. Ste. 533
North Dighton, MA 02764

Chapter 8

Prison Pen Pal Websites

"Put yourself in situations where you are tremendously outnumbered by the opposite sex." -Paul Hartunian

So many prisoners are worried about the costs of using an online prison pen pal website. I can understand that. But how much is the perfect pen pal worth to you? If you find your perfect pen pal then it's priceless and worth every penny you spent. The truth is, just as it is in life, online "you get what you pay for". There is one advantage that prison pen pal websites have over every other tactic in this book: The people who use these sites are specifically looking for a prisoner to write. Or at least they are open to it. They are presold on writing you! Whereas other avenues you'll have to sell them on writing a prisoner. This fact alone should be why you use prison pen pal websites. In this chapter, I'll tell you about my experiences using these websites and what I've found in my research. Done right, prison pen pal websites can deliver what you are looking for.

Unrealistic Expectations

The biggest obstacle that I've found is that most prisoners have unreal expectations when it comes to the number of response they are going to get off a prison pen pal site. They think (or hope) they'll get hundreds of hits on their page. Richard Coté, author of *Love By Mail*, wrote that his personal ads over four years brought in 199 responses, and that it averaged out to about 10 per ad that he place. That was in the late 1980's and early 90's, before internet dating. My own research has found that most prisoners get an average of one to six replies off their online prison pen pal ads. So if you go into this with the understanding that you are looking for the ideal pen pal you may just find what you're looking for? But if you think you'll get hundreds of responses, you'll be disappointed.

With the above being said, there are prisoners who do get bags of mail because of their notoriety. Prisoners like Scott Peterson and Charles Manson, get lots of mail and have flocks of females wanting to marry them. Prisoners on death row, have lots of free world supporter's and have better chances to get mail. In the early 2000's, online prison pen pal websites were raved about because guys were getting tons of responses. Now that the market is saturated, it's a little different. But have no fear because you can still have success if you use the right websites and write an effective ad. Since you learned how to write an effective ad in chapter six, let's examine which sites are best and which ones are complete waste of time and money.

My Prison Pen Pal Website Experiences

In 2003, I was placed on the now defunct website, *The Pampered Prisoner*, and also *Prison Talk Online* (PTO). I've also been on *Friends Beyond the Wall* (FBTW) twice, WriteAPrisoner.com, LostVault.com, JailMail.net, FriendsWithPens.org, PrisonInmates.com, PenPalsBehindTheWalls.com, and a few others. As I write this, I have existing profiles on five different prison pen pal websites. Of course you want to know about my responses right? I got two off *The Pampered Prisoner* and flooded with mail from my ad on PTO. PTO has since changed their format. Ill share my experiences on some of the other websites in a minute. But first I'd like to share with you some of my research about these websites.

In December, 2010, *Help From Beyond the Walls* used www.statbrain.com to compile stats about the number of people who view prison pen pal sites each day. The most viewed site was WriteAPrisoner.com with over 5,000 page views a day. Second was Meet-An-Inmate.com with over 4,000 page views a day. The only other site that got over a thousand page views was CellPals.com. Why did these sites get the most page views? Because they had the most Google links. Since google is the largest, and most used search engine in the world, when anyone does a search on Google for "prison pen pals", they'll most likely get directed to one of these sites. Listed on the next pages are what you'd get if you do a search on Google for "prisoner pen pal websites" in May 2015. The Google Search shows the first site to be Meet An Inmate.com. Based on all of this, here are my top 5 prison pen pal websites:

Meet An Inmate (meet-an-inmate.com)

PenACon (penacon.com)

Write A Prisoner (writeaprisoner.com)

FriendsBeyondTheWall.com (friendsbeyondthewall.com)

Inmate Classified (inmate.com)

That is just based on Google search and nothing else. (FYI: I have never been on *Inmate Classified* or *Meet An Inmate*, nor do I know a prisoner who has, so I can't pass judgement or review their services.)

One last thing about these "page views" or "hit counters". In the first four months I was on *Write A Prisoner* my profile received 1,500 plus page views. This averages out to about 375 page views a month. But this doesn't necessarily mean that 375 different people are seeing my profile each month. It could be people going from profile to profile then coming back to mine, that drives up the page views. I do know that I've kept my profile on the front page of the *Write A Prisoner* site by adding blogs, poetry, and extra photos, and still have only been seen by a few hundred people each month. Keep this in mind.

Google

prisoner pen pal websites

Web Shopping Videos News Images Search tools More

About 523,000 results (0.53 seconds)

Meet-An-Inmate.com - Male and Female Inmates Desire...
www.meet-an-inmate.com/
Meet-an-Inmate.com has been helping male and female inmates connect with the
outside world since 1998 and is ranked #1 among prison pen pal websites.
Meet an Inmate

The LARGEST & BEST Prison Pen Pal site on the Internet!
www.prisonpenpals.com/
Largest Prisoner Pen Pal Site on the Net - Male & Female Prisoner Ads ... The
purpose of this site is to find prisoner pen pals. ... Tell a friend about this site.

Prison Pen Pals at Write A Prisoner!
www.writeaprisoner.com/
WriteAPrisoner.com
We have thousands of pen pals in prison to select from. ... Unlike sites like Facebook
and Myspace, here you will be able to research all information on the ...

Prison Pen Pals - Write a Prisoner at Friends Beyond The...
www.friendsbeyondthewall.com/
2500+ Prison Inmates - Prison Pen Pal Photo Ads listed in 46 States! ... Prison Pen
Pals and Inmate Pen Pals ... Prison is a lonely world without a friend.

INMATE Classified Pen Pals in Prison
www.inmate.com/
Prison inmates looking for pen pals and new friends, to exchange pen pal letters and
experiences, find legal help and lawyers.

Prison Inmates Online - Write A Prisoner / Prison Pen Pals
www.prisoninmates.com/
Mar 7, 2014 - It's a great place to find prison pen pals or advocate for a prisoner. ...
write inmate letters, find pen pals, read other prison voices, and be a part of ...
You visited this page on 5/19/15.

LostVault.com: Prison Pen Pals - Free Pen Pal Ads for...
www.lostvault.com/
Free ads for prison pen pals. Post an ad online for free. Informative and fun forums
for those with a friend, loved one, or future friend in prison. Features a...

Loveaprisoner - Prison Inmate Pen Pals and Inmate...
loveaprisoner.com/
Love a Prisoner, Inmate Profiles, Inmate Pen Pals, Male and Female Personals...
Welcome to Loveaprisoner.com, a pen pal service dedicated to those in the....
Parents, please visit our Keep Kids Safe section to restrict access to adult sites.

Female Inmate Pen Pals: +: Write Female and Male Prison...
prisoninmatepenpal.com/
Female inmate pen pals. Write female and male prison inmates. Submit a listing for
an prison inmate friend, or loved one today.

DMOZ - Society: People: Pen Pals: Prisoners and Inmates
www.dmoz.org › Society › People › Pen Pals
DMOZ
Jul 15, 2014 - Ask A Convict - Prison pen pal site that also allows visitors to ask a

90

question of an ... Female Prison Pals - A free website, with no charge to view ...

Prison Is Lonely - LAsurim.org

Ad www.lasurim.org/
We Offer A Free Pen Pal Program Help A Prisoner And Sign Up Today!

Pen Pals | black and pink

www.blackandpink.org/pen pals/
Find an LGBTQ Prisoner Pen pal Today! To get started, please click the button below
based on your age:

Write an Inmate - Free Inmate Pen Pal Listings | Facebook

https://www.facebook.com/letters.to.inmates
Any inmates from Mass wanna be pen pals? I'm from New Bedford ... Free Inmate
Pen pal Listings - Florida Inmates - Male Inmates - my only son needs a pen pal.

PRISON PEN PALS - CONPALS InmateConnections.com...

www.convictpenpals.com/
Prison pen pals website. Write a prisoner through ConvictPenPals.com. Incarcerated
men and women seek pen pals for love, friendship, romance, art, ...

Prison Pen Pal Directory

www.prisonpenpaldirectory.com/
Oct 27, 2014 - Top ten prison pen pal sites ranked by traffic, If you are looking to list
an inmate on prison pen pal site check here first.

Inmate-Connection - Prisoners Seeking Pen Pals

www.inmate-connection.com/
Features bios of lonely male and female inmates looking for pen pals. ... Welcome to
Inmate-Connection.com, a website designed to make a difference in the...

The Radical Power of a Prison Pen Pal - Talking Points Memo

talkingpointsmemo.com/.../power-prison-pen pals-...
Talking Points Memo
Dec 12, 2014 - The term "pen pal"—sweetly alliterative and quaint—may evoke....
The Internet delivered the news: My friend had been executed in 2011.

Newest - Paper Dolls Pen Pals

paperdollspenpals.com/newest.asp
Looking for genuine pen pals to correspond with and/or talk with on the ... Prison can
be a very lonely place and I want to find friendly people to connect with.

Jailbabes: Female Inmate Seeking Pen Pals

www.cowtowninfo.com/ You'll find personals ads from women in prison, with and without photos, listed by state or in order of receipt. So when you search
prisoner pen pal websites for...

Prison Pen Pals - YouTube

www.youtube.com/watch?v=Mz08mLd3zyQ
Mar 3, 2011 - Uploaded by C. W.
WRITE TO PRISONERS: meet-an-inmate.com,
prisoninmates.com, friendsbeyondthewall.com, & www...

to Personal Pen Pal Ads - Prisoner Life

www.prisonerlife.com/personals-search.cfm
1 Prisoner Pen Pal Site on the Net - Male & Female Prisoner Ads - Photos Addresses,
Free!
Communicate
With prisoners and death row inmates, and learn...

Prisoner Pen Pal

Ad www.wow.com/Prisoner+Pen+Pal
Search for Prisoner Pen Pal Look Up Quick Results Now!

How do I find a Prison Pen Pal? | Yahoo Answers

https://answers.yahoo.com/question/index?qid...
Nov 21, 2010 - I would like to find a Pen pal who is in prison. ... How it works, can you
explain it to me and maybe provide a good website for finding a pen pal?

FemalePrisonPals.com - Female Prison Pen Pals
www.femaleprisonpals.com/
A free website, with no charge to view prisoner's mailing addresses.

The Business of Prison Pen Pals - Priceonomics
priceonomics.com/the-business-of-prison-pen pals/
Apr 7, 2014 - Lovell is the founder of WriteAPrisoner.com, a website that lists personal ads from prisoners seeking pen pals. A visitor to the site might decide...

Exclusiveprisoner - Prison pen pals and Inmate personal...
exclusiveprisoner.com/
ExclusivePrisoner.com is the best Prison pen pal website connecting inmates with pen ... Many of you coming here today have a close friend or family member ...

Home - Outlaws Online Prison Pen Pals
outlawsonline.com/
America's Most Wanted Seeks Prison Pen Pals The purpose of this site is for ... to go to the Department of Corrections website to read more about the inmate.

Websites for prisoners seeking pen pals blasted by victims...
www.usatoday.com/news/...03.../prisoner-pen pal-websites/...
Mar 11, 2012 - Websites offer prisoners a way to find pen pals, but victims object and some states have made using the sites illegal.

CellPals!: Prison Pen Pals
www.cellpals.com/
Free to browse inmates in prison who want pen pals and sometimes more. Male and female inmates including gay, lesbian and death row listings. ... Free Public Access Website this site is for nonjudgmental people! Contact Us Male Female...

Prison pen pals | Today | 9Jumpin
www.9jumpin.com.au/show/today/today-takeaway/.../prison-penpals/
Apr 27, 2015 - iExpress is a website that generates a personalized webpage, which allows people in prisons and hospitals to make a personal statement that ...

Prison Pen Pals / Inmate / Criminal Pen Pals - Singles Men...
www.convictmailbag.com/
While the majority of male and female prison pen pals on this site committed a crime warranting their incarceration in prison, that does not change the fact that ...

Prison UK: An Insider's View: Prison Pen Pals: Who Writes...
prisonuk.blogspot.com/2014/.../prison-penpals-who-writes-and-why.htm...
Sep 19, 2014 - Sometimes these pen pals are friends of friends, or even female prisoners in women's nicks. Others are involved in various prisoner support...

Womenbehindbars.com - Write Prison Pen Pals - meet an...
https://www.womenbehindbars.com/
Write prison pen pals at Women Behind Bars! Meet an inmate and begin a relationship with female prison pen pals.

Hot Prison Pals.com -- Welcome to the hottest prison pen...
www.hotprisonpals.com/
OT PRISON PALS. We care about your love life!
Leopard:Users:admin:Desktop:andrew_webb.jpg. TIM BROWN WINNER 2014 H.P.P. HOTTEST INMATE OF...

The Smart Woman's Guide to Understanding Prisoners and...
www.amazon.com › ... › Love & Romance
Amazon.com, Inc.
The Smart Woman's Guide to Understanding Prisoners and Prison Pen Pal Sites Kindle Edition by Lance Pough, Divine. Download it once and read it on your...

WriteAPrisoner.com - Wikipedia, the free encyclopedia
en.wikipedia.org/wiki/WriteAPrisoner.com
Wikipedia
Several states have placed a ban on inmate pen pal sites in response to these issues,

which the site owner has stated is a violation of the First Amendment.

Prison Pen Pals - JPay Forum
forum.jpay.com/prison-pen pals/
May 9, 2015 - 40 posts - 23 authors
Because we all need pen pals in our lives, whether free or away. ... Exclamation
Sticky Thread Sticky: Find An Inmate Pen Pal / Write An Inmate. Started by
Texas Dust ... Looking for a friend in Mi. Started by kendra552469...

Jewish Pen Pals
www.jewishpenpals.org/
Shalom New Pen Pal Friend. ... My volunteer job is the Pen Pal coordinator for the
6000+ Jewish men and women in prison who have been forgotten by their...

Ask a Convict: Free Prison Pen Pals
askaconvict.com/
Prison pen pal site that also allows visitors to ask a question of an inmate, receive
answers, and review other answers. Fee for inmate listing.

PRISON PEN PALS - Prison Talk
www.prisontalk.com/forums/forumdisplay.php?f=294
Prison Pen pal ads for inmates incarcerated in the states of (New Mexico - Not
Allowed), New York, North Carolina, North Dakota, Ohio, (Oklahoma - Not ...

Prison pen pals pack killer profiles - National - NZ Herald News
www.nzherald.co.nz/nz/news/article.cfm?c...
The New Zealand Herald
Oct 27, 2014 - A Facebook page where prison inmates are able to advertise for
female pen pals has been blasted by victim advocates who say it's creepy and ...

Pen Pal Correspondence Resources | Equal Justice USA
ejusa.org/prisoner/resources/Pen%2BPal%2BCorrespondence
PO Box 470, Montgomery TX 77356 / E-mail: cellpals2 [at] Hotmail [dot] com /
Website: www.cellpals.com CellPals is a prison pen pal organization on the...

Prison Ministry Resources
Ad www.wheatridge.org/
Inspiration and free resources for prison ministry - Come be inspired!
Sign Up Form - Who We Are - Sample Devo - Todays Devotion

Write a Prisoner

On the next few pages, I'm going to show you the profiles and ads I've posted in research for the ideas and strategies in my books. The first one is from WriterAPrisoner.com. You'll see my first ad with "Tall, Rich and Lonely" headline. That one didn't work. It only got me two responses. Both were gold diggers who wanted me to pay their bills. So I changed it up, added some blog posts, and a poem. That's when I started getting responses. I really like WriterAPrisoner.com, but the key to their site is to keep your profile in the "newest members" section by adding blogs, poetry and new photos every two months. That way, anyone who logs on will see your profile first before they have to search through every prisoner's ad on the website.

One other thing about WriteAPrisoner.com hits. They seem to be age-specific. What I mean is that most of the women who wrote me were in their 30's and early 40's (around the age I was went I went on the site). Whereas, on other websites, I got younger (college age) women or mélange of people. And I got quite a few foreign pen pals from the United Kingdom. I like, and recommend WriterAPrisoner.com. The truth is that if you can't get a response to your profile on WriteAPrisoner.com, there is something wrong with your ad!

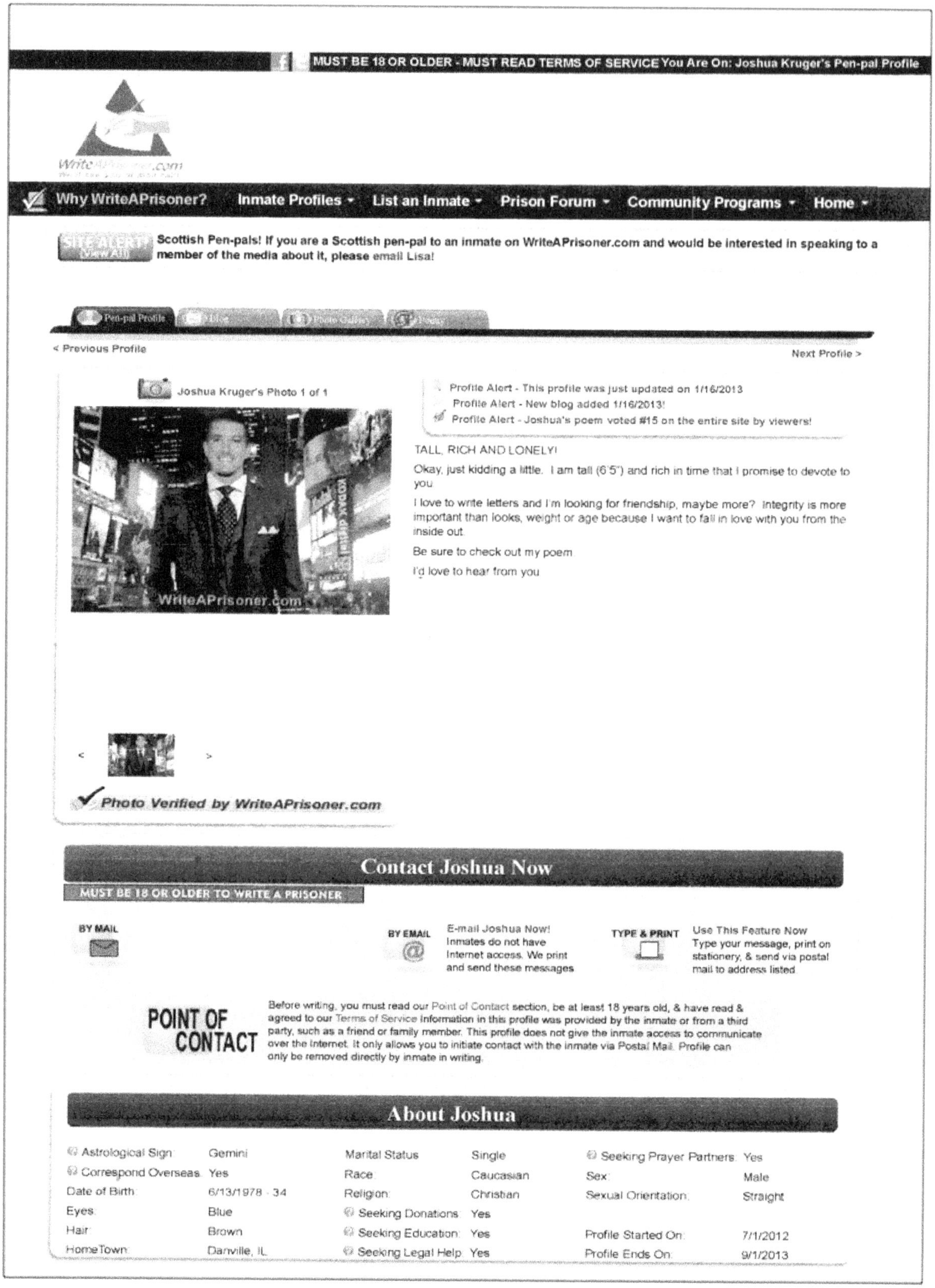

MUST BE 18 OR OLDER - MUST READ TERMS OF SERVICE You Are On: Joshua Kruger's Pen-pal Profile

WriteAPrisoner.com

Why WriteAPrisoner? | Inmate Profiles | List an Inmate | Prison Forum | Community Programs | Home

SITE ALERT! View All

Scottish Pen-pals! If you are a Scottish pen-pal to an inmate on WriteAPrisoner.com and would be interested in speaking to a member of the media about it, please email Lisa!

Pen-pal Profile | Blog | Photo Gallery | Poetry

< Previous Profile

Next Profile >

Joshua Kruger's Photo 1 of 1

Profile Alert - This profile was just updated on 1/16/2013

Profile Alert - New blog added 1/16/2013!

Profile Alert - Joshua's poem voted #15 on the entire site by viewers!

TALL, RICH AND LONELY!

Okay, just kidding a little. I am tall (6'5") and rich in time that I promise to devote to you.

I love to write letters and I'm looking for friendship, maybe more? Integrity is more important than looks, weight or age because I want to fall in love with you from the inside out.

Be sure to check out my poem

I'd love to hear from you

Photo Verified by WriteAPrisoner.com

Contact Joshua Now

MUST BE 18 OR OLDER TO WRITE A PRISONER

BY MAIL

BY EMAIL — E-mail Joshua Now! Inmates do not have Internet access. We print and send these messages

TYPE & PRINT — Use This Feature Now Type your message, print on stationery, & send via postal mail to address listed

POINT OF CONTACT

Before writing, you must read our Point of Contact section, be at least 18 years old, & have read & agreed to our Terms of Service Information in this profile was provided by the inmate or from a third party, such as a friend or family member. This profile does not give the inmate access to communicate over the Internet. It only allows you to initiate contact with the inmate via Postal Mail. Profile can only be removed directly by inmate in writing.

About Joshua

Astrological Sign	Gemini	Marital Status	Single	Seeking Prayer Partners	Yes
Correspond Overseas	Yes	Race	Caucasian	Sex	Male
Date of Birth	6/13/1978 - 34	Religion	Christian	Sexual Orientation	Straight
Eyes	Blue	Seeking Donations	Yes		
Hair	Brown	Seeking Education	Yes	Profile Started On	7/1/2012
HomeTown	Danville, IL	Seeking Legal Help	Yes	Profile Ends On	9/1/2013

Josh Kruger

Incarceration Information

| Earliest Release Date: | 07/30/2020 | On Death Row: | No | Serving Life Sentence: | Yes |
| Latest Release Date: | N/A | Incarcerated Since: | 1999 | Incarcerated For: | See Crime |

Official Links: This person is incarcerated in the Illinois Department of Corrections.

WriteAPrisoner.com Community Information: If you have questions or information to share about this particular Department of Corrections or prison, please visit our Illinois Forum.

Profile Resources

Driving Directions to Joshua's Facility

Print Joshua's Profile

Report an Address Change

Send Joshua a Greeting Card

Send Joshua Books Using Amazon.com

Send Joshua Games, Jokes & Trivia

WriteAPrisoner.com Paid Services:

Make Changes to Joshua's Profile

Purchase Credit for Joshua

Renew Joshua's Profile

Subscribe to Joshua's Profile:
We will email you when there is an update to this profile such as a profile or photo change, upcoming birthday, soon to be expired, and more!

Email Address
Your Name
Subscribe

Embed Joshua's Profile:
`<iframe height='375px' width='425px' frameBorder='0'`
(Show Preview)

Direct link to Joshua's Profile:
http://www.writeaprisoner.com/Template.aspx?i=z-k50216

Send Joshua Self-Help Information:
Select One

Profile Font Size: A- A+

Legal Notice: You must be at least 18 years of age to write to an inmate and have read our Terms of Service. This information may not be duplicated without written consent from WriteAPrisoner.com, Inc. (excluding media use). All information is provided by the member placing the profile or from a third party, such as a friend or family member of the inmate.

Bookmark Email Print Report Problem   Like 0   Tweet 0   Pin it

2000-2013 WriteAPrisoner.com, Inc. All Rights Reserved. Must be 18 to be viewing this website and have read our Terms of Service.

MUST BE 18 OR OLDER

WriteAPrisoner.com

WHY **WRITE A PRISONER?** | Inmate Profiles ▼ | List an Inmate ▼ | Prison Forum ▼ | Community Programs ▼ | Home ▼ | 🔍 SEARCH

You Are On: Joshua Kruger's Poetry

Please speak out! Some states have banned inmates from communicating with us and other organizations that help inmates find pen-pals. In response, we have started a petition against these governors, and we need your support. Please sign and share our petition today!

Personal Profile | Photo Gallery | Poetry

< Joshua's Previous Poem   Joshua's Next Poem >

Joshua's Poems

View original inmate poetry featured on WriteAPrisoner.com. Vote for the poetry you like, and visit the inmate's profile. Poetry provides a means for expression and communication. Many people choose to develop their creative skills while incarcerated. This section allows you to read original poetry written by inmates.

DREAMS OF REALITY

Last night I had the most beautiful dream
It was so real, or so it did seem
I woke up from my slumber and a visitor appeared
It was you standing there, your eyes filled with tears
I pulled you close, and whispered, 'Baby don't cry'
I'll always love you till the day I die
I held you and kissed the tears from your face
The tears dissolved and a smile took their place
We talked of tomorrow, our hopes and dreams
Of being together, always a team
We laughed and talked and made love through the night
Everything was perfect, everything was right
Then suddenly I awakened the sun on my face
And found myself alone, back here in this place
My dream was so real, I almost forgot
It left me thinking, and these were my thoughts
If you believe in your dreams you're certain to find
That dreams are a reality of your unconscious mind
So baby don't think we're apart forever
For tonight when I dream, we'll be together

Joshua Kruger K-50216
Joliet, IL

✓ VOTE FOR THIS

Share Joshua's Poem

Link to this Poem
Poem URL:
http://www.writeaprisoner.com
Poem code: copy it to your profile
<href

Options for this page: ☆ Bookmark ✉ Email to a Friend ⇪ Report

http://writeaprisoner.com/inmate-profiles/inmatePoem.aspx?f=z-k50216

Prison Inmates Online

Besides my ad on *Prison Talk Online* back in 2003, my profile page on *Prison Inmates Online* (PIO) has got me the most responses. I love their pages and all the stuff you can add to your page, especially YouTube videos. The $50 cost for the length of your incarceration is by far the best deal out there. They are my #1 pen pal website for all of these reasons.

The one caveat about the $50 cost is that email messaging service is included for the first year, but after that you're going to have to pay $25 a year to get the emails that people send you through the site. Do you have to do this? No. should you? Yes. You must make it the easiest for possible pen pals to contact you. And since my responses of PIO all came through their email messaging service, I recommend renewing your email service every year. Not only for first responses, but a continued online communication avenue, because your pen pals can use the email service to write you if they want, not just for the initial response. With college-age pen pals and foreign friends, this is great.

PIO also does Facebook shout outs every once in a while to get you responses. When they did mine I got several great pen pals that I still have today. PIO is another great website that has worked for me.

Joshua Kruger's Poetry

"I AM"

Posted by Joshua Kruger

I am a poet writing of my pain,
I am a prisoner living a life of shame,
I am your son hiding my depression,
I am your brother making a good impression,
I am your friend acting like I'm fine,
I am a wisher wishing this LIFE weren't mine
I am a man who thinks of suicide,
I am the boy pushing my tears aside,
I am a convict who doesn't have a clue,
I am the kid sitting next to you,
I am the one asking you to care,
I am your best friend hoping you'll be there!

By Joshua Kruger

Joshua Kruger

View All Entries
Write New Entry
Edit This Entry
Delete This Entry

Joshua Kruger   Photos (10)   Tattoos (4)

Tattoo Art
By Joshua Kruger
4 photos · 908 views · 0 comments

Joshua Kruger
#K50216   Like Share Be the first of your friends to like this   Favorite Message Me

Josh Kruger

PRISON INMATE

Favorite   Message

Albums (2)

> Featured Inmates: (34)
See All

Krina Johnson Ladoi Harrison William Ashby
Eduardo David Antoine Ebron James Richard
Paris Peterson Disabled Member Reginald Soria

Joliet
Map   Prison

Profile

Profile

Dear Lonely Women Seeking A New Friend,

Are you tired of the same old personal ads and lies?
Or guys who are lacking honesty, sincerity and respect?
Who don't shower you with attention, affection and appreciation?
Well, here are some things I promise you'll get from me: eyes you can look into and trust...a helping hand.... A heart that understands and doesn't judge...a supporting shoulder....a prompt reply to all your letters....and time devoted to you.

I'm a tall (6'5"), slim, witty, confident, athletic, Gemini who loves to write letters. I believe that prison will be a stepping-stone to success and try to always look for opportunities in life and not the obstacles. In November I was found NOT GUILTY of murder, but in January 2002 I was rearrested and charged again. Convicted and sentenced to life in 2003, my post-conviction petition was recently granted on appeal because of new DNA evidence which could lead to my freedom in two or three years. I'm very excited about this NEW EVIDENCE!!

I'm searching for a meaningful and lasting relationship with a special woman that might lead to marriage? If you want a faithful man committed to building a companionship based on harmony, friendship, and ultimately love, then maybe we should connect? Inner warmth is more important than your looks, weight, or age because I want to love you for who you are and not try to change you into someone else.

Maybe all of the above fits what you're looking for? If it is, don't hesitate to send me a message so we can begin getting to know each other. No matter what, may you be blessed in all that you do.

Yours for future happiness, Josh

Common Interests

Favorite Food	Pizza
Favorite TV Show	ESPN Sportscenter
Favorite Quote	"Women are the rainbows in the storms of life"
Favorite Music	Classic Rock N Roll
Favorite Movie	Heat
Favorite Book	Think and Grow Rich
Heroes	Felix Dennis, Nelson Mandela
Fluent in Spanish (Español)	No

Incarceration Details

Incarcerated Since	1999
Inmate Release Date	2099
Incarcerated For	Felony Murder
Serving Life Sentence?	Yes
Correspond Overseas?	Yes
JPay	Yes

Blogs

Browse Entries   My Entries   Write New Entry

What is Twin, Inc.?

Joshua Kruger

It's a corporation whose founding members were established by birth. If you browse my photos you'll see that I'm an identical twin. My brother's name is Joe. You'll also see that I have twin daughters. Their names are Brittney and Jessica. I don't get to see them, but they are still the motivating force behind everything that I do.

Our corporation is a unique one in that we have a special bond because we share DNA with each other.... And yet there's something missing: We don't have a First Lady!

Do you think you have what it takes? If you do, we would love to welcome you into our family and share with you all the special benefits we enjoy. So don't hesitate to contact me with your thoughts so I can stop the search. May you be blessed in all that you do!

Joshua Kruger

Here is a first. I got the following email off PIO:

PRISON INMATES ONLINE

Serving Inmates Since 2000
Contact: info@prisoninmates.com
8033 W Sunset Blvd #7000 - Los Angeles CA - 90046

0216

Pontiac IL 61764

11/15/2017
Brianna Trent

canton ohio 44705
USA

Hi Joshua I would love to get to know you better. I am a stay at home mom and that is basically my life I have 4 kids I own my own house and my family is wealthy . I am looking for a friendship some one to talk to you as I get lonely a lot . I hope you respond to me .

Submitted from: 75.179.24.166, Server: 75.179.24.166, Date/Time: 4:40.36 am, Windows, Internet Explorer, 10.0

After responding that night, the next week a member of the Internal Affairs Department showed up at my door and delivered the following letter. When I showed him the email she sent, he said "She must have a husband or something. She's trouble. Don't write her." Don't worry, I won't. Just a lesson that you got to be careful in the pen pal game.

Illinois
Department of
Corrections

Pat Quinn
Governor

S. A. Godinez
Director

Pontiac Correctional Center
700 W. Lincoln Street, P.O. Box 99
Pontiac, IL 61764

Telephone: (815) 842-2816
TDD: (800) 526-0844

MEMORANDUM

DATE: December 1, 2014

TO: Joshua Kruger K50216

FROM: Investigations & Intelligence Unit

SUBJECT: Correspondence

This Memorandum serves as notification that you are to immediately cease all communication with Brianna Trent of Ohio. Failure to comply with this notification will result in disciplinary action.

Be guided accordingly.

Investigations & Intelligence Unit
Pontiac Correctional Center

Inmate Connections (www.convictpenpals.com) (www.conpals.com)

This was a site I went on because there were several guys in my cell house who were on the sites and getting quite a few hits. So I signed up to see if it was true? I paid $115 to put up a deluxe website and front page placement for twelve weeks. This meant that for three months, my photo would be linked at the top of the first page visitors see after they enter the site. I knew that if I didn't get any responses from this placement, then it meant that the website didn't get any visitors and it was all a scam.

If you look at the profile I put up on the next page, you'll see that I said I'd write anyone and was open to gay/bisexual contact. Another prisoner told me he did this and got more responses. I had two thoughts on this. One, I was going to get flooded with mail from homosexuals. Or two, I wasn't going to get any hits because my ad sounded too desperate. I was already in the process of writing this book and wanted to experiment for your sake. You're probably wondering the results of this ad? Here's what happened.

Within eight days of being on this site, I got a hit from a gal in Cali, who had previously been writing another lifer. He got out and didn't want to mess with her anymore. So she went back online to find someone new and there I was. About a month later, I got another letter from a Latin woman, who is in the Navy! A few months later, I got another hit from a 34-year old woman from Texas. And I did a few a hits from homosexuals who liked my profile and wanted to write. I wrote them back and thanked them for writing, but politely declined to correspond with them. So this site works. My advice to you is that if you're willing to write anyone, say so. You'll get a lot more hits that way.

Joshua Kruger

Share / Save

Birth Date:	June 13, 1978
Incarcerated Since:	1999
Release Date:	N/A - Lifer
Convicted Of:	Felony Murder
Home Town:	Danville, IL
Race:	White
Religion:	Asatru
Height:	6'4"
Weight:	195 lbs
Wants To Write To:	Anyone
Sexual Orientation:	Straight
Open to Gay/Bisexual Contact:	Yes
Will Write Overseas:	Yes
Seeks:	Romance, Friendship, Legal Help, Donations

Hi there, hope you're having a great day. I'll be honest, I met some people on other sites in the past, but the connections just didn't happen. So I'm changing it up. Consider this my summer makeover.

Are you tired of the same old lies? Or people who are lacking honesty, sincerity and respect? Well, I promise to shower you with attention, affection, and appreciation. To always lend a helping hand...deliver a prompt reply to all your letters...and time devoted to you and you alone!

I'm a tall, slim, witty, confident, athletic, spontaneous and open-minded guy. I spend my time reading and writing. I just finished my first book, The Millionaire Prisoner: How To Turn Your Prison Into A Stepping-Stone To Succe$$. In my spare time, I like to watch fooball but would so much rather turn off the TV and write you.

Prison is lonely and I would like to meet some new people. I'm searching for a meaningful and lasting friendship, maybe more? Inner warmth is more important than anything else because I want to get to know you from the inside out! If this sounds like something you're interested in, don't hesitate to send me a message so we can become acquainted.

Print me a letter
Send me an email

Listed: 06/22/14

© Conpals LLC • Home

ExclusivePrisoner.com

I really don't like their pages and haven't got any responses. They have a great brochure, and sell their services well, but the proof is in the pudding. When I looked into the pudding, I didn't find any proof. Here's what happened.

I posted my ad in October of 2013, and in May of 2014, I wrote to them complaining that I hadn't got any replies, aka "hits". I asked them what happened to the compatibility factor and Facebook shout-outs? Their response came two months later. (See letter on next page.) As you can see, they hint at me scamming pen pals and being a "fly-by-the-night" pen pal writer. I wrote back and said "Watch this." Their response? Silence.

Here's the truth about this site in my opinion. This day and age, it's all about making it easy on the person responding to the ad. But Exclusive Prisoner doesn't do that. They don't allow users to email you their first response. Think about that. If you were in the free world and could write a note to the prisoner right that minute, then click and icon and have it sent, wouldn't you like that? But you can't do that with Exclusive. Instead, they'll have to sit down and write a letter via snail mail and most people, especially the younger crowd (Generation Y) just won't do that for a first response.

The only reason I went on the site was because *Inmate Shopper* rated them a "10". But that's really a bogus rating because George Kayer (now retired) never used Exclusive Prisoner. His review was based on talking with the owner and looking at the brochures. Is that really a fair review? If I was the owner and knew I was talking to the #1 prison-based reviewer there was, I'd make sure *Inmate Shopper* was "wowed". But I knew all of this ahead of time. I wanted to see for myself. $40 down the drain. Not one response.

It's a legitimate site. But it didn't work for me, and I won't recommend it to anyone else. Use it at your own risk. If you have had success with Exclusive Prisoner, be sure to let me know so I can update this section in future editions of this book.

Dear Mr. Kruger,

Thank you for writing us and letting know of your dissatisfaction. The fact that you were so successful on Writeaprisoner.com or any other website tells me that you have over saturated the market. The inmate viewing / pen pal crowd all peruse the same prison pen pal websites. It makes sense that if they keep seeing the same faces over and over they begin to suspect "fishing for money". We have received multiple complaints from pen pals who have been conned by a prison pen pal. When researching this, we found that the inmates had themselves posted on multiple sites with identical ads.

Scam:
Noun-
a confidence game or other fraudulent scheme, especially for making a quick profit;

Since we do just as our brochure says we do, we are not even close to being a scam or a fraud. We provide you with a venue to post your photo, your words and your info. We promote you on Facebook, Google+ and all the other major Social Media sites.

There are no guarantees. The fact is we have many more satisfied customers who have long standing pen pals to worry about the number of fly by night pen pal writers who come and go with each month. If pen pal services were foolproof, you wouldn't need multiple subscriptions and you'd only need to be posted for a week to be successful. The reality is, inmates are at the top of the dating pool or the social scene. It takes work and time.

With regards,

Mike Davis
Client Representative

Your profile will expire: **10/25/2014**

Sincerely,
Director, ExclusivePrisoner.com

ExclusivePrisoner.com
P.O. Box 533
Madison, AL 35758

Josh Kruger Member since 2013

Hi there! Are you tired of the same old personal ads and lies? Or guys who are lacking honesty, sincerity and respect? Who don't shower you with attention, affection and appreciation? Well, here are some things I promise you'll get from me: eyes you can look into and trust…a helping hand…a heart that understands and doesn't judge……a supporting shoulder….a prompt reply to all you letters…and time devoted to you and you alone!

By way of introduction, I'm a tall (6'5"), slim, witty, confident, athletic, spontaneous, and open-minded authorpreneur. I don't smoke and love kids and animals. I love to laugh and have fun in life. Some of my favorite movies are Wedding Crashers and The Hangover. I believe that prison can be a stepping-stone to success and try to always look for the opportunities in life and not the obstacles. My post-conviction petition was recently granted on appeal because of new DNA evidence; which could lead to my freedom in 5 or 6 years. I'm very excited about this NEW EVIDENCE!

Prison is a lonely place and I'm searching for a meaningful and lasting friendship that may lead to something more? If you want a faithful man committed to building a companionship based on harmony, trust, and ultimately love, then maybe we should connect? Inner warmth is more important than anything else because I want to get to know you from the inside-out. If this sounds like something you'd be interested in, don't hesitate to send me a message so we can see if your kiss will turn me into your prince? What do you have to lose?

Use one of the options below to contact me. May you be blessed!
Yours for future happiness,
Josh

Date of Birth **06/13/1978**
Age **35**
Gender **Male**
Sexual Orientation **Straight**
Astrological Sign **Gemini**
Race **Caucasian**
Religion **Asatru**
Hometown **Danville, Il.**
Marital Status **Single**
Education **Junior College**
Favorite Book/Author **Think and Grow Rich**
Favorite Activities **Writing letters, watching football, drawing, meeting new people**
I would like to receive letters from **Women**.
I am seeking Legal Aid.
I am seeking Donations.

Details of My Incarceration
Incarcerated Since **07/30/1999**
I am serving a life sentence.

More Photos
** click on thumbnail to view larger image **

FriendsWithPens.com

I only placed a six-month ad on their websites and didn't get any responses. I don't know if that's because I don't pay for everything else they offer, but I don't really like their profile pages anyway. You can judge for yourself.

Register | Login

Welcome Guest

Home | Forum | Browse Ads | Post Ad | FAQ

Admin: Logout | Tasks | Help

Home ▶ Categories List ▶ Inmates Looking For Pen Pals ▶ Men ▶ View Ad

<< >>

Authorpreneur Seeks Long-term Friendship! Add to HotList

Add to Editor's Pick | Email to a Friend | Print Friendly   Reply to Ad

Ad Posted: Saturday, December 29, 2012
Ad Expires: Thursday, June 27, 2013

User Information:

Posted by:	k50216
IP Address:	24.116.43.170
Name:	Joshua Kruger
Birth Year:	1978
Male or Female:	Male
Country:	United States
User Location:	Joliet
User Web Site:	Myspace or Facebook Page
All User Ads	All Ads by k50216

Ad Information:

Address:	
Address Line 2:	
City:	
State:	Illinois
Zip Code:	60434
Favorite Movie:	Oceans Eleven
Dream Job:	Bestselling Autho
Dog Person:	Yes
Cat Person:	Yes
Word that Best Describes You:	Spontaneous
# of Tattoos:	5
Are you an Artist or Musician:	Artist & Writer
Favorite Music Genre:	Classic Rock
Smoker:	No
Drinker:	No
Religion:	Christian
Favorite Season:	Summer
Favorite Food:	Pizza
Favorite TV Show:	ESPN Sportscenter

Your Penpal Ad Is Online
Please check to make sure
the spelling and content is
correct

Report if this ad is offensive Viewed: 21 times

Ad Description:

Text size: a a **a** **a**

Hi there. By way of introduction, I'm a tall (6'5"), slim, witty, optimistic, confident, athletic Gemini who loves to write poetry and letters. I love to laugh and have fun in life. Some of my favorite movies are Wedding Crashers, Shawshank Redemtion, and Western's. In my spare time I like to watch baseball and football, but would so much rather turn off the tv and write you.

...g this ad is that I would like to find someone that I can develop a friendship with. Prison is a lonely place and I would like to meet ...love to hear from you, so drop me a letter or send me an email at: millionaireprisoner@gmail.com

Joshua Kruger K50216
Stateville CC
PO Box 112
Joliet, IL 60434

*****You can reply to this ad. We will print it then mail it to the inmate. INMATES DO NOT HAVE INTERNET ACCESS. Make sure that you leave your address so that the inmate can write you back.

PenPalsBehindTheWalls.com

I really like their pages and I was able to add a music video to my page at no extra cost. But I haven't gotten that many responses which is a shame because I really like their pages. They were a new website and I don't know if they did any advertising to promote their site or not. If you know, let me know and I'll update this review in the next edition of this book.

Name: Josh Kruger
Nickname: J-Roc
Facility: Stateville Correctional Center
DOB: 6/13/78
Age: 34
Race: White
Gender: Male
Sexual Orientation: Straight
Height: 6'5
Weight: 195
Eye Color: Blue
Hair Color: Brown
Job Profession: Writer
Conviction: Felony Murder
Earliest Release: 7/30/19
Seeking: Friends

I'm a single, confident, witty, and open minded author looking to meet new people. I try to look at the bright side of things and believe that prison will be a stepping stone to success. In my spare time I like to watch football, read non-fiction books and write poetry. I'm interested in learning new things and I can be spontaneous at times. I love to laugh and hope to share some good times with you. I have no specific qualifications for you... except that you have inner warmth because I want to get to know you from the inside out. So if you want to begin a great friendship with an honest, faithful guy don't hesitate to drop me a line or two. If it's more convienent you can email me at millionaireprisoner@gmail.com I hope to hear from you soon. May you be blessed in all that you do~

20 Questions/20 Inmate Answers:

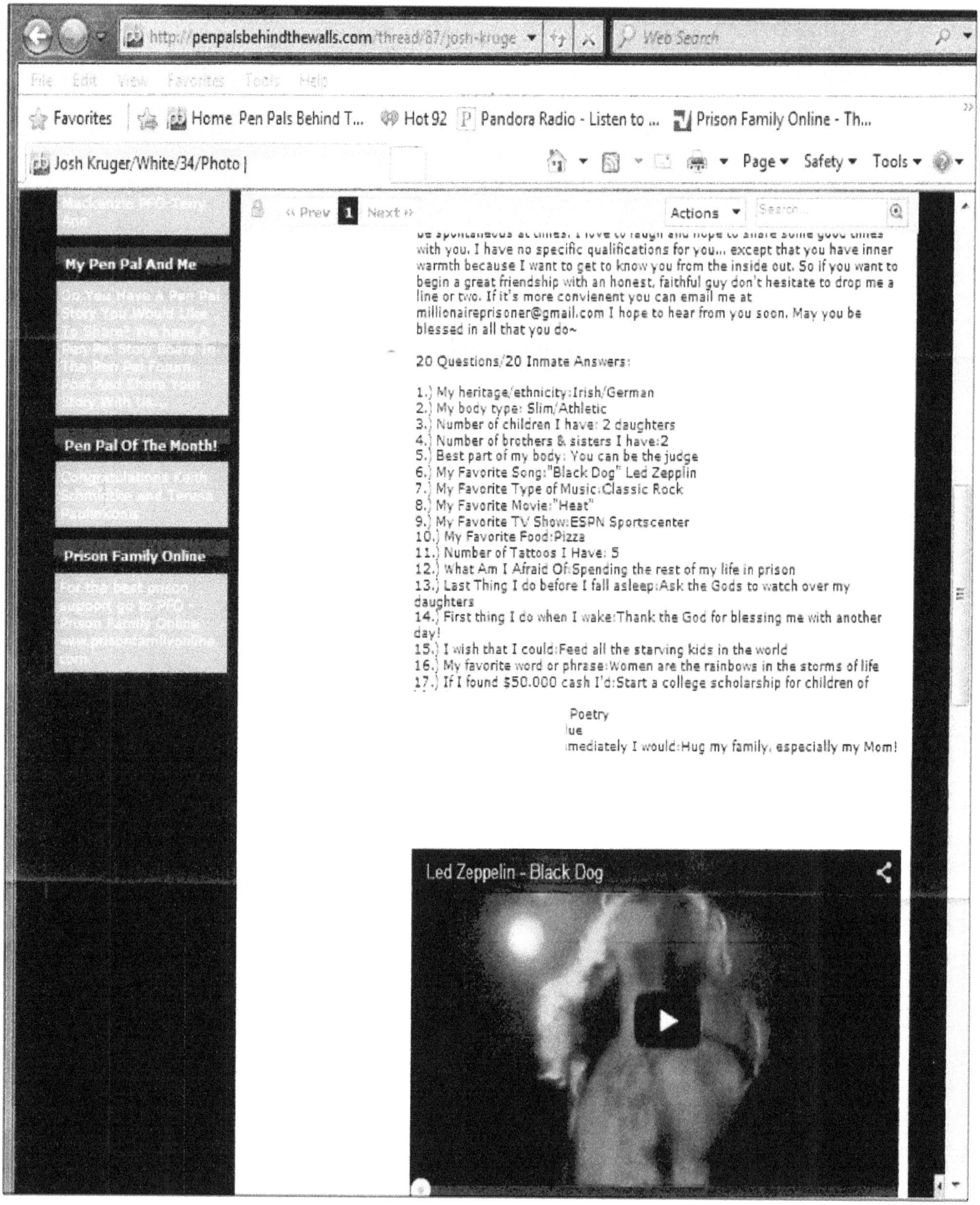

http://penpalsbehindthewalls.com/thread/87/josh-kruge

Favorites | Home Pen Pals Behind T... | Hot 92 | Pandora Radio - Listen to ... | Prison Family Online - Th...

Josh Kruger/White/34/Photo |

My Pen Pal And Me

Pen Pal Of The Month!

Prison Family Online

« Prev 1 Next » Actions

with you. I have no specific qualifications for you... except that you have inner warmth because I want to get to know you from the inside out. So if you want to begin a great friendship with an honest, faithful guy don't hesitate to drop me a line or two. If it's more convienent you can email me at millionaireprisoner@gmail.com I hope to hear from you soon. May you be blessed in all that you do~

20 Questions/20 Inmate Answers:

1.) My heritage/ethnicity:Irish/German
2.) My body type: Slim/Athletic
3.) Number of children I have: 2 daughters
4.) Number of brothers & sisters I have:2
5.) Best part of my body: You can be the judge
6.) My Favorite Song:"Black Dog" Led Zepplin
7.) My Favorite Type of Music:Classic Rock
8.) My Favorite Movie:"Heat"
9.) My Favorite TV Show:ESPN Sportscenter
10.) My Favorite Food:Pizza
11.) Number of Tattoos I Have: 5
12.) What Am I Afraid Of:Spending the rest of my life in prison
13.) Last Thing I do before I fall asleep:Ask the Gods to watch over my daughters
14.) First thing I do when I wake:Thank the God for blessing me with another day!
15.) I wish that I could:Feed all the starving kids in the world
16.) My favorite word or phrase:Women are the rainbows in the storms of life
17.) If I found $50.000 cash I'd:Start a college scholarship for children of

Poetry
ue
mediately I would:Hug my family, especially my Mom!

Led Zeppelin - Black Dog

V.I. Prisoners

V.I. Prisoners put me on LostVault.com (www.lostvault.com) and on their Facebook page (www.facebook.com/vipenpals) for $10. I know prisoners who have met wonderful people on LostVault.com and I wanted to try out their Facebook page to see what that was about. The results?

Within one week I got a hit from a homosexual in Arizona off LostVault.com he said the reason he wrote me is because I said I was an "open-minded guy" in my ad. Apparently, that can be taken as meaning open to anything? But I wasn't mad because it was research for this book. I knew my page on LostVault.com was being seen by someone. You may be wondering if I wrote the guy back. Yes, I wrote him back and thanked him for responding to my profile, but told him I didn't think we would make good friends. To be fair, that wasn't because he was gay. It was because his whole first letter was about some off-the-wall stuff, like prisoners selling their used boxer shorts after working out and outside showers? Whoa! That is definitely not my cup of tea. I've got homosexual responses off other sites as well, but never one of that ilk.

You don't need V.I. Prisoners to put you on LostVault.com. It's free to post on, so anyone can do it for you. But it only costs $3 through V.I. Prisoners. I used them because I liked their customer service. They had sent me a free "hotshot" photo when they sent a follow-up brochure package. I knew they were legit after that. And I didn't need a SASE to hear back from them. I don't know if they are still in business or not, but it would only cost you a stamp to find out. V.I. Prisoners (Out of business 2015)

V.I.P Pen Pals
3 seconds ago

Hi Friend,

Are you tired of the same old lies? Or people who are lacking honesty, sincerity and respect? Well I promise to shower you with attention, affection and appreciation. To always lend a helping hand...deliver a prompt reply to all your letters...and devote time to you and you alone!

I'm a tall, slim, witty, confident, athletic, spontaneous and open-minded guy. I spend my time reading and writing. This year I finished my first book, "The Millionaire Prisoner: How To Turn Your Prison Into A Stepping-Stone To Succe$$". In my spare time I like to watch football, but would so much rather turn off the tv and write you.

Prison is lonely and I would like to meet some new people. I'm searching for a meaningful and lasting friendship, maybe more? Inner warmth is more important than anything else because I want to get to know you from the inside out! If this sounds like something you're interested in, don't hesitate to send me a message. You can do so by writing to me direct using snail mail, or clicking through this link:

http://www.prisoninmates.com/joshuakrugerk50216

Like Comment Share

0 people reached   Boost Post

Josh Kruger

LOSTVAULT.COM
A RESOURCE FOR THOSE LOST IN PRISONS WORLDWIDE

LostVault.com Penpals

There are **2456** ads in **4** categories

HOME » PEN PALS - MALE » AD DETAIL

JOSH KRUGER (viewed 0 times)

Search

Name and Address:		**BIRTHDATE:**	June 13th
		AGE:	35
RACE:	White	**GENDER:**	Male
HEIGHT:	6'4"	**WEIGHT:**	195
EYE COLOR:	Blue	**HAIR COLOR:**	Brown
CONVICTED OF:	Felony Murder, Robbery	**RELEASE DATE:**	July 30, 2020
AD POSTED:	6/4/2014	**AD EXPIRES:**	5/30/2015

Description: Hi Friend,

Are you tired of the same old lies? Or people who are lacking honesty, sincerity and respect? Well I promise to shower you with attention, affection and appreciation. To always lend a helping hand...deliver a prompt reply to all your letters...and devote time to you and you alone!

I'm a tall, slim, witty, confident, athletic, spontaneous and open-minded guy. I spend my time reading and writing. This year I finished my first book, "The Millionaire Prisoner: How To Turn Your Prison Into A Stepping-Stone To Succe$$". In my spare time I like to watch football, but would so much rather turn off the tv and write you.

Prison is lonely and I would like to meet some new people. I'm searching for a meaningful and lasting friendship, maybe more? Inner warmth is more important than anything else because I want to get to know you from the inside out! If this sounds like something you're interested in, don't hesitate to send me a message. You can do so by writing to me direct using snail mail, or clicking through this link: http://www.prisoninmates.com/joshuakrugerk50216

113

FriendsBeyondTheWall.com

As you can see, FBTW has some great looking profile pages. They are my personal favorite for best design. But who cares about design when results are all that matters. I paid $138.95 to do a lot on FBTW. $39.95 went for a one-year "Skid Bid Deluxe Profile". I paid $75 to be listed in the "New & Featured Ads" section for the whole year. I paid $10 to put up an extra photo. I paid $10 to have an "Invisible Hit Counter" so the outside public couldn't see it. And I paid $4 to get a color, full-page printout of my profile. (See next page.) Why did I pay so much? Because a friend of mine, Emmanuel Grant, (who you've already met) had great success using FBTW and I wanted to make sure my ad was seen or possibly could be seen, with placement in the "New & Featured Ads" section for a year. So what happened?

Within the first few months I received several replies to my ad. I did receive one from a gay man and he said he responded because my profile says: "Seeks correspondence with anyone." Another response was from a single mother of three who works as a cook in a nursing home. But other than that, I haven't got any more replies. Here's what Cordelroe McMutuary in Michigan says about his experience with FBTW:

> *"I paid for a two year membership, it was costly considering my current circumstances, so after payment, I received a letter of confirmation informing me that my ad had been posted. I was so excited. A month later, I received a letter from a female. We seemed compatible right off. She claimed she felt compelled to write me and she enjoyed my sincerity. All of a sudden, out of the blue sky, she disappeared about 2 months down the line. My twisted theory, I believe she was working with the company running a scam. That's over the top right? (LOL)"*

Maybe, maybe not? I've heard stories about that happening. I've also received bogus addresses and fake emails off some prison pen pal websites before. Makes me wonder. I don't know if that's what did happen in his case. The people who contacted me off FBTW were real and it was I who discontinued the correspondence, not them. But I'm including his submission here so you can get another prisoners point of view.

FBTW is legit and has been around for years. You will get hits on their site if you follow all the rules in their brochure and this book. But you don't have to pay for all the extras like I did. It didn't pay off. Still in my "Top Five" though!

Josh Kruger

Friends Beyond The Wall

Presents ...

Composite Magic Photos
See What We Can Do
With Your Visiting Room Photos!

Before & After

Great Gift Idea! Click Here!

Joshua Wayne Kruger

Profile Information

DOB: 06-13-1978

RACE:

HEIGHT: 6' 5"

WEIGHT: 195

HAIR: Brown

EYES: Blue

EXPECTED RELEASE: 07-2020

Letter Writing Center:

3 Convenient Options
for response!

1) **Email Express**
(If facility rules allow)

2) **Print Express**

3) **Mail Call**

Click Below to Respond
Using One of the Above Options!
or write directly to the address listed!

Joshua Kruger

Hi friend, hope you're having a great day. I'll be honest, I met some people on other sites in the past, but the connections just weren't there. So I'm changing it up. Consider this my summer makeover.

Are you tired of the same old lies? Or people who are lacking honesty, sincerity and respect? Well, I promise to shower you with attention, affection, and appreciation. To always lend a helping hand... deliver a prompt reply to all your letters... and time devoted to you and you alone!

I'm a tall, slim, witty, confident, athletic, spontaneous and open-minded guy. I spend my time reading and writing. I just finished my first book, *The Millionaire Prisoner: How To Turn Your Prison Into A Stepping-Stone to Succe$$*. In my spare time I like to watch football, but would so much rather turn off the TV and write you.

Prison is lonely and I would like to meet some new people. I'm searching for a meaningful and lasting friendship, maybe more? Inner warmth is more important than anything else because I want to get to know you from the inside out! If this sounds like something you're interested in, don't hesitate to send me a message so we can become acquainted.

Sincerely,
-Joshua

*** Seeks Correspondence with: Anyone ***
Sexual Orientation: Straight

**Click Below to Send Letter or
Write Directly to Address Listed Above!**

Tips for Creating a Winning Profile

Now that I've told you a little bit about my experiences let me give you some more tips on putting your best profile up.

- Make sure you use a good, clear, up-to-date, close-up photo. Hopefully you're smiling in it. If you can, use photos doing something that you live, i.e. playing basketball or dancing. One prisoner I know used a baby picture and I used a photo of me as a kid. Be creative.

- Sell yourself, but do it softly, using words that stimulate the imagination. Use stories and anecdotes to paint word pictures.

- Be honest, positive, and exciting in your profile. Never complain about your circumstances. Show people that it will be fun to write you.

- Do you want a marriage? I wouldn't put that in your profile. Why? Because it will scare off a lot of potential pen pals. Instead, say you're looking for friendship. You will attract pen pals and over time you'll see if they have bad habits or if you are truly compatible or not. If you rush in, you may regret it later when you see the real side of your pen pal.

- Don't put too many limitations on who you're looking to meet or what you're looking for. Try not to sound judgmental or critical.

- Tell the best story about yourself in the least amount of words. You're paying for a word limit so make them count. Plus, the more you say, the better chance you have to turn the prospective pen pal off. Leave some mystery to your personality.

- Try and write something that no other prisoner will write on their profile, but make sure it fits your personality. My friend, Emmanuel "Top Flight" Grant, used this in his ad on *Friends Beyond the Wall*:

  "He can cook Italian and Mexican food."

  "He taught himself to drive cars and ride horses."

  "He sings beautifully in the shower."

  "He is Emmanuel Grant, the most interesting prisoner in the world."

  And it worked because he got the response he was looking for. Be original and creative.

- Be specific when describing your interest. Don't say "music" "sports" and "animals". Say "Hip-Hop, Oakland Raiders football and pit-bulls" if that's what you like. Don't be a generality!

- Do not allow your ad to be shuffled into the file. Keep it on the front of the site. If that means paying for placement, then do it. Your ad needs to be seen for you to get responses.

- Do not talk about money in your profile. A recent *USA Today* article described how prisoner Jerry Lee Beatty put his profile on VoiceForInmates.com and said: "I need finances for attorneys, art supplies, and some everyday essentials." That's a no-no. Build friendships first, then ask for help later.

Just a few tips for you to remember when setting up your profile.

Is Timing Everything?

Something else that you might consider is the time of year when you place your ad. People think about love and romance more in the spring and around Valentine's Day. They also think about friends and family during the Thanksgiving and Christmas holidays. I always get a spike in hits to my profile pages during the winter holiday season. Don't worry too much about the summer, because most people are outside, not inside at the computer. With a yearly service, your profile is up 24-7, 365. Then timing doesn't matter. Just make sure your profile is on the front page in February, and November through January.

Before you make a decision, do your own research. Talk to your fellow prisoners about the sites they've used. Review the rest of this book. Write the pen pal websites and request their brochures. Read them and see what you think. Just remember all the tips in this book and put your best foot forward. Let me know how you do and I might just include you in a future edition of this book!

ATTENTION: FEMALE PRISONERS

All of the strategies in the book work for female prisoners. I believe that women could have more success using them because there's always a shortage of female pen pals. And there are avenues that are not available to male prisoners, which are open to females. For instance, female prisoners get to place ads and photos in *Outlaw Biker* magazine. But you must stand out amongst the other girls who are advertising. Here are two ads that stood out to me from the March/April 2014 issue:

> Almost at the door but still single, no one to share my life with. Much saved up energy, sexuality and curiosity waiting to be set free. Needing a story, secure, mature man to swoop me up and carry me off into his sunset. Do you think that could be you, if so, I'm ready and waiting to hear from you. Write me at: Jamie McEvers in Ocala, FL.

> Chocolate Lovers Dream. Sexy sultry Shawna, fun loving free spirited inhibited. A for-real, never say never girl! Looking for outgoing individuals to write, have fun, share fantasies, life's up and downs. In a short time, this lady will be in the free world ready to catch up on all life has to offer. I am ready to hear from you! LaShawna Duval in Gatesville, TX.

These ads could be better, but they stood out from the rest. Remember that you are placing an ad in *Outlaw Biker*! So play up the fact that you're interested in sex, but also the biker lifestyle. Here's a great possible ad for a female prisoner to place in *Outlaw Biker*:

> Are you tired of riding alone? I want to wrap my long legs around you as your hog roars underneath us and the wind blows my hair. Coming home soon and ready to win all the rally contests! I'd love to hear from you. Write me at:

Combine that type of ad with a hot photo and you're bound to get responses. You've got to ask yourself: "if I was a biker, what would I want in my chick?" The magazine gives you the answer and my ad above plays into the biker lifestyle. *Pen Pal Success Rule: Tailor your ad to fit the medium you're posting your ad or profile in.* If you're a female prisoner, send your photo and ad submission for *Outlaw Biker* to:

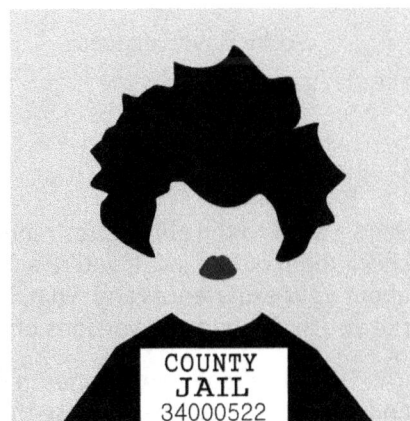

> SUBMISSIONS
>
> 5252 Orange Ave
>
> Suite 109
>
> Cypress, CA 90630

There are also websites specifically for women prisoners, not available to male prisoners. Here they are:

> Babes Behind Bars (formerly Jailhouse-Babes)
>
> 4246 Albert St, Suite #403

Regina, SASKATCHEWAN

S4S 3R9

CANADA

Women Behind Bars

Attn: Todd Muffoletto

PO Box 284

Hobart, IN 46342

Paper Dolls

PO Box 218

Oregon, WI 53575

Prison-Princesses.com

Foster-Hansen Holdings, Inc.

PO Box 864862

Plano, TX 75086-4862

Forgotten Females

c/o McLloyd Services

PO Box 3621

Wichita, KA 67201

Send a SASE to the above sites requesting information about their services or have your personal assistant check them out online. If you're a female prisoner deep in the pen pal game, I'd love to hear from you. Tell me about your experiences and what, if anything, you know about the above websites or any others. I'll be sure to put you in any updated versions of my books if I use what you submit. I look forward to hearing from you.

CAUTION: I've read news stories in the past where female prisoners were charged with new crimes for fraud and deceptive practices because they were promising sex to the guys who wrote them in exchange for money. These prisoners had to pay back hundreds of thousands of dollars and got more time added onto their sentences. So be careful about promising sex or any other favors in return for money. Use the strategies in this book to develop real friendships and you'll have everything you need in life.

Sheela Wood

Another avenue that I've seen prisoners using successfully to get pen pals is Sheela Wood's, Have-A-Friend

Club that runs in *National Examiner* and *Globe* magazines. A lot of women prisoners use this as well. Ads in Sheela Wood's Club are "coded ads". In a coded ad, your message is published but your address is withheld. The person responding must send their letters to the publisher with a fee so that the publisher (Sheela Wood), can send the letter to you. Because someone has to pay to respond to your ad, you know they are really interested in you. But with a coded ad format you will not get lots of response because of the aforementioned payment for responding. If you read the tabloids then you might find your special someone through this service. One of my cellmates did. If you're interested, send a letter of request for information about the service to:

Sheela Wood's Have a Friend Club

c/o The Examiner

Box 32

Rouses Point, NY 12979-0032

FREE Newspaper Pen Pal Ad

The national black newspaper, *San Francisco Bay View*, allows prisoners to place free pen pal ads in their publication. My comrade, Tim Smith, put me up on this resource. Your ad will run for three months and you'll also be listed on their website. You can also write articles and submit them to the *Bay View*. They list your contact info and you may get a pen pal that way? Check them out at:

San Francisco Bay View

4917 Third St.

San Francisco, CA 94124

www.sfbayview.com

($24 a year or $2 per month)

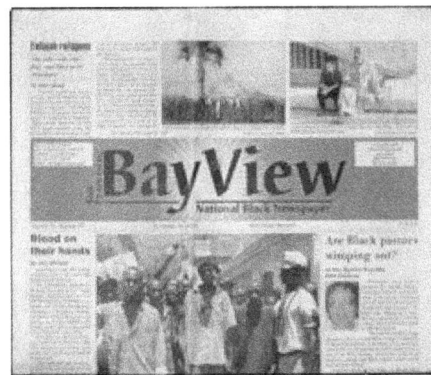

Remember to follow the rules from Chapter Six when writing your ad. There are no photos in the pen pal section of the *Bay View* so try to stand out from the rest of the ads. Ladies, place your ad because there's always a shortage of women's ads!

Answer Everyone Who Responds to You

Don't ignore them. They took the time to send you a note or answer your letter. Even if you don't want to write them you can write them in one of two ways:

"Thank you for writing. You appear to be a great person, but I have been swamped with replies and can't keep up. I want to wish you luck in finding your special friend. Thanks again."

Or

"Thanks for responding to my ad. To be honest, I've been overwhelmed with replies and can't keep up. But I have a friend who might be more your type. If you're interested in writing him, his name and number are _____. I'll tell him to maybe keep an eye out for your letter?"

I hope you find yourself in this position. Where you got too many pen pals to keep up with. But even if you don't like someone, still thank them for writing. It's the right thing to do and puts interest in the pen pal bank for good karma.

Thinking Outside the Cell

If you are allowed third party calls you can try a party line. Call home collect, then have other person call a "party line" using three-way technology. During the conversation with some of the women on the party line you can have them look up our profile page on WriteAPRisoner.com or other internet inmate pen pal websites, like Penacon.com. If the woman look you up and liked what she saw and they started corresponding.

Do not do this if you are not allowed third party calling, it can lead to being placed in the hole, losing your privileges or worse. But the key to the above strategy is having your profiles online and on different websites. If I could still take photos on visits I would post them on Instagram and Facebook. Then I would tell other people I meet, that they could check out my photos on these sites. Photos tell a story and the better story you tell, the more you'll sell. That translates to more opportunities to connect with new people and make lasting friendships. Remember, think outside the cell.

I hope this chapter helps you on your pen pal journey and you find success. Don't neglect prison pen pal websites along the way.

Chapter 9

Foreign Pen Pals

"When it comes to making new friendships or seeking a marriage partner...the world is literally your oyster!" -Richard N. Coté

A lot of prisoners that I've met over the years will not write overseas pen pals because of the extra postage costs. Other than that, the only other disadvantage of foreign pen pals is the time it takes to get replies. Let's look at writing foreign pen pals and some of the enticing benefits to writing overseas.

First off, it's never boring to write someone from another country. I had a pen-friend from Holland, and she sent me an English-Dutch dictionary. I began to learn to read and write Nederland's (Dutch). This process added some fun to our correspondence. Plus, she was very beautiful, which is always good! Another prisoner friend of mine had an English girl who would fly over twice a year and spend 10 days visiting him. She also sent him thousands of dollars a year to spend on commissary. So while some prisoners may shy away from foreign pen pals, you just might find what you are looking for if you're open-minded.

Here are some other things I've found over the years when it comes to foreign pen pals:

- India is one of the fastest growing and developing economies in the world. A lot of its people are computer literate and online on Facebook.

- In Malaysia and Singapore, the people are English speaking and educated. A lot of them want to come to America.

- Brazil is another fast growing economy and if you can learn to read and write Portuguese you might check that option out.

- My favorite place to write is Europe. Why? Because I find the women beautiful, they read and write English, and a lot of them are anti-prison. They don't believe in locking up convicts and throwing away the key. Also, their society is freer in its sexuality, and that is a major bonus!

Yes, I'm hyping up foreign pen pals, but let me caution you first on the two downsides of writing overseas.

1. Cost of Postage: For prisoners that are allowed to receive and or possess stamps, this isn't so much of a problem because you can just add the needed stamps to cover the extra postage. For a prisoner like me, who has to add a money voucher to cover the extra postage, it causes additional delays. I have to wait on the prison trust fund office to process the voucher, add the postage, and then post the letter. In some prisons, this process can take a while. I got around this problem by sending 10-15 envelopes at a time to the business office and getting them pre-stamped with the correct postage for overseas mail. That way, the letter can get sent the next day. If your prison doesn't allow you to possess stamps then talk to your counselor about getting this done ahead of time.

2. Response Time: It does take a lot longer to get replies to your letters because of the distance and some of the postal systems overseas. On top of that, your prison mail room may be super slow and add to the delays. Here's a rough guideline to how long it takes for someone overseas to get your letter from the day you posted it in the U.S. Mail:

- United Kingdom and Europe takes approximately 6 days;

- Mexico is approximately 6 days;

- Pacific Rim countries is about 10-14 days;

- Central/South America is about 12 days;

- Eastern Europe is about 12-14 days;

- Former USSR countries and Asia are about 18-30 days.

Remember that these times are only estimates and do not consider the time it takes the prison mail room to process incoming and outgoing mail. So you must exercise patience when writing overseas.

Foreign Pen Pal Clubs

There are numerous pen pal clubs from around the world that need you, the American, to help fill up their listing and publications. If you send them your name, address, age, languages that you speak (read and write), and your interest and hobbies, they *may* list you for free. But most of them do not offer you free sample or checking copies of their publications. Since most of these places get lots of letters requesting FREE listings, it can take quite a while, up to 6 months, for your listing to run. Just write them with your ad and then forget about it. When you get a letter out of the blue, you'll be pleasantly surprised. This is a great strategy for a woman prisoner to utilize because of the majority of the free requests will be from men. If a woman requests a free listing, her ad will be given priority, because of the shortage of women to list.

Here is a sample letter requesting a FREE listing:

Sample Letter Requesting FREE Listing

Intercambio International
Miquel Boggiano
Ave San Luis 516
Arecibo, Puerto Rico

Dear Mr. Boggiano:

I would like to be listed in your pen pal publication please:

Name
Address
City, State, Zip Code
U.S.A.

Age: 36   Ht. 6'5"   Wt. 195lbs

Interests: Pen pals, Futbol, Stamp Collecting

Thank you for your cooperation in this matter.
Respectfully Requested,

Josh Kruger

I know some prisoners who have had success with Asian pen pals, either through F.O.G. Corporation (Vietnamese women) or Pacific Islands Club (Asian Brides Overseas).

Foreign Newspapers

Another strategy you might consider is putting a classified ad in an English-language foreign newspaper. This is something I have considered because of the world becoming more developed and the internet leveling the playing field. Here's an ad I might run:

> American professional man, 36, 6'5", open-minded and caring with writing career, seeks college-educated woman, up to 40 yrs. old, for correspondence and friendship, maybe more? Photo, email to: millionaireprisoner@gmail.com.

It would probably do well if I placed it in the right newspaper. But you would have to see first if the newspaper would accept your classified ad. It would be easy to find out beforehand. Here's how:

1. Pick the country you want to advertise in?
2. Check to see if they have an English-language newspaper? (You can use InmateMag.com newspaper list)
3. Buy a sample copy of the newspaper and see if they run classifieds. If so, then...
4. Email the advertising department for their rates and see if they accept PayPal, U.S. money orders, or how they accept payment?
5. Send in your ad and placement and wait for response.

I took the liberty to peruse *InmateMags'* newspaper list to see what possibilities exist for this tactic and here is a partial list of English-language newspapers (and their circulation numbers) to help stimulate your mind:

- The Australian [Australia](314,000)
- The Herald Sun [Australia](540,000)
- The Age [Australia](250,000)
- The Daily Telegraph [Sydney, Aus.](250,000)
- Global Times[China](120,000)
- Business Standard[India](70,000)
- Daily News & Analysis [India](288,000)
- Economic Times [India](385,000)
- India Today [India](1,100,000)
- Irish Independent [Ireland](170,000)
- The Irish Times [Ireland](150,000)
- The Star 2 [Malaysia](90,000)
- Manila Times [Philippines](200,000)
- Moscow Times [Russia](50,000)
- The Expert [Russia](85,000)
- New Straight Times[Singapore](400,000)
- Today [Singapore](650,000)
- The China Post [Taiwan](400,000)
- The Nation [Thailand](60,000)
- Daily Express [England](1,100,000)
- Daily Mirror [England](1,800,000)
- The Sun [England](3.472.000)
- The Post [Zambia](80,000)
- Vietnam News [Vietnam] (????)

Any woman who responds would be a newspaper reader and internet user. It would be up to you to keep her interest and move the correspondence offline, if you wanted to? My advice is for you to try the other strategies in this book first, but if you want to stand apart you could try this one.

Tips and Tactics for Writing Overseas

Over the years I've learned some tips that can help you when it comes to writing overseas. Here they are:

- If you have email access and your overseas pen pal has email, go the email route. It's quicker, cheaper, and more hip for the younger pen pals.

- Get a good bilingual dictionary for the language that your pen-friend naturally speaks. Make sure it's a two-part type: "English to _____, _____ to English" variety. Some English words don't translate to other languages correctly and some foreign words don't convert to English. You want to find the right word.

- Never send sexually suggestive mail or photos to Islamic countries. There are strict laws about this for them and you don't want them to be arrested for something you said or sent.

- Never send money, money orders, stamps, or anything else of value without first wrapping it in another sheet of paper. People will steal them overseas. It's unfortunate that the mail system is not as good or reliable as ours.

- Always be respectful of your new friend's culture and customs. (Encyclopedias are good for finding information of this sort on their country.) If you're able to watch a documentary on their country or people, you should. This can help you understand a lot and give you bunches of points to write and talk about.

- Make sure you get the address right! Always write your return address in BLOCK LETTERS with "USA" underneath it:

> Name
> Address
> City, State, Zip Code
> U.S.A.

Different countries have different rules for their addresses. In Europe, the postcode goes in front of the city:

> Name
> Steenbreek 6
> 2481CH Woubrugge
> HOLLAND

In Germany the post code goes in front of the town:

> Name
> Surmstrasse 10
> 90478 Nuremberg
> GERMANY

In Great Britain and Canada, they put the postcode after the names of the shire or province:

> Name
> 98338 84th Ave
> Edmonton, Alberta T6E2G1
> CANADA

And always write the name of the country in BLOCK letters underneath everything. Make sure you get the country right. Use the latest edition of the *World Almanac and Book of Facts*.

Foreign pen pals can be fun and rewarding. I hope that you will not allow the extra postage costs to stop you from writing overseas. At least make sure you say your willing to write overseas pen pals on any prison pen pal website you post a profile on. You'll be surprised at the quality and increase in number of your responses.

126

Chapter 10

Is Online Dating an Option?

"Internet dating, although far from perfect, is clearly the most effective and efficient method of getting introduced to a large number of available singles." -Judith Silverstein

This chapter will be brief because I have no experience with online dating. Technically I do. Back in 2004 my brother's wife put me on PlentyOfFish.com but I didn't understand that with online dative, you have to be interactive. It's not for getting pen pals. And I didn't get any pen pals either. I might have gotten hits to my online dating profile, but I never knew about it because I had no one monitoring my page. If you choose to try an online dating website, you must have someone monitor your profile and make replies for you. I really do want to try it one day. The numbers back up the fact that single people are using online dating. In 2011, 40 million single people went online to find love. *Playboy* (Nov. 2014) reported that 22 percent of 25-34 year olds use online dating. The fact is that it's here to stay and now the de-facto way to meet the love of your life. If I was going to set up and online dating profile, I would come up with a template response that my assistant could automatically write for me. Something like this:

> "Thank you for responding to my ad. I'm encouraged by the prospect of getting to know you better. I believe in honesty and must tell you the truth. I have an assistant who handles my internet access because I'm incarcerated. To cut out the third part, I'd like to move our conversation offline to snail-mail. If you're open to proceeding in this manner, please email me your mailing address. I understand that trust is something we must earn, so if you want to obtain a post office box for me to write you at, that is fine also. I eagerly anticipate hearing from you again."

Yes, you are going to lose a lot of people by saying something like that. But you only want to talk to people who are open to communicating with a prisoner. I have my doubts about how many people want to do so on online dating sites? If you have any experience on them, feel free to let me know what happened and I might include your story in a future book.

Just to give you a glimpse of all the different types of dating websites, heres a list of some of them.

2017 Update - Plenty of Fish

In the beginning of 2016 I had my brother post me a profile on the online dating service PleantyOfFish.com. I used four photos and was able to put my personal bio like this:

- About: Non-smoker with athletic body type
- Details: 37 year old male, 6'4"
- Intent: Josh is looking for friendship
- Personality: Outgoing
- City: Menard, Illinois
- Ethnicity: Caucasian, Gemini
- Education: Some College
- Profession: Freelance Writer

I could also add my interests like this: STL Cardinals, UFC, Movies, Criminal Justice Reform.

I got a lot of hits to my profile. Women who lived in my prison's vicinity all wanted to meet me. There was my problem. They wanted to go on a date. Makes sense, it is called online *dating*. What did I learn from my experience? If I was to get out I would have no problem finding a date. Second, it's going to be real hard for a prisoner to come up using online dating because you can't go on the actual date!

For more about online dating you may want to check out Dan Slater's book, *A Million First Dates: Solving the Puzzle of Online Dating.*

Online Dating Sites

adultfriendfinder.com	kiss.com
americansingles.com	lavalife.com
ashleymadison.com	lovecity.com
asianfriendfinder.com	match.com
benaughty.com	matchmaker.com
collegeluv.com	matureuser.com
christianmingle.com	megafriends.com
christiansingles.com	mingles.com
date.com	myrightsomeone.com
datecraze.com	neodates.com
datingdirect.com	nevre.com
drdating.com	okcupid.com
dreammates.com	oneandonly.com
eharmony.com	overthirtysingles.com
emode.com	perfectmatch.com
epersonals.com	plentyoffish.com
facelink.com	realsinglesdating.com
friendsearch.com	sciconnect.com
friendster.com	singlesnet.com
glimpse.com	spiritualsingles.com
gay.com	thesquare.com
hifisoulmate.com	tinder.com
iwantu.com	ucandate.com
jdate.com	udate.com
jumpdates.com	usamatch.com

There are thousands more of them. Some are free, some you must pay to play. You're going to have to pay someone something to monitor your profiles, so use this tactic as a last ditch effort. Maybe in the next edition of this book, I'll be able to share my own experiences with online dating? As for right now, it's just not an option for getting pen pals.

online dating

PEN PAL TIP

Put your best photos on your pages. They are key to getting responses. Have a good, smiling shot for your bio photo.

Chapter 11

Social Networking: Is It Worth Your Time?

"Social media is either a time-wasting, woolgathering, yak-shaving waste of effort, or perhaps, just maybe, it's a crack in the wall between you and the rest of the world."
-Seth Godin

Every prisoner wants to be on a social networking site. Well, at least the ones who think it's the answer to their pen pal dreams. A lot of prisoners are in fact online using social media, especially the younger generation who are fresh off the streets. This chapter will try to cut through the myths and madness of social media and explain how you can possibly use it to get pen pals.

Social networking began back in 1995 with classmates.com. That site allowed people to catch up with old classmates from school. Of course. Now everyone has heard about Facebook, Twitter, Instagram and others. The idea behind social media is pretty simple. You create an online profile and then hook up and share with other members who have the same interests. Since that is exactly what you're trying to do with pen pals, maybe you should look into this? Or should you?

Facebook

This is the behemoth of social media. It has been reported to have a few billion users now that other countries like India and China are getting involved. You are most likely familiar with Facebook, either having used it, seen the movie *The Social Network* with Justin Timberlake, or just heard your fellow prisoners talk about it. One of the things that I like about Facebook is that once you set up a profile, it will automatically start trying to connect you with other people who share interest with you.

It has a "Networks" app, that allows you to join up with other people who you worked with, went to school with, live in your area, and so forth. Facebook also has "Groups" that have their own page and allow members to share photos, links and other tidbits. Here are 8 Facebook groups that you should consider joining:

1. 5,000 Friends in 40 Days

2. Letters to Inmates

3. Crowd Conversion Social Media Marketing

4. Ultimate Exposure

5. Internet Marketing University on Facebook

6. Ultimate Exposure! Grown Your Contacts List Instantly, Fast!

7. Social Income Group

8. Facebook Addicted

Can you really build a network using Facebook? Studies have shown that the average "Generation Z-er" has over 600 Facebook friends. My fellow prisoner, Big T, has over 400 friends; and Kenneth Hartman (author of *Mother California*) cultivated over 1,000 friends on Facebook, before the CDRC shut prisoner pages down. What could you do with 1,000 friends?

In the 2013 Holiday issue of Inmate Shopper, Tia Tormen wrote a great article about Facebook. That article is on the next coming up pages.

For those of you who have Facebook profiles from before you got locked up, you'll probably still want to keep up with your friends. I don't blame you. I just hope you got a sister or a friend that can constantly update your profile. For those of you who don't have a profile, and still wish to pursue Facebook as an avenue to build your contacts, I think you should read the following three books:

- *The Complete Idiots Guide to Facebook* by Joe Kraynak & Mikal Belicove

- *Facebook for Dummies* by C. Abram & L. Pearlman

- *The Ultimate Guide to Facebook Advertising, 2nd Edition* by Perry Marshall, Keith Krance, & Thomas Meloche

Whatever you choose, do your own research about using Facebook to get pen pals before jumping in head first. But it may just be as Tia Tormen has suggested, a waste of time and money.

2017 Facebook Update

After my online dating experience on PlentyOfFish.com did not work out I decided to try out Facebook. And that's where I hit the jackpot!

I wanted to use my Facebook profile to accomplish two goals:

1. Get free publicity for my books

2. Find a woman. I was able to do both.

I had my brother set a Facebook page called "Free Josh Kruger." I was able to do a lot of biographical info on there like this: sports teams I like, music I like, movies I like, TV shows I like, books I like, etc. I joined three different Facebook Groups: Letters Magazines to Inmates, Prison Inmate Pen Pals World International, and Pen Pals for Prisoners. But the real gold came when I punched in my high school years and hometown. That's when Facebook automatically started inviting friends I knew years ago to "friend" me. I re-met people who didn't know I was doing life in prison. I started posting weekly updates and little blogs to my page. One of the friends I had was watching my posts and gave her phone number to my twin brother. She then wrote me a letter and sent a photo. I'm still with her and I tell everyone I meet they should start with Facebook.

For one, it's free. Two, it automatically helps you find who may be looking for you and anyone from your past. Just be careful what you post. I wrote a blog about the prison being on lockdown due to a stabbing and Internal Affairs showed up trying to interrogate me. I have since taken my Facebook page down, but it's certainly a great avenue to find someone in your area or your hometown. I recommend it!

Twitter

This is the second most popular social networking site. It allows users to communicate in real time in 140 characters or less. Freelance copywriter Matthew Brennan (www.mathewbrennan.com) says: "Facebook is for talking with people you know, and Twitter is where you locate the people you should know". My comrade, Emmanuel "Top Flight" Grant, is working Twitter@graceforgrant. So a prisoner can definitely make it work for them. You want to find influential people on Twitter, follow them, and then retweet what they say. If they follow you back then you'll inherit their network. If you do set up a Twitter account, make sure you list your Twitter handle with the following directories: www.twiends.com, www.twellow.com, www.tweetfind.com, and www.justtweetit.com. For more on how to use Twitter, you might want to check out the following books:

- *Get Rich with Twitter* by Dennis L. Prince
- *Ultimate Guide to Twitter for Business* by Ted Prodromou

Google Plus

Google+ is Google's social networking site that they hope will one day rival Facebook in users. The one thing that I love about Google+, is that it's owned by Google. So anything you post will be available for someone, to possibly see, who Google searches. That in itself is why you should have your own Google+ profile. Social media expert Chris Brogan loves Google+ and wrote a book about it that you may want to read:

- *Google+ for Business: How Google's new Social Network Changes Everything*

Tia's Tips: #3 The facebook scoop

I've been in this biz for almost 5 now and I've watched business that promote Inmate Facebook ports pop up, then disappear just as quickly as they pop up. I think they disappear even faster than the photo companies out there. I've received report after report from guys who sent a biz money to build them a Facebook port, only to receive nothing in return. I'm here to give you the real scoop on having a Facebook port.

The question I receive most often is: *"Tia, will you set up a Face Book port for me? I can pay!!!"*
Short Answer. No. Long Answer: Facebook is an interactive, computer displayed, social networking port and in my opinion, is one of the biggest time suckers I've ever had the misfortune of joining. Besides that, you need to have access to a computer and probably don't.

Misconception #1: Facebook is Super-Exciting!
Uhhh, seriously? That's only because you can't do it from inside and you can't see it for what it is--a giant time sucking melting pot of social gunk. Facebook is actually pretty boring most of the time.
You can spend hours and hours of your day doing nothing but reading about what other people are doing. I would much rather be out there doing something, than sitting there reading about what other people are doing. UGH!
And, 99% of what people post is crap.
Examples: *"MandyW: My dog just took a dump right in my kitchen on the floor, now I have to scrub all the floors again! Waaaa!"* **BORING!!** And seriously, Mandy? You thought your friends needed to hear that? How about this one?: *"AlexP. My life is shit."* I see so many posts like this that it makes me want to barf. This person is just looking for attention. And by the looks of the replies people leave below her comment, she's getting it. If your life is shit, go out and do something to change it. Don't just sit there whining to your friends about it.
Ooh! How about this one: *"Geoff X wrote: "......"*
Seriously? WTF? Yes, that was his entire post. Basically he had nothing to say, but felt compelled to post something on his port (more attention seeking) so he posted just this → .....
Or they post just this: Yep. The entire post is just a big smiley face.   How exciting is that?

Misconception #2: FB will help me find pen pals.
Probably not. Why? Because you don't have a computer and therefore can't access your port on a daily basis in order to maintain your postings and search for people who want to write a pen pal. It takes hours and hours to hunt down people that you do know so you can add them to your friends list. Imagine the time it will take to try to find people you don't know.
On top of that, you need an email that you can access regularly, so you can set up a port. Unless you have a really cool friend that is willing to do this for you, who is seriously going to put in the time that is needed to do it right, for a reasonable cost?

When a Facebook port *might* be worth the money:
If you have a business or product that you're selling, then Facebook could be something you might want to consider as a business venue. But, you are going to drop a wad of money on an agent (someone on the outside to do it for you) in order to get your port up with your information, then help you get with lots of "friends" and other business that will read the posts your agent writes.

So seriously, Guys, unless you guys know of a reputable company that's been in biz for a while, that is offering FB ports for a reasonable fee, quit worrying so much about not having one. If you do know of a good company that sets up FB ports, let me know. I'll look into them personally.

If you're in the market for Pen Pals, my advice would be to find a pen pal company that uses Facebook as a business tool to help promote their pen pal clients . I've personally only seen one company do this so far.
Exclusive Prisoner has a Facebook/pen pal business page and I see them post pen pal ad's with photos of the pen pal, and an address of where to write them, on a daily basis. I do not know if there are other prisoner pen pal businesses out there that post their pen pal ad's on Facebook. (I am not endorsing Exclusive Prisoner and I know nothing of their success rate in regards to finding pen pals for prisoners by using FB.)
Just putting up a FB port with your, photo, name, and address does you absolutely no good. You need to be able to or find someone willing to promote it for you. No one can see it except for those people on your friends list. If you don't have someone willing to devote the time needed to a FB port, it's a waste of your money.
And seriously, it's not going to be anywhere near the same if you can't read the posts for yourself.

135

LinkedIn

 This is the social networking site for business people. If you offer services, are an author, or are looking for work, you need to be on this site. And you may want to read

- *The Power Formula for LinkedIn Success: Kick-Start Your Business Brand and Job Search* by Wayne Breithbarth
- *The Power in a Link: Open Doors, Close Deals, and Change the Way You Business Using LinkedIn* by Dave Gowel

Passions Network

Passions is a free online dating and social networking website. There are thousands of individual's networks inside the Passions community. Once you sign up for a "network Wide Membership", you can access the different networks. I was curious and looked to see what networks I would join if I was on Passions. Here are the ones for me:

- Inmate Passions
- Legal Passions
- Millionaire Passions
- Movie Passions
- Non-Smoking Passions
- Pen Pal Passions

- Reading Passions
- Skinny Passions
- Sports Passions
- Tall Passions
- Tattoo Passions
- Writers Passions

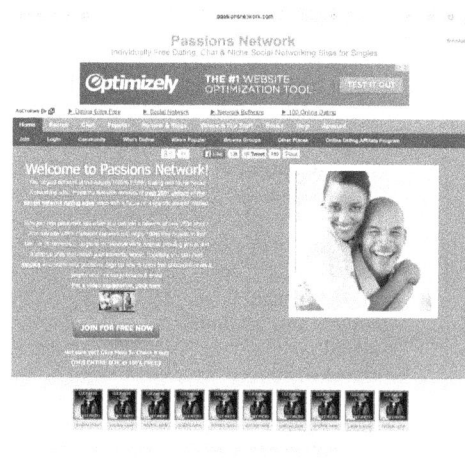

There are plenty of other networks inside the Passions network that you may want to join. Once involved, you'll be able to get "smiles" (kind of the same as a Facebook "Like"), find pen pals, and grow your list of contacts. This is probably your best shot, but of course, you'll need email and someone to help you interact online. Try this website first before all the others in this chapter.

MyJailBird.com

A few years ago, I saw the ads for this site in *Prison Legal News* and had my personal assistant set up a profile for me. I was disappointed. The only way to use myjailbird.com is through a third party sponsor. And all pages on myjailbird.com are private and can't be seen by the general public. Only those people who join myjailbird.com, can see it and become my friends. So I abandoned my profile and went back to writing. If anyone is using myjailbird.com to successfully build their network, send me a letter showing me how you're doing it so that I can share it with the rest of the prison world.

There are some of the major social networking sites, but there are plenty of others. Have you web savvy fiend check them out for you.

> *"You have to be a social media player if you want to be a player."* -R.W. Goldberg

Social Media Rules to Live By

If you do decide to take on the burden of social media, here are some things to remember.

- Put your best photos on your pages. They are key to getting responses. Have a good, smiling head shot for your bio photo. Use that same photo for all of your bio photos on all of your profiles.

- When writing your bio, fill out the section completely. Change it up every once in a while so your pages don't become stale.

- People are on social media sites to make connections, so don't be fake or phony. Keep it real and build friendships.

- Put your email address and your snail-mail address on your page so people can contact you. Then put your social network links in your email .sig.

- When sending email and/or messages, keep your posts short. People online don't read, they scan. So messages should be kept under 200 words.

- Share! If you find a website, photo or something that you think others will be interested in, then share it. Add value and people will love you for it. Remember to put "http://www." In front of the site name (nameofsite.com) so they can instantly click through to it. (i.e. http://www.nameofsite.com vs www.nameofsite.com (most sites services, will automatically make this a link, either way.)

- Engage as much as you can. Ask questions. Encourage interaction. Talk with your people, not at them. By using www.hootsuite.com, you can preschedule your social media posts ahead of time. So a prisoner could write a week's worth of posts, and have them sent out one a day!

- Remember to use hashtags! This is done by putting the "pound sign" (#) in front of key words. (i.e. #millionaireprisoner) Especially when writing about trending topics. That way anyone searching for that topic would have the opportunity to see your post as well.

- Use free websites *About.me* or *Vizify* to link all of your profiles and pages.

- If you don't want other people to see or read it, you're better off not posting it.

The above tips are only just a few that you need to know. If you are considering going online to use social networking sites, I suggest you research it first.

The
Art of
Social
Selling

FINDING AND ENGAGING CUSTOMERS ON TWITTER,
FACEBOOK, LINKEDIN, AND OTHER SOCIAL NETWORKS

Shannon Belew

You can start by reading the books I've already listed or this one:

The Art of Social Selling: *Finding and Engaging Customers on Twitter, Facebook, LinkedIn and Other Social Networks* by Shannon Belew

The key for a prisoner using social media is having someone in your network that can respond to all the messages and posts that you receive. Cultivate this person. Because if you don't, you're going to have to spend a lot of money paying someone to do it.

A Social Media Tactic for Getting Pen Pals

If I was going to leverage the power of social media to get pen pals this is how I'd do it. First, I would build simple pages on Facebook, LinkedIn, Google+ and Twitter. Then I'd build a blog that I wrote for 3 or 4 times a week and link that blog back to my social media pages. When someone left a comment on one of my blog posts, I'd send them a message and start connecting with them. This is how Freedom Jones (author of *How to Get Girls While in Prison*) met his girl. (By becoming a prisoner expert via blogging.) Maybe you could do the same? To do this it would be best if you registered your own domains like Chris Zoukis has done with www. chriszoukis.com and www.prisonlawblog.com. Then blog regularly through these sites and have your posts automatically fed to your social media pages. Just something for you to consider.

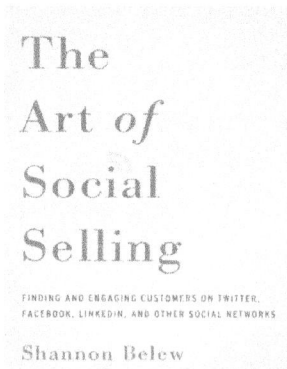

A Final Thought

For getting pen pals, blogging and social media may just not be worth the time for prisoners. But for the business minded prisoner trying to network, it may be the answer? If you'd like to read a different perspective about this whole thing, then check out *Social Media is Bullshit* by B.J. Mendelson. For now, I advise you to work the other avenues in this book first before you try out social media.

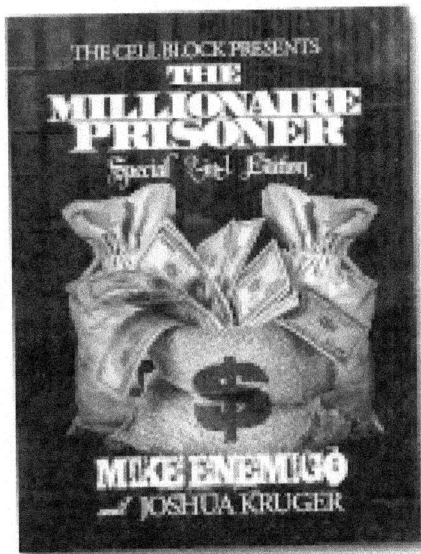

$29 each,
Free S/H with Tracking

CLEAR

Light Blue

Light Pink

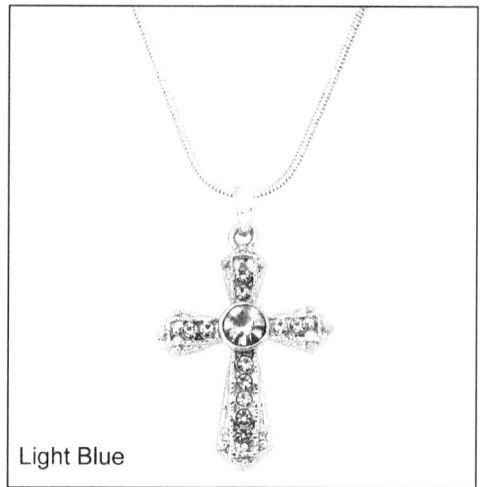

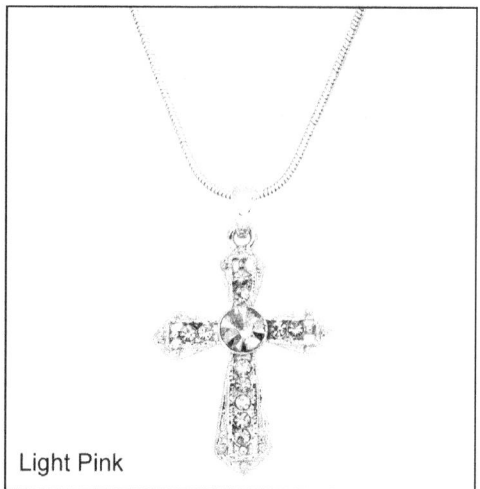

The classic emblem of faith is beautifully reimagined in this charm version necklace. The classic cross pendant rhinestone necklaces come in clear, light blue, or light pink.

The cross-pendant measures .75 inches in width by 1 inch in length and is embellished on the front with one large center stone and 10 smaller stones on the body of the cross. 18-inch snake chain, rhodium plated.

Each cross necklace arrives in a shiny metallic gift pouch and a small gift card. (include 30 characters to be added to the card). Each gift will be shipped in a decorative bubble envelope for safe shipping.

FREEBIRD PUBLISHERS

No Order Form Needed: Clearly write on paper & send with payment to:

Freebird Publishers 221 Pearl St., Ste 541 North Dighton, MA 02764
Diane@FreebirdPublishers.com www.Freebirdpublishers.com
We accept all forms of payment. Plus Venmo & CashApp!
Venmo: @FreebirdPublishers   CashApp: $FreebirdPublishers

PayPal
VISA DISCOVER BANK

140

Chapter 12

Pen Pal Mentorship with Celebrities

"The shortest route to success in any field of endeavor, and life in general, is to seek the company of those who have a great deal of wisdom." -Robert J Ringer

Most prisoners dream about having a celebrity in their network. It can be done, it just takes homework, a lot of writing, determination and patience. James Allridge III, was on death row in Texas. Before he was executed in 2004, he built a list of contacts using his artwork. He had the support of movie stars like Elizabeth Taylor and Robert Redford. Actress Susan Sarandon bought artwork from him and even visited him on death row. So it's definitely not impossible. You just got to know how to do it.

Any celebrities address can be found with an internet search. Have your personal assistant try whitepages.com if you know their hometown. Another great site for addresses and phone numbers is www.zabasearch.com. If they are a big enough celebrity, a simple Google search will get you their fan mail address. If you still can't find it, try www.celebrity-addresses.com, which has over 14,000 addresses. Once you get their address, write them a letter. Don't be a fan. (The word fan comes from *fanatic*, and has a negative ring to it.) Show knowledge of their recent work, and compliment them. Be respectful and be different. Take your shot. I said it before and I'll keep saying it: *It only takes one yes to change your life*. Never say no for the other person. How do you know they won't write back? You won't unless you try. Keep writing new people and asking questions. Don't become a stalker. Eventually you'll get that one yes you're looking for.

Resource Box

If you really want to pursue getting a celebrity in your network, then you should read the following books:

- *The Celebrity Black Book* by Jordan McCauley

- *Celebrity Leverage: Insider Secrets to Getting Celebrity Endorsements* by Jordan McCauley

Have someone check out his website at: www.celebrityleverage.com

---

But celebrities are not limited to just Hollywood and who's on TMZ. Every town has a celebrity. Every occupation has a celebrity. Even prison has their celebrities. Find these people and cultivate them. Yes, it takes work, but that's why it's called a net-work. Seek and you shall find. Ask and you shall receive.

Finding Favorable Mentorship

Someone once said, "If the king likes you, it doesn't matter who dislikes you." It sounded cool, so I wrote it down. Later on, it dawned on me that they were talking about favor. Favor has been defined as being friend to another, especially in regards to a superior, towards someone of lesser standing. I'm not talking about "favors" as in the exchange of gifts. With favor there is no debt. To better illustrate what I'm talking about, let me give you a few examples. This will help you understand its power.

In 2007, I began a writing campaign in which I wrote to all the authors of books, which I read in research for my first book, *The Millionaire Prisoner*. I wrote them telling them how their book had helped me and that I was writing my own book for prisoners. Notice that I was telling the truth. It wasn't some form of a jailhouse game. Their books had in fact changed my life and the way I thought. I wanted to share this with them. But did I really expect responses? No, but I hoped that someone I admired would validate my journey by giving me a reply. A few of them did write me back.

The famous motivational speaker and author, Zig Ziglar, sent me a copy of his autobiography: <u>Zig</u>. He's an inspiration to me and his books *Top Performance* and *Secrets of Closing the Sale*, have helped me on my journey. His autobiography was a great read and showed me that by helping others get what they want out of life, my prosperity would be given to me. If I had questions, I'd write Zig and he'd give me an answer. He showed me favor and is my mentor. It is with deep sadness that I tell you that Zig passed away in 2012. But his son is carrying on the Ziglar tradition and you should read Zig's last book, *Born to Win*. Zig Ziglar didn't have to send me books or write me back. But he understood that helping someone else up the ladder of success is the right thing to do. You need to find your own Zig Ziglar.

"Favor must become your seed before it can become your harvest." -Dr. Mike Murdock

The easier way to find a mentor is by writing to them. On the next page is a sample letter that you can use as a format. Once you get someone to answer one of your letters, here are a few things you can do to make it a profitable relationship:

1. Choose the right mentor. If you want to be a writer, you don't seek out someone who builds motorcycles for a living. You want someone that's successful in your chosen vocation.

2. Be honest with yourself and your mentor about what is happening. Seek to understand what your mentor has to offer, and what you hope to gain. Discuss this with your mentor, if possible.

3. Be open-minded and humble. Don't allow what you think you know to stop you from learning what you need to know. Don't brag about who's mentoring you to other prisoners either.

4. Have a hunger for learning. Always ask questions. Your mentor will not get mad or upset if they see that you're honestly trying to learn. Become a protégé, not a parasite. You want what's in their head, not anything they could hand out. If you ask the right questions you'll get the right answers.

Having a mentor will save you time and money. They should show you the errors in your ways and help you excel. One day you'll be able to show them how much their help aided you, on your journey. That will be the ultimate compliment.

Cultivating Favor

But favor is not just limited to your mentors. Because you can receive favor from anyone you need to follow a few steps in your everyday life to assist you.

First, always be respectful to those who have the power to bless you. Especially those in higher positions than you.

Second, be ready to accept the responsibilities that others ask of you. If someone asks for help, help them. Do this without expecting any form of payment from them. The Universe will pay you in kind for all that you do for others.

Letter Requesting a Mentorship

Dear (insert expert's name):

I hope this letter finds you in the best of health and spirits. I just finished reading your book, (insert their book title), and I can honestly say that it has truly changed my life. I am trying to learn more about becoming a success in (insert whatever it is), and would like for you to mentor me.

In making this request I would like to know what you've learned over the years, and I'm not out to get what you've earned. I would like to be a protégé and not a parasite. I don't want you to tell me, but to show me. I do understand that your time is valuable, so what I propose is sending you a letter here and there with any questions that I may have. Then you can answer them whenever you get some free time. If it's more convenient you can respond by emailing me at _____@gmail.com.

Once again, thank you for writing (insert their book title). I like the part about (insert something you like about their book). It was a great read. You can quote me on that in any promotions that you do. Thank you for taking the time to consider my letter and request. I look forward to hearing from you soon.

Respectfully requested,

(*Your Name*)

(*Your Address*)

Third, you must always prepare yourself when your time comes. Make your first impression a great impression. Let me share with you a few more examples of how prisoners cultivated favor. I found this story on the front page of the USA Today newspaper. James Churchill spent 10 years in prison for armed robbery in Michigan. Lt. Ralph Mason told him that if he could stay out of trouble he would help him find a job. Churchill did just that and Mason helped him get a job at an industrial plumbing company making $21 an hour upon his release.

In the same USA Today article, it was reported that Andres Idarraga spent six years in prison for cocaine and weapons charges. He approached A.T. Wall, the Director of Corrections in Rhode Island, for a letter of recommendation to Yale Law School. Idarraga had earned high grades at the University of Rhode Island and Brown upon release from prison. After a series of breakfast meetings, Mr. Wall, who is a graduate of Yale, decided to write the letter. That letter opened the door for Idarraga, and as I write this, he's in law school at Yale.

Both of the above former prisoners experienced the power of favor. Churchill received his from a police officer, and Idarraga got his from the director of the prison system. Sometimes in life you need help from unexpected sources. If you put yourself in the right position, you may get the letter of recommendation that you need.

Brian Hamilton knows firsthand the plight of a prisoner having had a cousin who died inside. Once the owner of his own landscaping business, Hamilton is now CEO of Sageworks Inc., a computer company that develops software for financial professionals and small businesses. In 2008, Hamilton founded Inmates to Entrepreneurs, a community outreach program that teaches prisoners how to start productive, low capital service businesses upon release. The key to the program is the goal of connecting released prisoners with mentors who can assist them.

Former prisoner Lawrence Carpenter did time for dealing drugs and armed robbery. Now he runs his own janitor service company that has 53 employees and provides services for businesses in several states. In 2010, Carpenter and Brian Hamilton went to the Eastern Correctional Institution in North Carolina to give a two-hour course on starting a business. They may be coming to a prison near you in the future. If they do, sign up. But you don't have to wait for someone to show up at your prison to get a mentor. Seek them out by letter, email, and through the books you read.

"Successful People rely heavily on their mentors. Ordinary people don't." - Robert G. Allen

---

Resource Box

For more on mentors, you may want to read:

* *Who's in Your Top Five? Your Guide to Finding Your Success Mentors* by Bertrand Gervais

---

If you do decide to start an account with Prisoner Assistant, you'll have the opportunity to post a profile on their website. You can see mine on the next few pages. I used it for more of a business type profile, than my pen pal pages. You should too. It could be an avenue to starting yon your journey to success.

Now that we've gone through the ways to get pen pals that I use, let's learn how to keep them!

Joshua Kruger

Joshua Kruger

Age	36
Date of Birth	06/13/1978
Gender	Male
Ethnicity	Irish-German
Religion	Neo-Pagan
Educational History	Some Junior College
Hometown	Danville, IL
Release Location	Las Vegas or a Carribean Island somewhere
Release Date	I am serving life so it's up to the appellete courts.

Profile

I'm a typical man's man. (Okay, that's what I tell everyone, but I'm really a Momma's boy at heart). I spend most of my time writing and reading nonfiction "How-to" books. I dabble in poetry and have had some published. Some of my favorite magazines are *Success, Inc. Entrepreneur,* and *Forbes*. My favorite TV shows are Shark Tank, The Profit, the Blacklist, and Hannibal. I like movies, especially Clint Eastwood westerns. I love watching college football, and basketball, and St. Louis Cardinals baseball. My musical tastes range from Led Zeppelin and Guns-N-Roses to Cage the Elephant and

Eminem. I have twin, 14-year old daughters that I do not get to see because of my incarceration, but dearly wish I could talk to them. Besides my daughters, some of the other things I miss the free-world are: Dairy Queen Blizzards, fried egg and cheese sandwiches, and a bigger bed, not in a little cot-like bunk (I'm 6'4"). I especially hate being on a 10-minute timer in the shower. (There's nothing worse than the water being cut off on you while you have shampoo in your eyes.)

As far as politics goes, I believe in lower taxes and less government intrusion into our daily lives. I know from an insider's view that America as a nation incarcerates way too many people and for the health of our country that needs to stop. I also don't believe that prisoners should be cut off from communicating with the free world. But really, I love life right now, and can't wait to get up in the morning to see what I can learn or accomplish. I know that prison can be a stepping-stone to success and we should always look for the opportunities in life and not the obstacles.

Seeking a Mentor

I'm looking for mentorship in wealth building through publishing ventures like a print magazine or newsletter, or E-zine; and how-to-use print-on-demand technology to publish books.

Future Goals

My future goals are to own my own business and to be very successful at whatever I do. To make up for all the time that wasn't spent with family and friends. I want to be able to show everyone that no matter what crime you commit and with the odds stacked against you, you can be a pillar of society. My goal is to make sure I never return to prison. I want to someday own residential real estate and my own home. These are goals that I've set to make a better future for myself and the people around me.

http://millionaireprisoner.blogspot.com

How Prisoner Assistant Has Helped Me

Prisoner Assistant has helped me reconnect to the free-world again. I no longer feel like a forgotten animal locked in a cage. Instead, now I know that with the help of Prisoner Assistant I can extend my reach via the internet and email. It gives me a sense of hope that maybe I can find some sort of redemption. But the world is now flat for me! Where before I saw only the 30-foot stone wall surrounding my prison, now I see a whole new world of opportunity.

Donations

Donations for the client will be accepted & deposited into their account. Please send a money order (NO CHECKS) made payable to the client's name. Send all donations to the following address:

482 Summit Wind Drive, Suite 704

Lake Harmony, PA 18624-0704

Or

UPDATE: Prisoner Assistant no longer provide services directly to clients. They have transioned into a company that services other prison service providers and will develop and market reenty programs.
Prisoner Assistant clients have been tranfered to
Lifetime Liberty Group, a Non-Profit Organization
122 Lakeshore Drive, Ste. 692, Lake Harmony, PA 18624-0692
www.lifetimelibertygroup.org - info@lifetimelibertygroup.org

Prisoners are looking for someone to help them with their legal appeals. But why wait for someone else? Take it upon yourself to find someone. That's what Anthony Faison did. In 1988 he and a codefendant were sent to prisoner for the murder and robbery of a cab driver. While inside, Faison wrote over 60,000 letters to attorneys, politicians, and anyone else who he thought might help prove his innocence. He found a taker in a Long Island, NY private detective. Faison and his codefendant, Charles Shepherd, were released in 2001 after 13 years behind bars and awarded $1,650,000! (www.truthinjustice.org/Faison) Proof that you don't have to wait on someone else to take action when you can write letters yourself.

"Energy and persistence conquer all things." -Ben Franklin

But when you do find someone willing to help you out with your criminal or civil cases, you should set up a legal defense fund. My friend, Illinois prisoner Jamie Snow, and his wife, set up a website www.freejamiesnow.com, and she coordinates all his legal stuff through the website. Snow writes his sites URL on the outside of all his outgoing envelopes and his family and friends write it on the money they spend. Guerrilla marketing at its best.

My info-cellpreneur comrade, Mike Enemigo, of The Cell Block publishing group, his team has an email address of freemikeenimigo@yahoo.com which helps get the word out.

Jody Cramer corresponds and visits death row prisoner Keven Cooper. She is an activist working to end the death penalty, and is the Executive Director of the Keven Cooper Legal Defense Fund. For more, check out www.savekevincooper.org.

You can do the same if you find the right person. If you are looking for legal help be sure to check that box on the website application. But if you or your pen pal have the funds available you should purchase your own website domain name: "free (your name) .com" or if on death row, save (your name)_.com". Then build your own website as a foundation for your defense and appeals. Good luck and never give up.

Angel Charm Bracelet

Cross Charm Bracelet

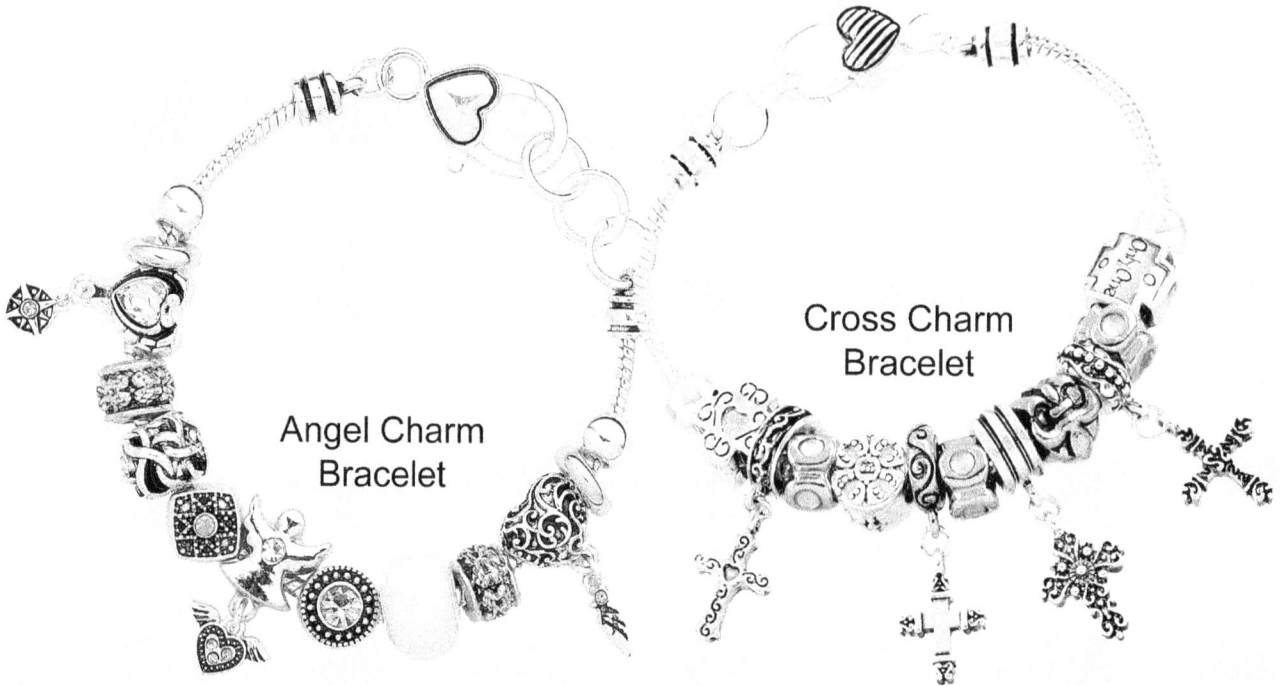

These beautifully crafted charm bracelets are always in style. They are the ideal gift for bridal, prom, anniversary ceremonies, baptism, communion, Easter, Mother's Day, Valentine's Day, or other celebration holidays.

ANGEL CHARM BRACELETS
Light blue rhinestone crystals, silver, and gold metal beads. Angel charms in silver dangle from the bracelet. One Size Fits All, 7" Chain with extra ring fit up to 8"
$25 with free shipping with tracking
Each angel charm bracelet arrives in a shiny metallic gift pouch and a small gift card. (include 30 characters to be added to the card). Each gift will be shipped in a decorative bubble envelope, for safe shipping.

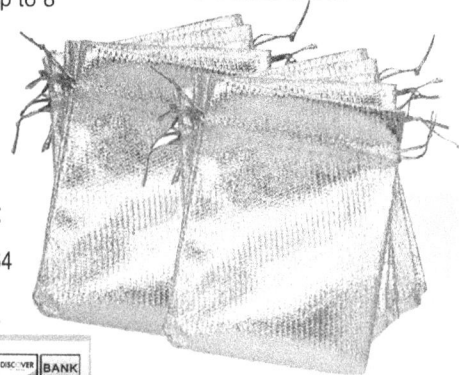

CROSS CHARM BRACELETS
Clear rhinestone crystals, silver, and gold metal beads. Cross charms in silver dangle from the bracelet. One Size Fits All, Silver Plated, 7" Chain with extra ring fit up to 8"
$25 with free shipping with tracking
Each cross charm bracelet arrives in a shiny metallic gift pouch and a small gift card. (include 30 characters to be added to the card). Each gift will be shipped in a decorative bubble envelope, for safe shipping.

FREEBIRD PUBLISHERS

No Order Form Needed: Clearly write on paper & send with payment to:
Freebird Publishers 221 Pearl St., Ste 541, North Dighton, MA 02764
Diane@FreebirdPublishers.com   www.Freebirdpublishers.com
We accept all forms of payment. Plus Venmo & CashApp!
Venmo: @FreebirdPublishers   CashApp: $FreebirdPublishers

PayPal
VISA   DISCOVER   BANK

Chapter 13

Turning a "Hit" into a Friendship

"In poverty and other misfortunes of life, true friends are a sure refuge." -Aristotle

Now that you've made contact you need to know what to do so you can stay in contact. This is, by far, the hardest part of the *Pen Pal Success™* system. It's where most prisoners mess up. It's where I used to mess up. Building a pen pal network is not about you and you only. If that is the attitude you show your acquaintances, they will not be your acquaintances for long. Remember that these people answered your ad, or responded to one of your letters. They have something missing from their life as well. You have to find out what it is and do it quick. Let's look at some things you can do to help you do this.

Because most of your contact will be done through mail, email and/or phone conversations, you need a system to keep track of things. First, write down your contacts info on a blank sheet of paper or 3x5 index card. Then list all the vital info that you know. If your contact is a celebrity or big shot in business, you could look them up in *Who's Who*, if your prison library has one. If not, a simple Google search will turn up lots of interesting stuff. What type of stuff do I write down? I keep track of where they went to school? What their pet's names are? How many kids? Age of children? Hobbies? Anything that I think is relevant. These files will be your pen pal network notes. Here's why I started doing it this way. The IDOC prison system forces prisoners to live out of two boxes. One is for correspondence/legal; the other is for clothes, food, cosmetics and other stuff. If I was to save all the mail that I received I would not have any more room in my correspondence box. So I keep notes on my pen pals and discard my mail. I only save very important documents, some cards and photos, etc. it also saves time when I want to look something up. Honestly, if I wasn't an author/ publisher and only did pen pals as a hustle, I would do it different. Then I would have a legal file folder for each pen pal and would get it out when I got a letter so I could review their file before I wrote back. Especially if I had a lot of pen pals.

No matter which way you go, the most important thing to remember is to keep your pen pal network notes up-to-date. Write down the date when you list info. Go over your notes periodically. They'll provide you with a wealth of information. When you write a letter, use your notes. If they have a birthday coming up, send them a card. And always write a little personal note in any card you send. Do not send e-cards. Use snail-mail. People (especially women) love them. (More about cards in a few chapters.) How else can you use your pen pal network notes? Do they have pets? Ask about them. Send articles about that type of pet that might help them out. Show them that you care. Understand that this is not about manipulation, but you want them to see that you are interested in them and their likes.

You are trying to build a friendship. Here are some more tips to remember when writing pen pals in your network:

- Do not ever gossip about other pen pals in your network to anyone else. Ever.

- Do not neglect your mentors when building your pen pal network. They can be an invaluable source of wisdom and ideas.

- Get a copy of *Chase's Calendar of Events*. It lists thousands of historical events by date. It's got famous birthdays and national/state events. Use it when you write your pen pals. You can really stand out by sending cards on special days that no one else knows about. Especially if these special days pertain to your new pen pal.

- Read and subscribe to newspapers and magazines. Cut out articles that may interest your pen pals. Send it to them when you write letters or cards.

- Try out new stuff, hobbies, and TV shows that your pen pals are interested in. use it for general conversation fodder. Talk to your pen pals about what they love and they'll love you for it. And you may find that you like it also.

- Answer all mail promptly. Answer online communication as soon as possible. Show people that you value them and their time.

Not every pen pal you get will stay your pen pal. Sometimes, things just don't work out. People change. Don't beat a dead horse in trying to keep writing them. Seek out new people to write. If it's meant to be, it will be.

"Expand your network by one quality person a day, forever." -Mark Victor Hansen

Run a Friendship-Centered Pen Pal Program

Because I'm a big advocate that you should develop long-term pen pals, I want to help you do that. Becoming a great pen-friend and having a long-term pen pal is easy if you're friendship-centered and not profit-centered. Yes, I know some of you are reading this book looking for "the game." Pen pals are your business! I'm not stupid. But I can tell you that if you develop some real friendships first, then you will have everything you want in the long run.

Of course that takes time, but once you have a friend that writes regularly, you'll be in a better position to get the help you need. What do you do if you've never done this? Pretend. Pretend like you do care. Pretend that if you don't make this friendship, you won't get out of prison. That way you'll do your best. Every prisoner could do it, if their freedom depended on it. Take your time and don't rush things. Time spent doing your best, putting together the best letter, will pay off in the long run.

> *"It takes time to succeed because success is merely the natural reward for taking the time to do anything well."* -Joseph Ross

So many other prisoners are running game, that if you just take your time to do it right, you will stand out. Trust me, I learned this the hard way. There are plenty of pen pals that I got back in the early 2000s that I wished I still had today. A lot of them I lost because I didn't take my time and tried to rush things. Others I lost because I didn't give it my best. I do things different now. So should you. Think true friendship first. When a farmer plants a seed, he doesn't get a harvest overnight. Neither can you get a pen pal harvest overnight. Put in the time and work and you'll get your harvest. Always remember this on your pen pal journey.

Pen-Pal Network Note Sample Form

Name_____Nickname _____

Address _____

State _____ Zip Code _____

Phone # _____ E-Mail _____

Age _____ Height _____ Weight _____

Eye Color _____ Hair Color _____

Occupation _____

School _____

Children _____

Pets _____

Interests _____

Hobbies_____

Favorite Book _____

Favorite TV Shows _____

Favorite Music _____

Birthday_____ Astrological Sign _____

Date of 1st Contact _____

What media was used? Website? Ad? _____

Any Health Issues? _____

Impressions _____

_____

Any Rules? No-No's? _____

Religion _____

Politics _____

Using Horoscopes

Anytime you can frame your friendship in a bigger picture, you should. Horoscopes allow you to give your pen pal correspondence a sense of destiny. What's better than having the stars aligned behind you? As soon as you know your pen pals birthday, you can use this strategy. Here's how.

Look for the horoscopes in any magazine, newspaper, or TV guide that you have or read. Or you can subscribe to horoscope guides from the prison magazine services. Read yours and your pen pals astrological sign. Anytime it says something that even remotely pertains to her/him, you or both of you, it should be sent with a note saying something like this:

> "I normally don't pay attention to this kind of thing, but as I was reading the latest issue of _____ , I came across the horoscopes. I couldn't help but smile as I read ours. Looks like I'll be paying much more attention to this now that the stars are aligned behind us."

Then you attach the horoscope that you're talking about to the letter, note or card. Do not write it out yourself. Let them read it in its original form and it will carry the weight of the sun behind it. For example, I'm a Gemini. If I was writing an Aquarius I just met, I could send the horoscope on this page.

After the first time you do this, you can just say, "Hey babe, I found another one. Crazy how close these things are. Makes you wonder huh?", and just send the horoscope. You won't be able to do it all the time, but when you do get to do it, it will be rewarding. Horoscopes are something to have fun with and shouldn't be taken too seriously.

Aquarius (Jan. 20-Feb. 18):
Looking to meet new people? This is the time to do it! Accept as many invitations as you can, and you'll find new friends.

Pisces (Feb. 19-March 20):
If you've been thinking about getting a new job, this is the time to look. You may be ready to expand your skill set, so think big!

Aries (March 21-April 19):
Traveling for the holidays will bring you perspective. You may find you are grateful for how you're living and how your life has turned out.

Taurus (April 20-May 20):
If you're making a big purchase with someone, ensure you both know the details. It will prevent problems in the future.

Gemini (May 21-June 20):
This is a great time to meet that new potential partner, Gemini. If you're attached, your relationship will go through a much-needed renewal.

Leo (July 23-Aug. 22):
You could be feeling listless this season, but taking time to appreciate the festivities will bri you out of your funk. People wa to see you shine.

Virgo (Aug. 23-Sept. 22):
You'll be busy making sure everything goes according to plan. Even though you're knowr for your organizational skills, lea some room for changes.

Libra (Sept. 23-Oct. 22):
A short trip will rejuvenate you now like nothing else. Once you're back to normal, you'll be able to enjoy everyone in your lif a lot more.

Scorpio (Oct. 23-Nov. 21):
You could have undergone som value changes and those will be evident now more than ever. Do be afraid to stand your ground, Scorpio!

Chapter 14

Getting to Know Your Pen Pal

"Make your friends your teachers and mingle the pleasures of conversation with the advantages of instruction." -Baltasar Gracian

This is the most important phase of getting pen pals. Getting to know your pen pal is the phase that pick-up artist's call "mid-game". And it's the phase that you need to master to have true pen pal success. Why? Because if you can give your pen pal what they want out of life, they'll give you what you want. Let me ask you a question: Who is your new friend's ideal pen pal? The answer is the key to your success. Find out. Then become that dream pen pal. In this chapter, I'll give you some times on how to find out the answer.

A great book that all prisoner should read is *Reading People: How to Understand People Their Behavior – Anytime, Anyplace* (www.readingpeople.com) by Jo-Ellan Dimitrius, *Ph.D.* She became super famous as the jury consultant on the O.J. Simpson legal team that helped get him acquitted of double murder. In Dr Dimitrius' book, she says that there are three key characteristics that can help you learn a lot about someone.

1. Compassion

2. Socioeconomic background

3. Satisfaction with life

I believe that these areas are especially important for any prisoner trying to get to know about a possible pen pal. Here's why:

- You want to find pen pals that are compassionate because you need a little empathy about your situation. A person who believes that prisoners should be locked up and forgotten about, is not going to make a good pen pal for you. You want to find those that believe people make mistakes and can change. Or those that hate the criminal justice system.

- How a person was raised and what environment they were raised in determines a lot about them. It can explain why they do certain stuff. This is why it's not good to prejudge people until you find out about how they were raised.

- Depending on what your pen pal goal is, a person's satisfaction with life is key to your success or not. For instance, I'm not in the least satisfied with my life. But I've met pen pals who were content just to work a normal 9 to 5, making minimum wage and just want to write letters. That's not what I want and we don't make good pen pals. I need someone who is either successful that I could learn from, or someone that is hungry for success that I can discuss goals and dreams with. So finding out about their life can help you determine if they'll make a good pen pal for you.

The easiest way to find out these things about your new pen pal is to ask. In either the first or second letter that you write you should say something like this:

> "I believe asking questions is the best way that we can get to know each other. So I would like to ask you some questions. Feel free to do the same. No topic is taboo with me. If I ever ask a question and you feel it's a topic that is off limits and you don't want to answer it, just let me know and we'll move onto something else, ok? Here are my questions: ..."

I normally only ask three questions per letter, and I start out with the basic getting-to-know-you stuff before I move into deeper topics. This is key, it gets your pen pal comfortable with the idea of answering questions. It also lets them talk about themselves, which everyone loves to do. Try to keep track of the questions that you ask and are asked. If someone asks you a question that you've never been asked before, write it down. You may want to ask it of someone else in the future. In my personal experience, here are some rules to remember in your first few letters:

- Don't ask about politics until you're well acquainted with your pen-friend.

- Don't ask about sex until your pen pal brings it up.

- Don't ask about religion unless you met your pen pal on a religious website or they bring it up.

- Don't ask about their past relationships. (You want your pen pal thinking of the present and possible future.)

Here are some questions that I like to ask:

- What is your nickname and the story behind it?

- What's important to you in a friendship? Relationship?

- What do you want out of life?

- If I had a magic wand and I could make anything disappear for you, what would you choose and why?

- What did you have before that you wish you could have now?

- What kind of books do you like to read?

- If you didn't need money, what would you do for a living?

- What are three wishes for your soulmate?

- What is something that your co-workers would be surprised you have in your home?

Here's something else you can do if you want to get personal revealing stuff. Play the "confession game". Tell them that you want to really bond by sharing something about themselves that no one else knows? That way you'll have secrets together. Remember, you're a salesman. Your pen pal is your customer. Your goal is to find out what your customer wants and then give it to them.

Resource Box

If you aren't good at coming up with questions, then you'll want to get a copy of:

- *4,000 Questions for Getting to Know Anyone and Everyone* (Random House Reference, 2004) by Barbara Ann Kipfer

It's a great tool and lists questions by topics like childhood/school, family/friends, fun/sport, habits, love/sex, outlook, and politics.

When your pen pal starts answering your questions, you'll be able to ask follow-up questions to elicit more information. An easy question to ask to get to the bottom of something is: "I can understand what you're saying, but what is most important to you about _____?" But what do you do if your pen pal says something you don't like or disagree with? Don't argue with them. You can use this language: "I hadn't thought of it that way. When did you first begin to see it that way?" or "I'm curious, what experience convinced you of that option?" if it's something that really bothers you then you'll have to consider ending your correspondence, because you never want to drag something out or try and change someone. It's better for both parties to call it quits.

What's in Your Favorite Five?

On most pen pal and online dating websites you should list some of the things that interest you. For pen pals that you are getting to know, it can be fun to share your "favorites". I have been using this strategy for years. Here's how it's done. In the third or fourth letter, I'll have a separate piece of paper with the heading "Josh's Favorites" and list some of my favorite things. (A sample version of how I do it is below.) Normally what happens after I send my favorite list, is the pen pal will do her own list and send it back to me. It's a cool and easy way to get some quick facts about favorites in front of your pen pal's eyes. Try it out by doing your own and you'll see that your new friend loves it.

Josh's Favorites

"We are shaped and fashioned by what we love." - Goethe

Fav Food: Pizza (Pepperoni, ham & bacon)	Fav Snack: Iced honey buns
Fav Breakfast: Fried egg w/ cheese on toast	Fav Ice Cream: Chocolate Chip
Fav Soda: Orange Crush	Fav Cake: Chocolate w/ vanilla icing
Fav Color: Blue	Fav Musician: Eminem
Fav Book: *The Millionaire Prisoner*	Fav Book (Fiction): *The Racketeer*
Fav Movie: Heat w/ DeNiro, Pacino	Fav Music Group: Led Zeppelin
Fav TV Show: Sports Center	Fav Shoe: Nike
Fav Sport to Play: Baseball	Fav Sport to Watch: Football
Fav Turn-on: Woman in the Shower	Fav Place: Outdoors
Fav Magazine: *GQ*	Fav Newspaper: *USA Today*
Fav Website: www.bookfinder4u.com	Fav Historical Person: Nelson Mandela
Fav Hobby: Writing letters	Fav Role Model: Felix Dennis
Fav Watch: Movado	Fav Suit: Armani
Fav Car: Aston Martin	Fav Animal: Shark
Fav Team: St. Louis Cardinals	Fav Game: Poker
Fav City: Las Vegas	Fav Place: Caribbean
Fav Item of Clothing: Brand new socks	Fav Month: June
Fav Memory: Grandfathers antique store	Fav Store: Amazon.com
Fav Quote: "I'd rather sit on a pumpkin by myself than share a velvet cushion."	

Using Stories to Demonstrate Value

Another way to allow your new friend to get to know you is by telling stories about your life. People love stories, and if you can learn to paint word pictures that elicit emotional responses in your pen pal, then you can develop a bond. Essentially, you want to move them in a heartfelt way. I do know some prisoners who use this strategy to try and get pity and sympathy from their pen pals. I don't like that because it's a form of manipulation and can backfire. I'd rather try and get empathy. There's a difference. With empathy, the other person can put themselves in your shoes for understanding. In pit and sympathy, you take a "woe is me" stance so that the other person feels sorry for you. Some of you reading this may say "so what?" You are free to use this book however you wish, it's your life. But I speak from prior experience when I say that it's better to play the game the right way and treat others the right way if you want great success. Let me get off my high horse and get back to using stories to demonstrate value.

The first rule is to use real-life incidents from your life. You do not make stuff up, but you want to highlight the good stuff. For instance, a lot of my new pen pals will ask me about my family. I could answer with the usual run-of-the-mill stuff: "I have a sister, twin brother, one nephew, etc." or I could use the question as an opening to tell a story about me and my family that can illustrate some form of value. What do I mean by value? I mean the emotional response your pen pal will get when seeing *worth* in you. Because women are more emotional than men, your stories should show your vulnerability, compassion, and humanity. (For women prisoners, your stories should show vulnerability, compassion, and hint at sexuality.) When using stories, do not complain about the bad stuff that happened to you. Not about your situation, the lames around you, or the wrongs at your prison. Instead, keep it positive! Why? Because, your pen pal wrote you because something is missing in their life. They have a need they want filled and it's your job to fill it. (After you find out what it is.) You can't do that if you're complaining. So try to use stories that are positive if you can.

Trance Words

After you have been writing your pen pal for a while you can find out their "trance" words. Go over your pen pals letters and find the words they use repeatedly. Not words like "I", "you", "me", or "us" but big words like "security", "love", "honestly", "comfortable", "sincerity", etc. after you get these words, use them 2 or 3 times in your letters. Tell stories that illustrate these words. This is kind of like optimizing your content for online search engines (SEO). But these "keywords" are what your pen pal is searching for and they are always evaluating what you write. So put these key words on paper a couple of times in your letters and you'll love the results. Don't overdo it or they'll see that you are just playing a game and trying to trick them. Drop the word naturally in your letters.

What's in Your Playlist (MP3)?

Another way to share with your pen pal is by telling them what some of your favorite songs are on your playlist. A lot of you have MP3 players and can have hundreds, if not thousands, of songs available. By sharing your favorite ones, you'll allow you pen pal to be moved by the music that you like. And after they see your list, when they hear one of your songs, they'll think of you. Of course, that's who you want them thinking about! All you have to do is write 20 or 30 of your favorite songs like this:

Some of My Favorite Songs

Katy Perry – "Firework"	Mariah Carey – "We Belong Together"
Eminem – "Supernova"	Diddy w/ Dirty Money – "Coming Home"
Black Eyed Peas – "Can't Get Enough"	Trey Songs – "Love Faces"
Nickelback – "Somebody"	Fabulous – "You Be Killin' 'Em"
R. Kelly – "Love Letter"	Sean Paul – "Temperature"
Bruno Mars – "Amazing"	Black Crows – "Hard to Handle"
Scorpions – "No One Like You"	Bon Jovi – "I'll Be There"
Lady Antebellum – "I Need You Now"	Ke$ha – "Your Love"
Usher – "Oh My Gosh"	Nelly – "Just a Dream"
Rihanna – "S & M"	Miranda Lambert – "Gun Powder & Led"

When doing your song list, here's some stuff to remember. If your pen pal is younger, then use newer songs, in the Top 40 hits genre, if you like some of those songs. Just mix it up. It helps if you like different kinds of music. Use songs that you like so you aren't being phony. This is just another tip you can use to liven up your letters and share with your new friends.

Using a Nickname for Your Pen Pal

In his book, *The Plan*, master seducer Tony Clink (also author of *The Layguide*, www.layguide.com), has a great way to come up with a nickname for your woman. Here it is:

1. Think of something yummy (sugar, butter, chocolate) or something descriptive of food (sweet, spicy, creamy, and/or hot).

2. Think of the part of her appearance that stands out compared to other women, or even better, something about her appearances she clearly loves and use one word to describe it.

3. Put the two words together and you've got a romantic, endearing and sexy nickname.

Tony likes to tease the woman with a hint about the nickname during a phone conversation, so her curiosity will run wild about the nickname. Then, the next time you two talk or see each other, shell beg you to find out the nickname. Try it out for yourself. I did, and I can tell you, it works!

If you still can't use the above formula to come up with a good one, here are some nicknames to spark your imagination. Or you can just steal one of these.

Angel Heart	Snuggle Bunny
Baby Doll	Pumpkin
Baby Girl	Sweet Cheeks
Big Mama	Sugar Lips
Cuddle Bug	Pooh Pooh
Cuddle Cakes	Sugar Plum
Duchess	Muffin
Flower Child	Diamond Girl

Funny Face	Hot Lips
Honey Bunch	Princess
Honey Pot	Queen

In the past I have used "Honey Bun". Here's how I told her that was my nick name for her:

> "I've come up with a nickname for you love. It's "Honeybun". Because you're sweet and scrumptious. When I was in the free-world, every time I stopped at a gas station for gas, I would get an iced honey bun and chocolate milk. It was something I had to have. A treat I couldn't pass up. You are now that treat I want to devour every day. ☺"

I like to use the nickname when I open the letter with a simple, "Hey Honeybun,". Don't overdo using the nickname, just try it once or twice in your letters. How do you know if she likes it? When she signs her letter with it! Don't worry if she doesn't ever sign her letter with it though. Do keep opening your letter with it. Unless she hates it, then stop. Most times she'll like it.

By the way, every time my girl went to a gas station and saw an iced honey bun or chocolate milk, guess who she thought of?

Final Thought

That's basically how I get to know my pen pal. I mainly use the questions and favorites tricks. Over time, you'll learn to be able to read between the lines and pick up on things that your pen pal isn't saying. Just don't assume too much. Sometimes things are not what they seem to be or what you think they are. Go with the flow and speed, which your new friend sets. Don't press. Building a friendship takes time. Allow it to happen and you can achieve long-term pen pal success.

PEN PAL TIP

Make your pen pal feel important. If they share something they've accomplished, write and let them know you're proud.

Chapter 15
Nice Guys Finish With All the Pen Pals!

"Goodness is the only investment that never fails." -Henry David Thoreau

The worst thing you can do on your pen pal journey is to offend people. Nobody likes the person who puts them down, belittles them, or cracks jokes at their expense. To become a *Pen Pal Success*™, you must learn the art of having tact. Most prisoners don't have tact, but in this chapter, I'll give you a few tips about how to do better in your letters when dealing with your pen pals.

What is Tact?

Tact is the art of making a point without making an enemy. It's the ability to tell a woman she needs to lose weight without offending her. It's knowing when to be silent. Tact is especially useful in a building friendship with pen pals.

> *"The most important single ingredient in the formula of success is knowing how to get along with people."* -Teddy Roosevelt

How to Have Tact

One of the easiest ways to better deal with people is to become genuinely interested in others. Everyone is interesting if you take the time to get to know them. But the key is to do it with *genuine* interest. When you ask your new pen pal questions about what they like, dislike, and need, get ready to hear their answers. When they respond, try to put away all thoughts about your wants, need and desires. Only think about this other person. Train your mind to look for the positives in them. Make your letters about them. I can't write that enough.

> *"Every man I meet is superior in some way."* -Emerson

Next, you need to learn to listen to what is being said and what is not being said. This is easier when having a face-to-face conversation, than a correspondence. But it's a trait you'll need to learn as you go along. You can learn about other people, places, or things that are interesting. With the written word, you should pay attention to what words are being used, how they are written and in which context that they are to be taken in. You also should remember who is writing them, their age, and their socioeconomic background. All of these things play part in who they are as a person. It's also why using the same tactics on different people doesn't always work. People are different and should be treated different. Heres a simple trick to show people you're interested in what they write.

When you get a letter from a pen pal, answer it by saying, "As you pointed out in your letter…"Then write about what they wrote about. Or, use "like you said…" Same thing. When you write about what interests them it will do two things. First, they'll like you. Everyone likes the person who is interested in them and their likes. Second, they'll start to look forward to and value your letters. So write about what they like and write to you about.

Another tip is to compliment them. Make them feel important. If they share something they accomplished, write "Wow, I'm amazed how you _____. I could never do it." or, a simple "Congratulations." We can never get enough praise or pats on the back. Of course, I understand that prisoners have a hard time at this. Prison is a place where everyone is trying to one-up the other guy. But you have to get rid of that mentality when writing your pen pals.

> *"Kind words can be short and easy to speak, but their echoes are truly endless."* -Mother Teresa

What Not to Do

Sometimes life is more about what you don't do than what you do. One of these things that should never be done in your letters, is telling them they're wrong if you are trying to influence or convince them of a point. If you do, they will do everything they can do to prove they're right. Even stop writing you. Instead, you can write something as simple as this: "I can understand why you feel as you do, and if I was in your shoes, I would feel the same way." Then write your point calmly, respectfully, and clearly. But if it's some trivial matter, let them be right. Don't try and win all the little battles, only to lose a pen pal.

Also, never give criticism unless it's invited. Never do it when you're angry either. Ask yourself: "Is what I'm about to say going to help or hurt?" If you must give constructive criticism, try and put it into personal examples with words like "This worked for me when..." or "I found it easier to..." Try to criticize the mistake and not the person. Once you give your answer to their problem, let it be. Don't harp on it. Remember, don't give constructive criticism unless asked for it.

You must become good with language. The ability to write well, will aid you on your journey. As the saying goes: The right word can turn an enemy into a friend, and the wrong word can turn a friend into an enemy.

> *"Language is the principle conveyor of understanding, and so we must learn to use it, not crudely but discriminatingly."* -Owen D. Young

A lot of prisoners tell jokes and make wisecracks at the expense of others. Don't do this in your letters. Do not make jokes about race, religion and/or creed. At least not until they do so. There are plenty of clean jokes that are just as funny as dirty or crude ones.

> *"It is a wise thing to be polite; consequently, it is a stupid thing to be rude. To make enemies by unnecessary and willful incivility, is just as insane a proceeding as to set your house on fire. For politeness is like a counter - an avowedly false coin, with which it is foolish to be stingy. A sensible man will be generous in the use of it."* -Arthur Schopenhauer

A Fable of Tact

We've all heard of or read the fables of Aesop. He was a great storyteller, and a Greek slave, who told fables 600 years before Christ. Aesop's fables are recorded in history and are just as relevant today as they were back when he told them. One fable of his is perfect for this chapter. The wind and the sun began arguing about who was stronger. They made an agreement, that whoever could strip a traveler of his clothing would be declared the stronger of the two. So the wind went first. But the winds violent gusts only made the traveler hold his clothes tightly around him. Eventually the wind go tired and let the sun try. The sun shone with a moderate warmth at first, which made the traveler take off his coat. Then, the sun blazed fiercely. Because the traveler couldn't stand the heat, he stripped off his clothes and went to bathe in a nearby river.

The moral behind Aesop's fable is that warmth is better than force when trying to persuade someone. How can you influence someone if you're offending them? Being tactful is your warmth and you should use it liberally. You never know who's going to write you. You never know who they know. Build friendships first, at least treat them like a possible friend because you just might surprise yourself.

> *"Treat everyone as if he is a valuable customer. He is or he could be if he's treated like one."* -Zig Ziglar

---

Resource Box

If you want to really learn about mastering tact, then I highly recommend that you get copies of these two classics:

- *How to Have Confidence and Power in Dealing with People* by Les Giblin
- *How to Win Friends and Influence People* by Dale Carnegie

Friendship Coupons

When I was writing Alyssa, my college girl from Georgia, she sent me some little coupon/certificate things. One said "You are entitled to a free kiss!" Another had "Free back rub." Then another had "Free hug" on it. She sent me about 10 of these with different things on them. We were supposed to send them back and

forth periodically to each other when we wanted a special thought or an added bonus to our letters. I took her idea and made up my own coupons. I had "Free drawing", "Free card", "Free love letter", "Free poem", "Free romance letter" & "Free gift". And we could only redeem a card once in a two-month period. She loved it and we used our coupons for a couple of years. When I went to segregation, my cellmate stole my coupons. He didn't take anything else, except those. He could have just made his own, but he stole mine. A few years ago, I happened to read Paul Hartunian's book, How to Be Outrageously Successful with the Opposite Sex. In that great book, he had actual pictures of his coupons and I smiled knowingly. This tactic works. Make up your own cards or have the prison artist make up some for you. Try to use thick, construction-type paper, because you will be passing them back and forth and want them to last. Get creative and think of things your friend will like. Put those on your card coupons. Your coupons don't have to be big. Ours were only the size of a business card. It's the thought that counts. Remember to use these!

Top 10 Reasons Why...

Sometimes in your letters, it's not so much what you say, but how you say it. And sometimes, it's both. Within the first couple of months of corresponding, I will use a "Top 10 Reasons Why" list. Here's how I did it with one of my pen pals:

"I feel like the luckiest guy in the world. Well, at least this carousel world I live in. You're a prize pen pal catch! In case you don't believe me, let me count the reasons why:

1. You have a job. (Always a plus!)
2. You like sports. You actually like them and aren't acting.
3. You have a great personality.
4. You're beautiful. (Another bonus!)
5. You're down-to-earth and low-maintenance.
6. You're not stuck-up or snobbish.
7. You have your own house. (The third bonus!)
8. You're drama free.
9. You're funny
10. You picked me to write.

Then every letter after that one, any time you compliment her/him with something different from your list of 10 reasons, highlight it in your letter. I normally use the next line and use the next #:

11. You have great taste in music.

That's all you have to do. Just write the next number and your compliment. They'll know what the # stands for and they'll love you for it. Of course, this means you must keep track of your "reasons". But if you do, you'll get lots of smiles on the other end. And smiles turn into feelings. Good feelings. Try it out, you'll see.

How to Rekindle a Lost Correspondence

Sometimes things just don't work out and you lose contact. Other times your pen pal is just busy and has forgotten to write you. Of course I'm speaking about new pen pals. If a long-term pen pal quits writing after a few years of correspondence, then something is probably wrong. But in the beginning, if I don't hear from a new-pal after 30, I'll send a "Thinking of You" card with a note saying:

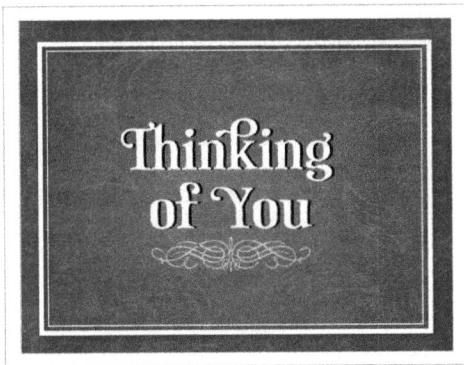

"Hi, I haven't heard from you in a while and hope everything is okay with you out there? Maybe it was something I wrote or said that has caused your silence, and if that is so, I offer my most sincere apology. I just wanted you to know that I was thinking of you and wishing you the best."

Over the years I have used this tactic to start up a few friendships that I thought were over. One time the girl had been moving out of state and had never got my letter. Another time, the woman was in a car wreck. The one thing you need to remember is that life happens at full speed in the free-world. Don't take it personal if someone stops writing. And never write a letter in anger cursing out a pen pal for not writing. Why? Because I've had three pen pals come back after years of not writing me. Because I was able to let things go peacefully, they said they missed my letters and wanted to write again. Sometimes, you don't know what you have until it's gone. The best thing for you to do when someone stops writing is to use the above card tactic and then forget about it. Move on to the next prospective pen pal. If they do come back, they do. If not, their loss, not yours. Use the rest of the strategies in this book to make lifetime connections.

JIMMY CHOO Perfumes Sprays

JIMMY CHOO ILLICIT 3.3 oz. **#265526** $78.99 PLUS 8.95 S/H

JIMMY CHOO FEVER 3.3 oz. #312774 . **$79.99 plus 8.95 s/h**

JIMMY CHOO BLOSSOM 3.3 oz. **$69.99 plus 8.95 s/h**

JIMMY CHOO FLASH 3.3 oz. **$69.99 plus 8.95 s/h**

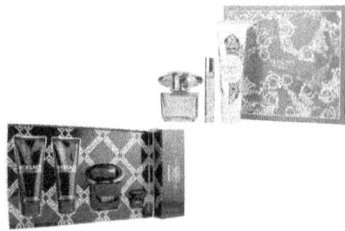

VERSACE BRIGHT CRYSTAL

Eau De Parfum Spray 3 oz and Shower Gel 5 oz and Eau De Parfum Rollerball 0.3 oz Mini by Versace **#310985$96.99 plus 8.95 s/h**

VERSACE CRYSTAL NOIR

Eau De Parfum Spray 3 oz. Body Lotion 3.4oz and Shower Gel 3.4 oz and Eau De Travel Parfum .17 oz by Versace **#166076 $96.99 plus 8.95 s/h**

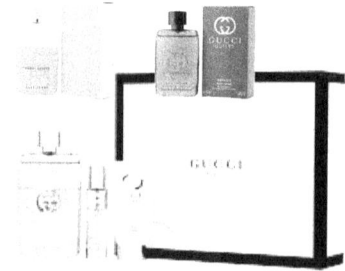

GUCCI GUILTY POUR FEMME SET

Eau De Toilette Spray 3. oz and Body Lotion 1.6 oz. and Eau De Parfum Spray 0.5 oz. by Gucci **#377830 $182.99 plus 8.95 s/h**

SPECIAL EDITION-GUCCI GUILTY LOVE Parfum Spray 1.6 oz. **#361101 $124.99 or 3. oz 168.99 plus $8.95 s/h**

GUCCI GUILTY ABSOLUTE Parfum Spray 1.6 oz. **#236552 $109.99 plus $8.95 s/h**

MUGLAR ANGEL GIFT SET & ALIEN GODDESS SET

ANGEL Eau De Parfum Spray Refillable 1.7 oz. and Body Lotion 3.5 oz. **#279575 $129.99 plus 8.95 s/h**

ALIEN GODDESS Eau De Parfum Spray Refillable 2. oz. Body Lotion 3.5 oz. **#139953 $179.99 plus 8.95 s/h**

MARC JACOBS DAISY GIFT SETS

DAISY-Eau De Toilette Spray 3.3 oz and Body Lotion 2.5 oz and Pen Spray **#0000M1 $149.99 plus 8.95 s/h**

DAISY DREAM or **DAISY LOVE** or **DAISY SO FRESH** or **DAISY SUNSHINE:**

Eau De Toilette Spray 3.3 oz and Body Lotion 2.5 oz and Pen Spray .33 oz **#00000M2-5 $149.99 plus 8.95 s/h**

D&G LIGHT BLUE GIFT SET

Eau De Toilette Spray 3.3 oz. and Body Cream 1.73 oz. and Travel Spray 0.33 by Dolce & Gabbana **#120682 $107.99 plus 8.95 s/h**

D&G Shower Gel 6.7 oz. **$71.99**

D&G Body Cream 6.7 oz. **$82.99**

D&G Parfum Spray 1.6 oz **$69.99**

Each complete order add $8.95 s/h

For the MAN in you life

VERSACE SIGNATURE

Eau De Toilette Spray 1.7 oz and Hair & Body Shampoo 1.7 oz and Aftershave Balm 1.7 oz **#192576 $66.99 plus 8.95 s/h**

VERSACE EROS FLAME

Eau De Toilette Spray 3.4 oz, Shower Gel 3.4 oz and Mini Travel Spray .33 **#3588881 $177.99 plus 8.95 s/h**

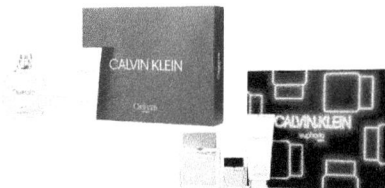

CALVIN KLEIN GIFT SETS

OBSESSED-Eau De Toilette Spray 4 oz and Hair and Body Wash 3.4 oz and Deodorant Stick Alcohol Free 2.6 oz by Calvin Klein **#311313 $97.99 plus 8.95 s/h**

EUPHORIA MEN-Eau De Toilette Spray 3.4 oz and After Shave Balm 3.4 oz. Travel Spray .5 oz. by Calvin Klein **#37866 $74.99 plus 8.95 s/h**

Euphoria Men Body Spray 5.4 oz **$19.99 plus $8.95 s/h**

BVLGARI MAN IN GIFT SETS

MAN IN BLACK or **MAN WOOD ESSENCE** or **MAN GLACIAL ESSENCE**

Eau De Parfum Spray 3.4 oz and Aftershave Balm 3.4 oz Pouch by Bvlgari **#327970 $132.99 plus 8.95 s/h**

BVLGARI MAN MINI VARIETY

3 piece men's mini variety with Bvlgari man in black & man extreme & man black cologne and all are minis **#327970 $99.99 plus 8.95 s/h**

Chapter 16

The Art of Giving Gifts

"In suggesting gifts: Money is appropriate, and one size fits all." -William Randolph Hearst

This is a topic that most prisoners shy away from. I wrote about it in the "Yield" chapter of my first book, *The Millionaire Prisoner*, and in the November/December 2013 issue of <u>Corcoran Sun</u>. But the truth is that successful people give their time, money, knowledge and many other things. This principle doubly applies in the pen pal game.

> *"A good man thinks it's more blessed to give then to receive."* -Aristotle

Joel Osteen says that to get greater living, you must do some greater giving. Some of you have heard of planting seeds, or sowing and reaping. I read that $50 worth of seeds will produce $1200 worth of fruits and vegetables. That illustrates the truth behind the maxim: "You reap what you sow". What are you sowing? What kind of harvest do you expect to reap? Every successful prisoner has built their prosperity by first planting a seed. Joseph Robinson sowed words and time into his book, *Think Outside the Cell*. Bernard Hopkins sowed time in training while inside and once he got out, he became a world champion. My friend Emmanuel Grant sows words into letters and reaps a pen pal harvest. Everyone sows and reaps. To reap success you have to sow positive seeds. For pen pal success, that means playing the game the right way.

Proper Way to Sow Seed

Yes, there is a proper way to do it. Let's look at how a farmer does it. First, the farmer gets the right attitude. Then he tills his field in preparation for the seed. He plants and waits. He expects a harvest. So he prepares the barn for the harvest. When the time is right, he goes back out into the field and brings the harvest in. throughout all of this process, the farmer is working. He is giving to get. What are you giving to get pen pals? Are you expecting, but not doing the working? Remember it's called net-working! When Michael Santos, author of *Inside: Life Behind Bars in America*, wanted to get a mentor, he would write a hundred letters. His harvest was several college professors who wrote him and visited him in prison. Are you prepared to sow your time and effort into one hundred letters? If you do the work, you may just get your harvest.

Sometimes it may feel like you'll never reap your pen pal harvest. But remember how a farmer does it? He puts dirt on his seed. The seed has to push through that dirt. Well, prison is our dirt. If we can push through by reaching out, our friendships can bear fruit. The other part is that you have to wait. Everything has a season. You can't rush your harvest. This is the biggest mistake I see prisoners make when it comes to pen pals. You can't expect her to send you money or gifts in the third letter. You have to build trust. That takes time. It will come. Patience is a virtue in all things.

The Law of Expectation

Sowing is only half the process. The other half is reaping. Do you expect to reap a pen pal harvest? You should. The investment banker does. The fisherman does. The newlywed couple does. When you purchased this book, you expected to reap pen pal success. I know some people say you're not supposed to give to get. That may be true for small favors and gifts that you do for others, but it's foolish to plant a seed then rape your harvest by expecting nothing in return. What do I mean? I hear prisoners all the time talk negatively about their pen pal dreams. Why do any of the work if you are just going to spit on it? Bless your work and expect it to bring you a tenfold return. The universe is watching and listening.

Giving Gifts to Your Pen Pals

I can see some of you cringing at the thought of spending money on someone else. That's not part of the game you say. You don't "trick off". Then there are some of you who have been "tricking off" for years and will continue to do so. But I hope to show you some ways that you can give quality, thoughtful gifts to the people in your life and spend the least amount of money to get the best results. (FYI: for years I did not use any gifts because I felt that if I started sending gifts, then my pen pal would come to expect it. I didn't want that to happen so I didn't use anything but my letters. Over time, I've softened a bit and now use strategically timed gifts. And since my pen pals don't expect these gifts, they carry much more weight when I do send them.) Gift giving is a high standard to live up to, but with the following tips and tactics you can master this strategy.

Cards are Your Secret Weapon

In her fantastic book, *What Women Want Men to Know*, Dr. Barbara DeAngelis suggests using cards with your mate to show affection. She even uses an acronym for cards: <u>C</u>ertificates of <u>A</u>ffection <u>R</u>eaping <u>D</u>eposits of <u>S</u>ex. I've found that she's right and cards are a great resource in the pen pal game. But you don't want to use just any card. Try and use cards that utilize the three T's: Tailored, Timed, and Thoughtful. Here's what I mean.

Tailored means "custom-made". In effect, you send a card created just for that person. If you could send that same card to another person, then it isn't specifically tailored to your pen pal. The card itself could be a generic Hallmark, but your note inside would be what makes it special for that person. Personally, I don't like generic

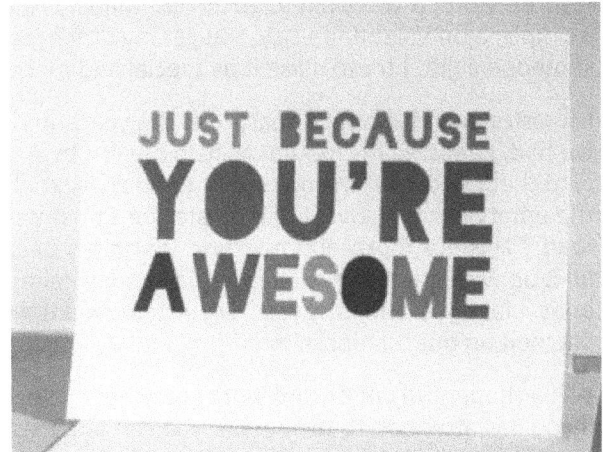

Resource Box

If you have trouble writing little notes, then you'll want to get a copy of this great book to help you out: *The Art of the Handwritten Note* by Margaret Shepherd

---

cards. Instead, I use homemade cards with artwork done just for my pen pal. If their favorite flower is a tulip, then get a card done with tulips on it. If their favorite color is green, then get a card done in green.
If you are not good at art, then befriend the prison artist who does do great cards. Make a deal with him to buy cards, four or five at a time, for a discount. Think of cards as an investment in the friendship (or love) account you're building with your pen pal. And always include a special little note for the person inside the card. Even if it just says "Thanks for the Wonderful Visit", it will go a long way.

The Second T: Timing

When sending cards and gifts, try and keep up with the holidays and special occasions. Everyone sending Christmas cards (and you should also), but if you really want to stand out, send Thanksgiving Day cards. A simple card saying: "I'm thankful for a friend like you", will allow you to get a leg up. Don't forget birthdays either. Remember to utilize *Chase's Calendar of Events*. It has all kinds of stuff you can use to send cards for and about. The second part of timing is sending cards and gifts so that your pen pal gets it on time. To be safe, you should err on the side of caution and make sure it arrives earlier than later. So try to be aware of how fast (or slow) the mail processing is at your prison and how long it takes to get to your pen pal. Plan ahead to be safe. Sending your cards and gifts out early, helps when your pen pal is writing other people, or has lots of family members. Everyone remembers their first.

The Last T: Thoughtfulness

Cards aren't the only gifts that you could, or should, send. You can use flowers, jewelry, stuffed animals, gift cards, book and magazines. This is where the last "T" comes in: thoughtfulness. If you've been paying attention in the beginning of your letter writing, and asking the right questions, then you should know what your pen pal likes. So if your friend likes vampires, get them the latest vampire book they do not have. If they love stamp collecting, then some rare, out-of-country stamps might be best. Another great gift is a magazine subscription to their favorite mag. It's like getting multiple gifts for the price of one. Or you can get them a gift card to their favorite store. If you want to go all out, then have a dozen red roses delivered to your pen pals doorstep or workplace on Valentine's Day. You get my drift? I send out lots of cards, but I use gifts sparingly. When I do give someone a gift, I try to make it as special and memorable by being thoughtful. Let me give you an example.

My sister and I had fallen apart over the years, and since it was mostly my fault, I wanted to rebuild the bond we had. I enlisted my mother to help me out by getting the biggest box she could find. Then I had her tape a card that I wrote on the bottom of the box. Next I had her wrap the empty box and give it to my sister for Christmas. The card read: "This box represents our past. It's empty because I want to fill it up with great new memories, instead of rehashing the old ones. I love you and miss you." My sister loved it and we have patched up our relationship.

Will a thoughtful gift or card work every time? No, it won't. But if you pay attention to the details, you can tailor your gift to have the biggest impact. I hope these three T's will stimulate your imagination and get you to think outside the cell.

Using Poetry with Cards and Gifts

Women love poetry. There's just no getting around it. My poem on WriteAPrisoner.com, "Dreams of Reality", has gotten me more hits and comments than anything else I've done online. But, I also use poetry in my letters and cards. (FYI: I don't use it all the time, because I don't want my pen pal to begin to expect it all the time.) Even if it's not my original poem, I still use it by prefacing the poem with a line like this:

I found this poem in a book in our prison library which expresses everything I feel right now. As you read it, pretend it is mine, because it truly says what I hope to convey."

Then I put in the poem. Sometimes, I try to end my letters with poems when I do use them so that they have the powerful effect of being the last thing my pen pal has on her mind. But there are two main reasons why I like using poetry to my letters and cards to women:

- Women are ruled by their emotions and good poetry stirs emotions and gives pleasure at the same time.

- A good poem speaks in metaphors and allows the woman to imagine what I'm feeling without me actually saying it.

So what makes a good poem to use with pen pals? The ones I like to use, have three key attributes. They have rhythm, they rhyme, and they use words that produce images. Reread my poem, "Dreams of Reality", and

you'll see what I mean about the above keys. Out of the three, rhythm and images are the most important. Poetry doesn't have to rhyme. There are many forms of poetry that don't. But, I prefer it because it sounds like music and I k now that music moves people. But what does good music also have? *Rhythm*. That is the key. You want your pen pal to feel the rhythm in your words. Think about your daily conversations. There's a natural rhythm. When you come across someone who doesn't speak with the right rhythm it throws you off, doesn't it? That's because life is full of rhythm and rhythm is life. I'm not going to get all esoteric on you, but it's the truth. When it comes to poetry, I like using those that have rhythm in my letters and cards. Even if you're not good at writing poetry, here are several tricks of the trade to use and remember:

- Obtain a copy of *Pearls of Love: How to Write Love Letters & Love Poems* and *Love Poems for Cards & Letters*, both by Ara John Movesesian. These are classics and you will constantly refer back to them.

- Go to your prisons library and check out any poetry books they have. Write down the poems you like or even parts of some that you can use in your own letters and cards. (FYI: *Inmate Shopper* showcases prisoner poetry books and buying a few of them would be a good investment.)

- Subscribe to *Poets & Writer's*, *American Poetry Review*, and other periodicals that publish poetry if you can.

- Read all the prison newspapers and newsletters to look for poetry. I've found great poetry in *The Angolite*, *The Prison Mirror*, and *The Echo*.

- Ask your fellow prisoners if they have any poetry you can read. Copy the ones you like. (Tell them you want to copy them ahead of time so there isn't any problem.)

- Invest in a good rhyming dictionary. You can normally find good ones in *Edward R. Hamilton* book catalogs, in the reference section.

- When you have free time, practice rewriting the poems you like, so that they fit your own situation. If you find some that don't rhyme, try and rewrite them so that they do. If you do find some that are in "free verse" (no rhythm), rewrite them so that they do.

- Lastly, you can use parts of song lyrics to help you out. A lot of prisoners use whole songs in their letters and there's nothing wrong with it. I like listening to slow jams and stealing bits and pieces from different songs to use in my poems. Do the same.

There you have it. Some tricks of the trade to help you get started. Poetry can be a secret weapon in your pen pal arsenal. Especially when you put it inside the cards you send. Who knows, you could be the next Ovid or Lord Byron? If you do come up with a great original poem, make sure you put it on your pen pal website profile page. This will help you get more responses!

A Few More Thoughts on Gifts

You have to be extra careful when using some of the prison-based gift services and catalogs. Here are some things I've heard over the years and that you should keep in mind.

- Some companies don't keep products in stock, but instead "drop ship" the items ordered. What this means is that the company works with a wholesales and just does the marketing and order processing. The wholesaler actually fills and ships the orders with the original company's address label on the gift package. Sometimes you'll never know if the company is using a drop shipper or not. Elijah Ray was a great prison gift company that operated for a long time on a drop ship basis.

- I like using a personal assistant to shop for me online. That way, I can find something unique and tailor it for my family member or friend. I've used Prisoner Assistant, Inc. to send flowers via 1-800-Flowers.com, to my Mom for Mother's Day. I've used "Help from Outside" to send flowers also. Both provided great service. You can also find personal assistants on Craigslist.com and www.

ivaa.org (International Virtual Assistants Association).

- One of my comrades, "Shyboy", would send gifts (flowers or jewelry with a personal card) every time he got $1,000 or more from a family member, friend or pen pal. I say do it every time you get anything of value. You want to reward what you like. If someone sends you $10-50, send a "thank you" card. If someone sends you some books and magazines, send a card. If they send $100, send flowers (if they're female). Show your appreciation and gratitude. Bless them and they'll bless you.

- If your pen pal or friend has children, then don't forget to get the kid(s) something. Small gift cards ($20 or less) to the kids favorite store is a good gift. If they are real young, then a stuffed animal in their favorite character can be great. Freebird Publishers (www.freebirdpublishers.com) offer many great gift lines of high quality that you might want to use? They also carry the full line of Swarovski Crystal jewelry, by Touchstone. Swarovski Crystal transforms everything it touches out of the ordinary, making it a staple on the red carpet worn and by Hollywood.

- Be careful with jewelry. Never send imitation or fake jewelry, because you'll be taken as cheap. That would do more harm than good.

Just remember the three T's when deciding what to give. I like gift cards the best. That way the person receiving it can just get whatever they want from the store they love. I have too many bad memories of all the gifts I got as a kid that I hated. They should have just got me a gift card so I could get what I wanted. You don't have to spend a lot to make a huge impression. Use cards and reward what you like. You can't go wrong if you follow the tips in this chapter. You reap what you sow.

"We make a living by what we earn – we make a life by what we give." -Winston Churchill

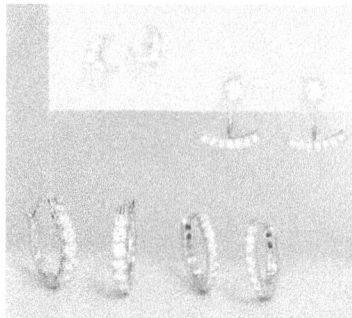

178

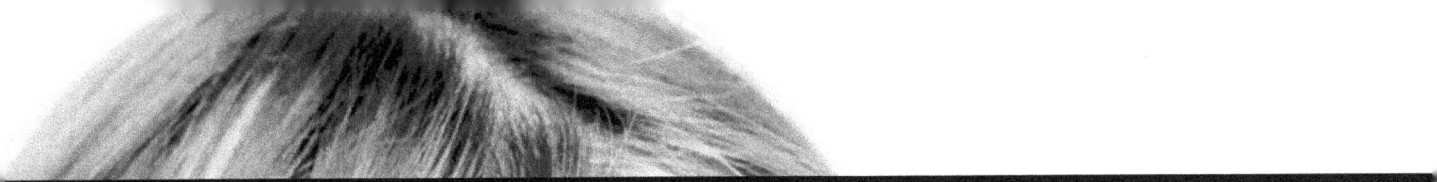

Chapter 17

Is Sex Talk Taboo?

"When it comes to sex, the exception is more common than the rule.
No two people are alike sexually." -Leil Lowndes

Talking and Writing About Sex?

Of course I know that a lot of you want to bring up sex in your letters with your pen pals. As a prisoner, you just don't get to have fun like you used to. You are horny and want to write about it and talk on the phone with your pen pal about it. I completely understand. But there's a time and place for everything. I do want to caution you on the fact that just like the rest of this book, this chapter is written only from my own experience and perspective. When it comes to matters of sex, you proceed at your own risk.

First, deicide what you really want pen pals for? If it's for sexually explicit letters only, then say so in your ad. Most women won't respond to an ad like that. Yes, there are women who love sex and only want a casual sexual relationship. But those women most likely will not be looking for it on a prison pen pal website. I would advise you not to mention sex in your profile. If you feel that you must, then do it discreetly. Because what you actually write may not be how people read it. They may read too much *into* it. Instead of saying "having sex", "f**king", or "getting down & dirty", use words like *passion, intimacy, kissing* and *physical relationship*. These words work and sound better than the other "lewd" versions.

Even if you don't write about sex in your profile, you are probably going to want to discuss it with your pen pal. Here's my rule about sex. Only write about it if you are prepared to lose that pen pal, or your pen pal brought it up. *Timing* is everything when it comes to writing about sex. If it's too soon, you're going to lose your pen pal. If they don't want that type of correspondence, then they will either admonish you not to write about it again, or stop writing you. So the timing has to be right. For us guys, the time is always right for sex. But for women, it's not so simple. Most of my women pen pals are willing to discuss sex with me, if they considered me relationship material. The ones who thought of me as a friend only, didn't want to discuss sex. That gives you an idea of timing again.

Now there's a difference about harmless flirting by using double entendre and innuendos, than writing explicit sex kites. At first, you need to err on the side of caution and broach the matter of sex lightly. You could ask about past relationships, or tell a joke and see what kind of response you get. Or you could just ask about it like I do sometimes: "Can I write you about *anything*? Is there a topic that is off limits for us?" your pen pal will let you know. You have to treat each pen pal differently, because no two people are alike. One of my pen pals said she hated how prisoner's wanted to write about sex before they even got to know her. Another one wrote about it in her second letter saying she had only been with four guys. Of course, it should go without saying that if you had sex with your pen pal before, then it is okay to bring it up whenever you feel like it.

Whatever you do with a new pen pal, just don't write explicitly about sex at first. Be more discreet. Ask your pen pal questions about it in a way that allows them to answer without having to give up personal information about themselves. Here are some:

- Do you believe in love at first sight?

- Do you think that guys think about sex too much?

- Do you believe that physical companionship is an important part of a long-term relationship?

- If men needed to know one thing about sex, what would you tell them?

These questions aren't that bad. See how your pen pal answers them. That will tell you a lot about how comfortable they are discussing sex with you. Always end any question block with "Feel free to ask me any questions that you have." A lot of the time, you'll get the same questions in reply. I prefer not to answer my own questions in the letter I'm writing. I've seen prisoners do it like this:

- Do you believe in love at first sight? (I do.)

- I don't do this because I don't want my answers influencing my pen pals answers. Other prisoners feel differently about it. You be the judge.

- Once you get past some harmless opening questions, you could move on to more explicit ones:

- Do you like oral sex?

- Have you ever had a "ménage à trios"?

- What is your sexual fantasy?

- What is your pet peeve about sex?

- Do you masturbate? Use a vibrator?

- What is your favorite position?

I could go on and on, but you get the point. Be forewarned though. You may not like the answers you get. I once had a pen pal write me that her fantasy was to get ravished by five guys at once. Let's just say that I didn't look at her the same after that.

A Few More Thoughts on Sex

Here are some more observations when it comes to talking about sex from my 15 years' experience in writing pen pals. Women from Europe, are more open about sex, than American women. Younger women (college-age) discuss sex more often than older women. And West Coast girls are more open than small-town, Midwest women. Now I know I just stereotyped women in general, but that has been my experience. It also depends on how you came in contact with your pen pal. Are you answering a swinger's ad or an adult X-rated pen pal request? If you are, then you can write about sex right away. If not, just be careful about when you write about sex. (For women prisoners: you can write about sex quickly because guys love sex! Unless he's overly religious or a prude, then you must be careful.)

How to Get Free Erotic Photos

A lot of prisoners purchase nude or semi-nude photos from prisoner-service companies. I never have and I never will. I have developed a few magic words that I've been using for years to get erotic photos from my pen pals. You can use these words in a letter as well. But remember, do not try this on your pen pal until you have written for a while and they are comfortable with you.

If you have wrote about sex, or she has wrote you an explicit letter, then you are free to use these words. The following is how I do it:

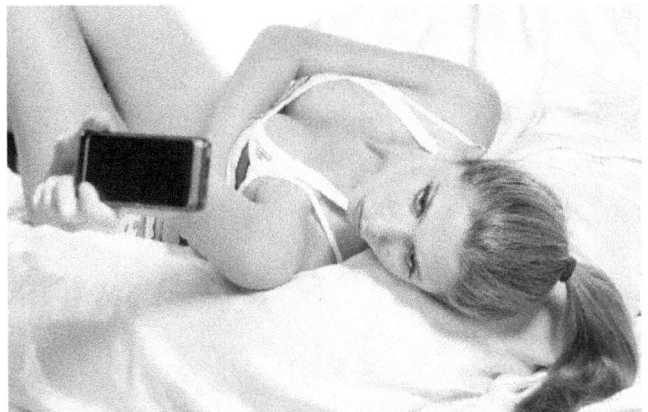

"As my birthday approaches I have been contemplating what I would like this year. Most prisoners would automatically say they want money, but I have something else in mind. We've been together for [*insert time frame*] and I really like where we're going as [*put what you call the relationship*].

But I must confess something to you. I have always had a problem with sex and masturbation. As a prisoner, I can't have sex, but as a man, I still must release my sexual tension. Normally I would look at pornographic magazines to stimulate my mind, but I have not looked at them since we started our correspondence because I felt I would be cheating on you. I would be lying if I said that I have not masturbated since we've been writing, I have. And I've thought of you while doing it. But I've always wanted some erotic photos of you that I could look at while imaging I'm with you. I feel this would be more intimate for us.

So that is what I would like for my birthday – some erotic photos of you. Not naked photos, but maybe some sexy lingerie or bra and panty shots? What do you think? I eagerly anticipate hearing your response on this subject! ☺"

That's all you have to write, then sit back and wait to see what happens. If she (or he) has never taken sexy photos then you must ease them into it. Don't try and get them to do anything elaborate at first. Just a few photos of her in a bra and panties will get her comfortable with the idea. Then you can slowly get her to do more in her photos.

Your pen pal may say that they don't have anyone to take the photos. You can get around this by telling her that they have cheap cameras with timers on them. She could set the timer, then hop on the bed for a quick pose. I've had a few pen pals do it that way at first. The only caution is that you must have already developed a bond with your pen pal before you crack on her about some sexy photos.

Most women will be turned on about the idea of you looking at their photo while you get off. They may say "That's gross", but really they are just as turned on as you. They just don't want you to think they are easy when it comes to sex, the erotic photos you get this way will mean much more to you than photos of some stripper you don't know. Remember, to get something you've never had, you've got to do something you've never done.

Chapter 18

The Next Level - Phone & Visitation

"You can't hear her, touch her, smell her, or taste her in a letter. But you can on a visit."
-Shyboy

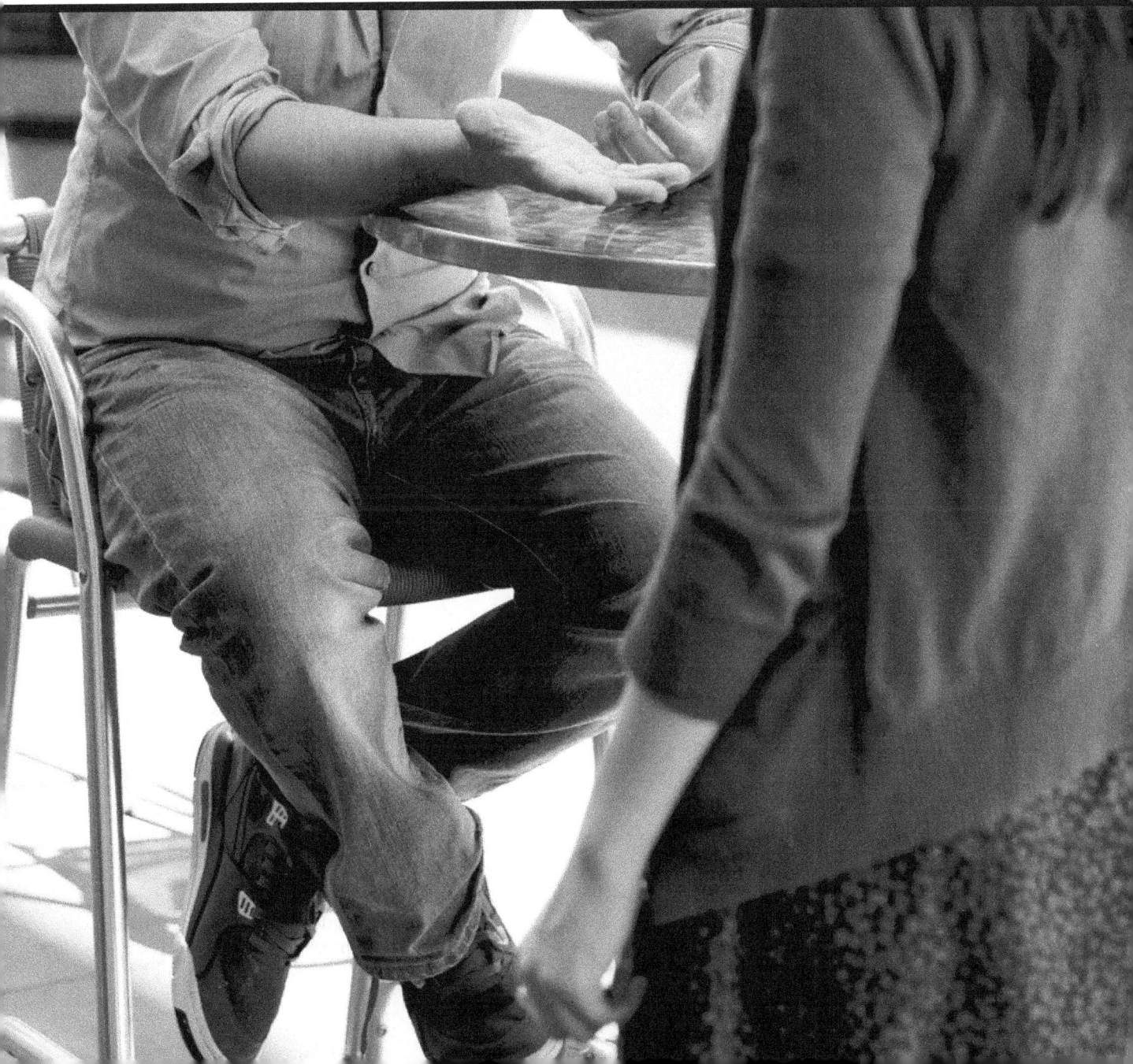

There may come a time when you and your pen pal want to move beyond just writing letters back and forth. The next level is talking on the phone and having visits. I have pen pals that I've never talked to on the phone and never seen in person. But all my long-term pen pals I've either talked to on the phone or seen in person in the prison visiting room. When you have been writing someone for years, you definitely want to hear their voice and see them in person. It's a natural progression. In this chapter, I will deal with some tips and help both your phone conversations and your prison visiting room experiences to be profitable for both parties involved.

Playing Phone Tag

Most prison systems allow prisoners to make collect calls. Some of you even are allowed phone cards, so you don't have to call collect. That can be a huge advantage in the pen pal game. Your pen pal may ask you at a certain point if you have phone privileges, or give you her phone number. When that happens, you must explain in detail all the rules regarding using the phone at your prison, so they will know how it works. (FYI: It's even better if you can send them a copy of the rules along with your letter to further prove what you're saying.) The main obstacle regarding phone calls is who is going to pay for the collect calls. Personally, I have never paid one of my pen pals phone bills. I know some prisoners who do. I don't. That's not to say, I wouldn't in the future, if I had a pen pal helping me with my business or legal stuff. But if we are just writing letters, then if you feel that I'm worthy of talking to you, I believe as the free world person, you should pay the bill. I would pay my daughters cell phone bill if I was able to call her collect, but that's a different story. How you ask? Well, she is 14, so I should if I want to, talk to her. Hey, if you are a rich prisoner and don't mind helping out with the phone bill, then do what you want. What I try to do is caution my pen pals about the cost of one call and how many times I'll be able to call. Then I work it out with her to set up a calling plan. Remember Alyssa, my college girl in Georgia? I'd call her twice a week on Monday and Wednesday mornings when on the exercise yard. She paid the bill. That worked out fine. I've had cellmates who called their pen pals every day. To me, that's overkill. Are we still in grade school? Calling your wife or baby mama every day is okay, but a pen pal you don't really know is a little much. And it caused problems when they couldn't get the phone or the prison went on lockdown. But I'm not here to tell you how many times to call. All that matters is that someone is paying the phone bill and communication stays open. I'd rather be able to call once a week than not be able to call because the number is blocked. I think you would too. So set up a calling plan that they can afford and makes everyone happy. Now that I got that out of the way, here are some tips to remember when using the phone:

- Become an active listener. Ask questions that get them to talk about themselves. While they are talking, do not interrupt them. Wait for them to finish before you ask them to clarify something. Remember to say things like: "As you just said..." and "Like you said about..." Show them you're actively listening.

- Try to have a plan ahead of time before you call. You don't want to hear silence on the other end. Even if you just have some simple bullet points on a piece of paper that you want to talk about is good. Use them.

- Stand up when you talk. It gives your voice a more full sound over the phone. And smile when you are talking to them. Trust me, you can hear the smile in the voice.

- Be positive, funny, and exciting. Tease your phone pal playfully. Don't be mean though. You want the phone conversations to be a pleasant experience for them. Because if it's not, they're not coming back for more!

- Talk about stuff in your letters and their interests. Try to stay away from the prison politics and don't complain all the time about your situation. I've had pen pals ask me how I deal with it, being a lifer. I'll always say "Hey, I got you in my life, so I feel free and prison can't touch me." Or some other corny line like that.

- Here's something I learned from pick-up artist Mettow. Use her trance words (the words she is always using). Slip them into your conversations, but don't overdo it.

- Men should use the language of romance novels. Women should use the language of *Playboy* and *Penthouse*. Don't use words that you don't understand though.

- Remember that every call is a sales event because you are a salesperson. So make it a soft sell and build trust with your friend.

- Speak slowly and spell out anything important. You are in control and if they misunderstand something, it's your fault.

- Take notes about what is said. When the phone call is over with, you can write about it. I always write that night. Especially if I say that I'm going to send something, look something up, or explain more. I'll say: "As we discussed on the phone..." then go into my spiel about whatever it is about.

- Guys, ask her how she feels? If she says she's having trouble with something, then say "Do you want to talk about it? I'm here to listen." That will go a long way. Remember to listen to what she's saying.

- Do NOT make a call when you are angry. I've violated this rule several times and said things I've regretted. Wait until you calm down and have thought things through.

If you are lucky enough to use phone cards, then you have more opportunities to build your network. You can call anybody, but it doesn't mean you should. If you do have some phone numbers of pen pals, then here's how you should play it.

- Let them know how you got their phone number first. Then say who you are. After that, ask them if they have time to talk? If not, ask when you can call back? Be polite and try to get another time to call.

But phone cards open up the door to getting mentors and business people on your team. Here's how you can do it.

1. Write a letter, asking for a mentorship or other information to the person you're trying to network with.

2. Wait a week or two and call this person's office. Say something like this: "Hi, this is Josh Kruger. I'm calling to follow-up on my letter to _____ so that I can arrange for delivery of my book, *The Millionaire Prisoner*." Even if you don't have anything to send, you could say that you're looking for some information.

3. If you are talking to a secretary or assistant, be polite and ask for a time when you can call back when the boss will be in.

4. If you get voicemail, then leave a message saying who you are and when you'll call back.

5. Remember to be patient, persistent, but not pesky. You want to be a protégé and not a parasite.

6. Always have a plan. No matter what type of phone call you are using, it's costing someone money. Respect their time and make it profitable for you.

The phone can be a great tool in your arsenal if you use it right. Don't overdo it, don't yell at the other person on the other end, and don't play games on the phone. Use the tips in this chapter to aid you and your friendships will have a stronger bond.

Resource Box

If you want to learn more about the art of selling on the phone, you should check out these books:

- *How to Manage and Execute Telephone Selling* by Bernie Goldberg

- *Selling on the Phone: A Self-Teaching* Guide by James Porterfield

- Telephone Marketing: How to Build Your Business by Telephone by Murray Roman

---

Visitation

Just like with the phone system, most prisons also offer some type of visitation. You should let them know all the rules regarding visiting room and prison policies. A lot of prisons have strict rules about what they can wear and bring in. I don't agree with half of those rules, but we have to deal with them. It's better to address them ahead of time with your pen pal. Especially if they've never come to a prison to visit a prisoner. If they have never visited a prison before, then here are some things you should explain in detail beforehand:

- How long will they have to wait for you? Do they wait in a special area or in the visiting room?

- Will they get searched? Patted down? Go through metal detectors?

- What can they bring into the prison? Money for the vending machines, if any? Books for you? Etc.

- Will you be able to touch each other or be separated by glass or some other partition?

- How long will the visit last? Can they get up to use the restroom or do they have to ask first?

- Are your conversations recorded? Are there cameras in the visiting room?

- What are the visiting days and hours? How many people can come at once?

I try to write all of this out in one letter and I send a copy of the rules and regulations regarding the visiting room, if I can. My main visitors are family members who have been coming to see me at different jails and prisons, since 1992. Each prison has its own rules, some writing and posted, some are unwritten "you know better" type stuff, common sense. I've had visitors suspended, harassed and just got into arguments with guards who are having bad days. I've also gone to see my brother in prison on numerous occasions. So I know both sides of the fence. It's harder on our loved ones then us. We are used to shakedowns, lockdowns and all the waiting around. Our pen pals aren't used to this stuff and anything we can do ahead of time to prepare them for this goes a long way. Sending that letter about all the crazy visiting room rules is a must. But what do you do once you are on a visit?

Rules of the Visiting Room Game

These are the tips and tactics I've learned over the years. But they are not the Ten Commandments. Different prisons have different rules, and each pen pal is different. Just use these things as a form of guidance on your pen pal journey. They will help.

- Don't make the first visit too romantic. Instead, have fun. Play cards if you can. Keep your conversation light. Break the ice and natural nervousness.

- Prepare before your visits. Go over your letters or at least some of the latest ones you've received. Ask questions about their travel to the prison or any hassle at the prison.

- Dress neat, clean hair and trimmed nails. Brush your teeth and pop a peppermint or candy beforehand.

- Don't look at the other women/men in the visiting room. Keep your eyes on her/him. If they mention something about someone else, say that he/she is better looking! Or say, "I didn't notice." Make them feel like they are the only ones in the room.

- When your visitor is talking, listen. Look at them and lean slightly forward, arms open. Don't cross your arms in a defensive posture.

- If your pen pals laugh is different, say "I love the way you laugh." If they do something else (flick of their hair, hand movements) say that you love that too.

- If you can eat in the visiting room, remember your manners. Don't talk with your mouth full, keep your napkins handy. Try to eat slowly if you can, and share. Especially if they brought their kid(s).

- If your prison allows it, then you should hold their hand once you two are on that level. If you can play cards, play "speed." Your hands will naturally touch and it's a competitive game. Let them win.

- Your visitor(s) are the star of the show. Make them feel that way. They are going out of their way to come inside a prison to see you. Reward them for doing so.

- Look into their eyes. Smile a lot. Laugh at their jokes. Flatter and praise them. Show your appreciation by making them feel special.

I had a cellmate who got his buddy to hook him up with his sister. He saw me going on visits every week and asked me a question about kissing his girl. He hadn't yet. I told him to try this: When you get up to leave and give her a hug, let her go. If she looks back when she's walking out, call her back to you. As soon as she gets back to you, pull her close and kiss her. He did it and it worked. Sometimes you just have to go with the flow. I had one girl kiss me on the first visit and others made me wait. I also have visitors who I have platonic friendships with and don't have to worry about that type of thing. Do what feels natural or say "I wish I could kiss your beautiful lips." See what they say. Just take your time and let things progress naturally.

After your visit, you should send a "thank you" card or letter. Say you enjoyed the visit and look forward to seeing them again. You can call later on to make sure they got home alright if they have to travel quite a way. It will mean a lot to them.

What Not to Do

There will come a time when someone misses a visit. Stuff happens, cars breakdown, kids get sick. When the inevitable happens to you, whatever you do, DO NOT snap on your pen pal. DO NOT write an angry letter saying "Where the F*@% are you?" DO NOT call and interrogate them about their whereabouts. Be calm and wait it out. It's best if you talk about this ahead of time. I've told my family and friends not to tell me when they are coming. That way I don't worry if they don't make it. Now there's no pressure on them to force it. They still come to see me and it's easier on everybody. It may be different at your prison. Especially if you have to get prior approval and or preschedule your visits. If a visit is missed, don't go crazy. Life still goes on and everything will be okay. You can say "I'm glad you're okay, I was worried about you." But no cursing or acting like they owe you. Remember this.

I hope you do get to the point where you're talking on the phone and going on visits with your pen pal. It can really help the time fly and give you something to look forward to. When you do get to that point, remember the tips in this chapter as you move forward on your journey.

TOUCHSTONE
CRYSTAL BY SWAROVSKI

A

B

D

C

Our premium collection – Sterling Silver plated in rhodium or gold for extra shine and tarnish protection paired with Zirconia provides exquisite sparkle and beauty.

A. Ring True Necklace
9064N / $99; 15" to 18".
B. Go To Necklace 9062N / $69;
15" to 18".
C. Go To Earrings 9063E / $59
D. Signature Necklace 9060N / $79;
15" to 18".

Josh Kruger

TOUCHSTONE
CRYSTAL BY SWAROVSKI

A

B

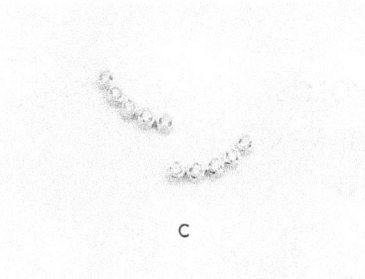

C

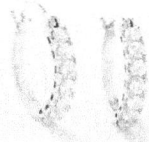

D

E

F

G

H

A. Extra Extra Necklace 9028N / $99;
15" to 18".
B. Tiny V Necklace 9032N / $69;
15" to 18".
C. Urban Climber Earrings 9004E / $42

D. Small Talk Earrings 9027E / $65;
½" inside diameter.
E. Luminous Earrings 9074E / $79
F. Legacy Earrings 5705EF / $62

G. Millionaire's Club Earrings
5548EF / $52
H. Monte Carlo Earrings
5678EF / $47

Box 541
North Dighton, MA 02764
www.touchstonecrystal.com/freebird

189

ℹ

PEN PAL TIP

If you're at a loss for words
on how your pen pal makes
you feel, use a quote.

Chapter 19

Making it Forever

"A good marriage would be between a blind wife and a deaf husband." -Montaigne

There may come a time when you feel like your pen pal is *"the one."* Or you may have other motives for trying to lock-up your new friend. Prisoners do have a constitutional right to marry. See *Turner V. Safley*, 482 U.S. 78 (1987). But just because you have the right to do something, doesn't necessarily mean you should do it. My brother was married for over 7 years to a girl he met while inside federal prison. She was good for him and took care of him until the last year or so, when he filed for divorce. I've also read about success stories in prison marriages. Billy Wayne Sinclair met reporter Jodie Bell and married her by proxy while in prison. They went on to coauthor *A Life in the Balance* and *Capital Punishment* together. He is in the free world with his wife now. So is Michael Santos, author of *About Prison*. His wife and he are partners. There are many more examples that I could write about. But after watching Prison Wives Club on TV and seeing how my fellow married prisoners act, I don't know if I ever want to put myself, or her, through the hassle and torment of a prison marriage. You may be different? In case you are, I hope this chapter can help you make the best decision on your pen pal journey.

The Most Important Selection You Can Make

In *Think and Grow Rich*, Napoleon Hill wrote that the most common cause of failure is the wrong selection of a mate in marriage. So the question is how do you know if your pen pal is the one or not? To find out, you can start with the questions I put in my first book, *The Millionaire Prisoner*. Try to answer them truthfully. Here they are:

- Am I willing to give my pen pal time devoted solely to them?
- Are they willing to devote time solely to me?
- Is what I love to do also what they love to do?
- Do I impress them with the things I do?
- Do they ask me questions about my plans or goals?
- Do we continue to bond and become closer?
- Do they learn from their mistakes?
- Do they hang around the wrong people and places?
- Do they accuse me before hearing my side of things?
- Have they had a string of bad relationships?
- Does my pen pals parents know about me? Like me?
- Does my pen pal overreact to small problems?
- Do they have a good job, or going to school for a career?

- Do they have self-discipline and motivate themselves?

- Do they have an inferiority complex?

- Would I like to have children with them?

- Would I be willing to spend the rest of my life with them if they never changed?

- Have I introduced them to my family and friends?

- Are they grateful when receiving a gift?

- Do they respect where I've been and going?

- Do I find it hard to talk to them?

- Do we discuss things together, before we make major decisions?

- Can I trust them with my money?

- Can we trust each other with our secrets?

- Can I trust my pen pal with my friends, when I'm not there?

"A husband or wife is the greatest environment influents for any man or woman." -W. Clement Stone

If answering these questions truthfully and you still feel that your pen pal is that special someone, then try a trial commitment. I even come up with a special "Certificate of Commitment" that I've used in the past. Trust me, women love this certificate. I've sent it to two different women and both of them signed it. The key is to know when to send it. You can't rush things. It was years into my correspondence before I sent the certificate. I suggest discussing the perils of a prison marriage with your pen pal. The main one being the financial burden that your free world pen pal will be under, due to the costs of phone calls, travel for visitation and legal fees. On the next page is the certificate. You don't have to be looking for marriage to use it either.

Pen Pal Success
Certificate of Commitment

This agreement, entered to as of this ____ day of _____ 20__, between _____ (hereinafter referred to as _____), incarcerated in the _____ Department of Corrections, and _____ (hereinafter referred to as _____), residing at _____ _____, united as a couple and partnership by and through love as soulmates.

WHEREAS, the parties are familiar with each other intimately and desire to fulfill each other's wants and needs, and to create a harmonious relationship together.

WHEREAS, the parties wish to have said relationship performed subject to the mutual obligations, covenants and conditions herein.

NOW, THEREFORE, in consideration of the foregoing premises and the mutual covenants hereinafter set forth and other valuable considerations, the parties hereto agree as follows:

1. Grant of Rights. (*your name*) grants, conveys and transfers to (*your pen pal*) certain limited, exclusive rights as follows:
   a. To use (*his/her*) last name as any married spouse would;
   b. Claim that (*he/she*) is (*his/hers*) as a (*husband/wife*);
   c. In the United States, and under common law;
   d. Until death do they part.

   Grant of Rights. (*your pen pal name*) grants, conveys and transfers to (*your name*)certain limited, exclusive rights as follows:
   a. To claim that (*she/he*) is (*his/hers*) as a (*husband/wife*);
   b. In the United States, and under common law;
   c. Until death do they part.

2. Duties of the Parties. (*your pen pal name*) grants, conveys, and acknowledges that (*he/she*) must perform certain duties under this agreement, as part of (*his/her*) obligations to (*your name*). these duties are as follows:
   a. To assist (*him/her*) in achieving (his/her) dreams and/or goals;
   b. To support (*him/her*) emotionally through letters, phone conversations, photographs and visitation at the prison;
   c. To invest in the business ideas and plans (he/she) creates;
   d. To support (him/her) sexually through erotic letters, erotic phone conversations, erotic photographs, and conjugal visits, should the opportunity present itself;
   e. To support (*him/her*) financially through periodic gifts to (*his/her*) trust fund account at the prison;
   f. To support (*his/her*) educational growth by purchasing books, magazines and newspapers for (*him/her*) and sending them to him, via U.S. Mail;
   g. To support (*his/her*) legally, by assisting (*him/her*) in acquiring an appellate lawyer and expert witness(s) to assist in securing (*his/her*) release from prison and overturning (*his/her*) conviction.

   Duties of the Parties. (*you*) grants, conveys, and acknowledges that (*he/she*) must perform certain duties under this agreement, as part of (*his/her*) obligation to (*your pen pal*). These duties are as

194

follows:

a. To assist (*him/her*) in achieving (*his/her*) dreams and/or goals;

b. To support (*her/his*) quest to _____ ;

c. To support (him/her) emotionally through letters, phone conversations, and visitation when (she/he) comes to the prison;

d. To support (*him/her*) sexually through erotic letters, erotic phone conversations, erotic photographs, and conjugal visits, should the opportunity present itself;

e. To support (*him/her*) financially by suggesting ways and means for (*him/her*) to invest, and make more money, along with building a business

f. To support (*his/her*) educational growth by sharing books, magazine articles and newspapers with (*him/her*) via U.S. Mail;

3. Waivers and Defaults. Any waver of a breach or default hereunder shall not be deemed a waiver of a subsequent breach or default of either the same provision or any other provision of this agreement.

4. Entire Agreement and Modification. This agreement represents the entire agreement between the parties. All modifications of this agreement must be in writing and signed by both parties.

5. Governing Law. This agreement shall be governed by the laws of the state (country) of _____.

WHEREAS, the parties enter into this contract willfully and willingly. No one has made them to sign this certificate of commitment by threats, force, duress, coercion, fraud, or trickery. The parties are not under the influence of drugs or alcohol and suffer no mental illness at the time of signing this contract.

IN WITNESS THEREOF, the parties has signed this agreement as of the date first set above.

S/_____
(Your name)

S/_____
(Your pen pals name)

The Rules of a Successful Prison Relationship

I have not been married while inside or out, but I have been involved in some serious relationships. One of those was with the woman who became the mother of my twin daughters. We started out as friends from school and church, then we became pen pals when I got locked up. Eventually I paroled and moved in with her. From that experience and my other serious pen pal relationships, I want to give you some rules to live by to make your relationship the best it can be. Don't forget to use every other tip and tactic in this book as well.

Rule #1. Don't hesitate to admit that you are in the wrong.

Rule #2. Don't prolong disputes and arguments.

Rule #3. Compliment and praise your partner every day.

Rule #4. Plan your finances together.

Rule #5. Leave petty prison stuff out of your relationship.

Rule #6. Appreciate each other's difference.

Rule #7. Prove to your partner that you trust them.

Rule #8. Keep your relationship interesting and exciting.

Rule #9. Never stop showing your partner appreciation.

Rule #10. Remember that the partner your writing may not be the same once you get out. Anybody can be anything in a letter.

Yes, only ten rules. But being in a prison relationship with someone in the free world is tough. Is it worth it? Yes, it is! I'm thankful for all the women who have wrote me over the years, especially the long-term correspondences that I've had. And I look forward to some more in the future. If the right woman comes along, I might marry? We'll see about that. I wish you the best in your search for your special someone.

> *"By all means marry. If you get a good wife, you'll be happy. If you get a bad one, you'll become a philosopher."* -Socrates

If you do decide to marry, you'll have to learn the rules about the process at your prison. Don't hesitate to let me know if one of these tips or tactics in this book helped you meet your soulmate. I'd love to hear that and may even put your story in a future edition of this book.

Chapter 20

Your Rights, or What's Left of Them?

"One doesn't prove that a law is right or moral merely by stating that it _is_ a law. To say that laws are necessary to protect individuals sounds all right until you realize that most laws interfere with the freedom of individuals..." -Robert J. Ringer

The Law As It Stands

There have been discouraging developments in a few states, like Louisiana and South Carolina, which have passed laws banning prisoners from using social networking sites. California asked Facebook to shut down all of its active prisoner pages. Indiana has recently banned its prisoners from advertising for pen pals. Some Florida and Missouri prisons have strict guidelines about prisoners using services to get pen pals. These laws and rules present problems for the success-minded prisoner. Here are some cases that you may want to get and study so you know what is and what isn't legal.

Your right to communicate by mail is guaranteed by the First Amendment of the U.S. Constitution. See *David v. Goord*, 320 F.3d 346 (2nd Cir. 2003); *Morrison v. Hall*, 261 F.3d 896 (9th Cir. 2001); *Zimmerman v. Tribble*, 226 F.3d 568 (7th Cir. 2000). But this right can be restricted by prison officials. Incoming mail is governed by the "reasonably related" standards. See *Thornburgh v. Abbott*, 490 U.S. 401 (1989). Outgoing mail is governed by *Procunier v. Martinez*, 416 U.S. 396 (1974). It's unconstitutional for the prison to bar you from writing people you didn't know before you came to prison. *Owen v Lash*, 682 F.2d 648 (7th Cir. 1982). And it's bogus for them to require prior approval of everyone you write. *Guajardo v. Estelle*, 580 F.2d 748 (5th Cir. 1978); *Finney v. Arkansas Board of Correction*, 505 F.2d 194 (8th Cir. 1974). They can use a list of people you are banned from writing. *Samford v Dretbe*, 562 F.3d 674 (5th Cir. 2009). Letters between prisoners in different prisons have been legally banned. *Turner v. Safely*, 482 U.S. 78 (1987). Some prisons do not allow you to write parolees. *Nasir v. Morgan*, 350 F.3d 366 (3rd Cir. 2003). You are allowed to write to the media and the press. *Kimberlin v. Quinlan*, 199 F.3d 496 (D.C. Cir. 1999); *Pell v. Procunier*, 417 U.S. (1974)

When it comes to responding to personal ads and using pen pal services the courts have said that prisoners do not have a right to do so. See *Rodriquez v. Ames*, 224 F.Supp.2d 555 (W.D.N.Y. 2002); *Lucas v. Scully*, 71 N.Y.2d 401 (N.Y. 1988). Placing an ad in a newspaper is protected speech for a free world person. See, e.g. *New York Times Co. v. Sullivan*, 376 U.S. 254 (1964). But not so much for a prisoner. *George v. Smith*, 507 F.3d 605 (7th Cir. 2007)

When prison officials do censor your mail they have certain guidelines they are supposed to follow. *Murphy v. Missouri Department of Corrections*, 814 F.2d 1252 (8th Cir. 1987); *Martin v. Kelley*, 803 F.2d 236 (6th Cir. 1986). A repeated pattern of delaying mail is unconstitutional. *Zimmerman v. Tribble*, 226 F.3d 568 (7th Cir. 2000). But brief delays are not. *Martucci v. Johnson*, 944 F.2d 291 (6th Cir. 1991).

Some of the mail restrictions that have been upheld are that prisoners have no right to possess stamps. *Johnson v. Goord*, 445 F.3d 532 (2nd Cir. 2006). Mail that discusses escape plans is banned and can be censored. *Gaines v. Lane*, 790 F.2d 1299 (7th Cir. 1986). Prisoners are not entitled to receive blank greeting cards in the mail. *Avery v. Powell*, 806 F.Supp. 7 (D.N.H. 1992). And prison mail room clerks can open and inspect your non-legal mail for contraband. *Martin v. Tyson*, 845 F.2d 1451 (5th Cir. 1998); *Bumgarner v. Bloodworth*, 768 F.2d 297 (8th Cir. 1985).

But there have been plenty of restrictions that have been struck down. You have a right to write religious leaders. See *Walker v. Blackwell*, 411 F.2d 23 (5th Cir. 1969); *Peek v. Ciccone,* 288 F.Supp. 329 (W.D.MO. 1968). You also have a right to write people and businesses that will post this on the internet for you. See *Canadian Coalition Against the Death Penalty v. Ryan*, 269 F.Supp.2d 1199 (D.AZ. 2003); *Cassels v. Stadler*, 342 F.Supp.2d 555 (M.D.LA. 2004). Officials may not ban your outgoing letters because they are critical about the prison or warden. *Todaro v. Bowman*, 872 F.2d 43 (3rd Cir. 1989); *McNamara v. Moody*, 606 F.2d 621 (5th Cir. 1979). But you should not be overly obscene or racist in your letters when complaining about prison officials. See *Leonard v. Nix*, 55 F.3d 370 (8th Cir. 1995).

This book is about pen pals and general correspondence. But if, and when, you do write attorneys, your letters are given more confidentiality. *Evans v. Vare,* 402 F.Supp.2d 1188 (D.NV. 2005). The prison cannot read your clearly marked "Legal Mail." *Reneer v. Sewell*, 975 F.2d 258 (6th Cir. 1992); *Lemon v. Dugger*, 931 F.2d 1465 (11th Cir. 1991). And it can only be inspected in your presence. *Marriweather v. Zamora*, 569 F.3d 307 (6th Cir. 2009); *Al-Amin v. Smith*, 511 F.3d 1317 (11th Cir. 2008); *Castillo v. Cook County Mail Room Dept.,* 900 F.2d 304 (7th Cir. 1993). But you have to show an "actual injury" to your legal claim to get any kind of rhythm. *Lewis v. Casey*, 518 U.S. 343, 351-53 (1996); *Gardner v. Howard*, 109 F.3d 427 (8th Cir. 1997). You may be better off alleging a First Amendment violation, instead of an Access to the Courts claim. *Denius v. Dunlap*, 209 F.3d 944 (7th Cir. 2000); *Poole v. County of Otero*, 271 F.3d 955 (10th Cir. 2001).

There may come a time when your pen pals want to donate books and magazines to you, and you have a right to read. *King v. Federal Bureau of Prisons,* 415 F.3d 634 (7th Cir. 2005); *Prison Legal News v. Lehman*, 397 F.3d 692 (9th Cir. 2005). Prison officials have more leeway in censoring publications but still must follow standards set forth by the United States Supreme Court. *Thornburgh v. Abbott*, 490 U.S. 401 (1989). When they do censor a publication you are entitled to procedure safeguards. *Krug v. Lutz*, 329 F.3d 692 (9th Cir. 2003). You are supposed to receive notice of the censorship and so is the person/publisher who is sending you the publication. *Jacklovich v. Simmons*, 392 F.3d 420 (10th Cir. 2004). A lot of prison systems went to a "publisher only" rule and the courts have upheld these rules. *Jones v. Salt Lake County*, 503 F.3d 1147 (10th Cir. 2007); *Hurd v. Williams*, 755 F.2d 306 (3rd Cir. 1985); *Zaczek v. Hutto*, 642 F.2d 74 (4th Cir. 1981). But you should be able to get newspaper and magazine clippings without violating these rules. *Lindell v. Frank*, 377 F.3d 655 (7th Cir. 2004); *Allen v. Coughlin*, 64 F.3d 77 (2nd Cir. 1995). I cannot say it enough, learn your prisons rules and your states laws regarding correspondence and publications. To be aware is to be alive.

Telephone Privileges and the Law

Prisoners do have a right to use the telephone. *Johnson v. State of California*, 207 F.3d 650 (9th Cir. 2000); *Washington v. Reno*, 35 F.3d 1093 (6th Cir. 1994). But pre-trial detainees have more telephone right than prisoners, and rightly so, because they haven't been convicted yet. *Lynch v. Leis,* 382 F.3d 642 (6th Cir. 2004); *Johnson-El v. Schoemehl*, 878 F.2d 1043 (8th Cir. 1989). Convicted prisoners have not been so lucky in challenges to the prison phone system. *Jeffries v. Reed*, 631 F.Supp. 1212 (E.D.WA. 1986); *Robbins v. South*, 595 F.Supp. 785 (D.MT 1984); *Wrinkles v. Davis*, 311 F.Supp.2d 735 (N.D.IN. 2004). If you go to segregation, you don't have a right to use the phone. *Benzel v. Grammer*, 869 F.2d 1105 (8th Cir. 1989); *Armstrong v. Lane*, 771 F.Supp. 943 (C.D.IL. 1991). And the use of preapproved call lists have generally been upheld in court. *Pope v. Hightower*, 101 F.3d 1382 (11th Cir. 1996); *Arney v. Simmons*, 26 F.Supp.2d 1288 (D.KS. 1998); *Carter v. O'Sullivan*, 924 F.Supp. 903 (C.D.IL 1996). Prisons can record your telephone conversations. *Martin v. Tyson*, 845 F.2d 1451 (5th Cir. 1998). If the prison lets you know in some way that your calls are being monitored and you use that phone, you consent to the recording. *U.S. v. Workman*, 80 F.3d 688 (2nd Cir. 1996). So be careful what you talk about, with your pen pal, on the phone.

Visitation Rights and Myths

The U.S. Supreme Court in all its learned wisdom struck a blow to prison visitation rights. See *Overton v. Bazzetta*, 539 U.S. 126 (2003). After this decision you had better learn your prisons rules regarding visitation. But a permanent ban on all visitation with anyone may violate the Constitution. *Kentucky Dept. of Corrections v. Thompson*, 490 U.S. 454 (1989). Prison systems are allowed to require that visitors be pre-approved. *Ramos v. Lamm*, 639 F.2d 559 (10th Cir. 1981). And have valid identification to get in. *Ross v. Owens*, 720 F. Supp. 490 (E.D.PA. 1989). Religious clergy may have more rights to visitation than regular visitors. *Kikumura v. Hurley*, 242 F.3d 950 (10th Cir. 2001); *O'Malley v. Brierley*, 477 F.2d 785 (3rd Cir. 1973). If you are a LGBT prisoner, you cannot be restricted from visitation because of your sexual orientation. *Whitmire v. State of AZ*, 298 F.3d 1134 (9th Cir. 2002); *Doe v. Sparks*, 733 F.Supp. 227 (W.D.PA. 1990). You don't have a constitutional right to contact visits.

Block v. Rutherford, 468 U.S. 576 (1984). If you're in segregation, your visiting privileges may be different than general population prisoners. *Beck v. Lynaugh*, 842 F.2d 759 (5th Cir. 1988). The same for protective custody prisoners. *Taylor v. Rogers*, 781 F.2d 1047 (4th Cir. 1986). Death row prisoners typically have different visiting procedures as well. *Smith v. Coughlin*, 748 F.2d 783 (2nd Cir. 1984); *Card v. Dugger*, 709 F.Supp. 1098 (M.D.FL. 1988). No one has a right to conjugal visits. *Hernandez V. Coughlin*, 18 F.3d 133 (2nd Cir. 1988). These are the federal cases on visitation. Your state may have additional rules and procedures that give you more rights. I have included the rules for my prison (IDOC), just in case you'd like to compare them to your prisons rules and regulations.

Resource Box

If you do feel that your rights have been violated you should *Shepardize®* or *KeyCite®* the cases in this chapter to get the most up-to-date case law in your circuit. If you can afford to do so, you should also get a copy of the following books.

- *Prisoners' Self-Help Litigation Manual, 4th Edition* by John Boston and Daniel E. Manville. Available for $49.95 (shipping included) from Prison Legal News, P.O. Box 1151, Lake Worth, FL 33460.

- *Battling the Administration: An Inmates Guide to a Successful Lawsuit* by David J. Meister. Available for $34.95 (shipping included) from Wynword Press, P.O. Box 557, Bonners Ferry, ID 83805

ADMINISTRATIVE CODE
TITLE 20: CORRECTIONS, CRIMINAL JUSTICE, AND LAW ENFORCEMENT
CHAPTER I: DEPARTMENT OF CORRECTIONS
SUBCHAPTER e: OPERATIONS
PART 525 RIGHTS AND PRIVILEGES

The General Assembly's Illinois Administrative Code database includes only those rulemakings that have been permanently adopted. This menu will point out the Sections on which an emergency rule (valid for a maximum of 150 days, usually until replaced by a permanent rulemaking) exists. The emergency rulemaking is linked through the notation that follows the Section heading in the menu.

SUBPART A: VISITATION

•Section 525.10 Applicability
•Section 525.12 Definitions
•Section 525.15 Responsibilities
•Section 525.20 Visiting Privileges
•Section 525.30 Clergy Visitation
•Section 525.40 Attorney Visitation - Adult Division
•Section 525.50 Attorney Visitation - Juvenile Division (Court Agreement)
•Section 525.60 Restriction of Visitors

SUBPART B: MAIL AND TELEPHONE CALLS

•Section 525.100 Applicability
•Section 525.110 Definitions
•Section 525.115 Responsibilities
•Section 525.120 Processing of Mail
•Section 525.130 Outgoing Mail
•Section 525.140 Incoming Mail

•Section 525.150 Telephone Privileges

SUBPART C: PUBLICATIONS

•Section 525.200 Applicability
•Section 525.202 Definitions
•Section 525.205 Responsibilities
•Section 525.210 General Guidelines
•Section 525.220 Publications Review Officer
•Section 525.230 Procedure for Review of Publications

SUBPART D: MARRIAGE OF OFFENDERS

•Section 525.300 Applicability
•Section 525.302 Definitions
•Section 525.305 Responsibilities
•Section 525.310 Request for Permission to Marry

AUTHORITY: Implementing Sections 3-2-2, 3-7-1, 3-7-2, 3-8-7, 3-8-8, 3-10-8, and 3-10-9 of the Unified Code of Corrections [730 ILCS 5/3-2-2, 3-7-1, 3-7-2, 3-8-7, 3-8-8, 3-10-8, and 3-10-9] and Section 1-3 of the Juvenile Court Act of 1987 [705 ILCS 405/1-3] and authorized by Sections 3-2-2 and 3-7-1 of the Unified Code of Corrections [730 ILCS 5/3-2-2 and 3-7-1]. Subpart A is also implementing a Consent Decree (Tillman vs. Rowe, #77 C 1008, N.D. Ill., 1977). Subpart C is also implementing a Court Agreement (Ryan vs. Walker, #04 C 4635, N.D. Ill., 2006).

SOURCE: Adopted at 8 Ill. Reg. 14598, effective August 1, 1984; amended at 9 Ill. Reg. 10728, effective August 1, 1985; amended at 11 Ill. Reg. 16134, effective November 1, 1987; amended at 12 Ill. Reg. 9664, effective July 1, 1988; amended at 14 Ill. Reg. 5114, effective April 1, 1990; amended at 14 Ill. Reg. 19875, effective December 1, 1990; emergency amendment at 16 Ill. Reg. 3583, effective February 20, 1992, for a maximum of 150 days; amended at 16 Ill. Reg. 10439, effective July 1, 1992; peremptory amendment at 17 Ill. Reg. 1666, effective January 22, 1993; expedited correction at 17 Ill. Reg. 11903, effective January 22, 1993; peremptory amendment at 17 Ill. Reg. 8069, effective May 27, 1993; amended at 20 Ill. Reg. 15960, effective January 1, 1997; emergency amendment at 21 Ill. Reg. 641, effective January 1, 1997, for a maximum of 150 days; amended at 21 Ill. Reg. 7139, effective May 31, 1997; amended at 27 Ill. Reg. 8039, effective July 1, 2003; amended at 30 Ill. Reg. 14843, effective September 1, 2006; amended at 35 Ill. Reg. 5400, effective April 1, 2011; amended at 37 Ill. Reg. 1645, effective February 1, 2013.

SUBPART A: VISITATION

Section 525.10 Applicability

This Subpart applies to all correctional facilities within the Department of Corrections.

(Source: Amended at 27 Ill. Reg. 8039, effective July 1, 2003)

Section 525.12 Definitions

> "Chief Administrative Officer" means the highest ranking official of a correctional facility.
> "Department" means the Department of Corrections.
> "Director" means the Director of the Department of Corrections.
> "Offender" means a person committed to the Department or to the custody of the Department.

(Source: Amended at 27 Ill. Reg. 8039, effective July 1, 2003)

Section 525.15 Responsibilities

a) Unless otherwise specified, the Director or Chief Administrative Officer may delegate responsibilities stated in this Subpart to another person or persons or designate another person or persons to perform the duties specified.

b) No other individual may routinely perform duties whenever a Section in this Subpart specifically states the Director or Chief Administrative Officer shall personally perform the duties. However, the Director or Chief Administrative Officer may designate another person or persons to perform the duties during periods of his or her temporary absence or in an emergency.

(Source: Amended at 20 Ill. Reg. 15960, effective January 1, 1997)

Section 525.20 Visiting Privileges

a) The Chief Administrative Officer of each correctional facility shall establish regular visiting hours.

1) All rules and regulations pertaining to visiting shall be posted and made available to visitors and offenders.
2) Visitors who travel great distances to visit an offender may request extended visits. These requests should be

submitted sufficiently in advance to the Chief Administrative Officer for consideration.

3) Visitors shall be subject to search in accordance with 20 Ill. Adm. Code 501.220.

4) Visitors may be permitted to wear religious headgear if:

A) There are no safety or security concerns; and
B) The headgear has been removed and thoroughly searched; and
C) The visitor has indicated that the headgear has religious significance; and
D) Either:

i) The headgear is a kufi, yarmulke, turban, habit, or fez; or
ii) A written request to wear headgear other than those listed in subsection (a)(4)(D)(i) of this Section was submitted to the Chief Administrative Officer at least ten days prior to the visit and the Chief Administrative Officer approved the request. Failure to submit a timely request shall result in denial of the request.

5) All offenders' visits shall be subject to monitoring and recording at any time by departmental staff, unless prior special arrangements have been made for confidential attorney visits or other privileged visits. For purposes of this Section, a privileged visit means any conversation or communication between visitors that is protected by a privilege of law or by decision, rule, or order of the Illinois Supreme Court. Notices stating that visits are subject to monitoring and recording shall be posted in places in which offenders are normally permitted to visit and in the offenders' orientation manual.

6) Visits may be restricted to non-contact visits by the Chief Administrative Officer for reasons of safety, security, and order. This may include, but not be limited to, restricting visits to non-contact visits for offenders known or believed to be engaged in gang activity.

A) Offenders who are assigned to an adult closed maximum security or who are in disciplinary segregation or who are extremely high escape risks shall be restricted to non-contact visits.
B) Offenders found in possession of illegal drugs or who fail a drug test shall be restricted to non-contact visits for at least 6 months.
C) Offenders involved in gang activity or found guilty of assault against a Department employee in accordance with 20 Ill. Adm. Code 504 shall be restricted to non-contact visits for a period of at least 6 months.

b) At the time of admission to a reception and classification center, an offender shall submit a list of proposed visitors to designated facility staff. A visiting list shall be established after verification, review, and approval by the Chief Administrative Officer. Permission to visit may be denied due to the safety, security, or operations of the facility. Visitors must be approved in order to visit.

1) Department staff may interview or request background information from potential visitors to determine whether the individual would pose a threat to the safety or security of the facility or any person or to the order of the facility.

2) Visitors 17 years of age or older must be on the approved list in order to visit.

A) An individual 12 years through 16 years of age who is not a member of the offender's immediate family may only visit with the written consent of his or her parent or guardian. Immediate family shall include children, brothers, sisters, grandchildren, whether step, adopted, half, or whole, and spouses.
B) When visiting, anyone under the age of 17 years must be accompanied by an approved visitor who is 17 years of age or older, unless prior written approval has been granted by the Chief Administrative Officer.
C) Visitors under 12 years of age may only be permitted to visit:

i) When accompanied by a parent or guardian who is an approved visitor;
ii) When prior written consent has been given by a parent or guardian who is in the free community for the child to visit when accompanied by an approved visitor designated in writing who is at least 17 years of age; or
iii) As otherwise approved by the Chief Administrative Officer.

3) In determining whether an exception shall be granted pursuant to subsections (b)(2)(B) and (C), the Chief Administrative Officer may consider, among other factors, the proposed visitor's age, emancipation, and relationship to the offender; whether a legal guardian has been appointed for the proposed visitor; the inability of an approved visitor to accompany the proposed visitor; and any applicable court order.

4) A proposed visitor who has been convicted of a criminal offense or who has criminal charges pending, including, but not limited to, an individual on bond, parole, mandatory supervised release, or probation or an ex-offender, may visit an offender only with the written approval of the Chief Administrative Officer. In determining whether to approve or deny a request, the Chief Administrative Officer may consider, among other matters, the following:

A) The nature, seriousness, and the date of commission of the offense.

B) The proposed visitor's criminal history.
C) The proposed visitor's relationship to the offender.
D) The date of discharge from parole, supervision, or probation or of completion of service of a term of incarceration.

5) The number of approved visitors may be limited by the Department due to operations and security reasons. Any limitations imposed shall be conveyed to offenders.

6) Offenders may request to change the names of requested visitors no more frequently than monthly except in emergencies or to add or change attorney names.

7) A visitor may be disapproved at any time by the Chief Administrative Officer in accordance with this Subpart.

(Source: Amended at 27 Ill. Reg. 8039, effective July 1, 2003)

Section 525.30 Clergy Visitation

Clergy and religious leaders from religious groups may visit offenders during regularly scheduled visiting hours and during other hours as approved by the Chief Administrative Officer subject to safety and security concerns.

(Source: Amended at 27 Ill. Reg. 8039, effective July 1, 2003)

Section 525.40 Attorney Visitation – Adult Division

a) Licensed attorneys and any investigators, law students, or paralegals working under their supervision may visit an offender during regularly scheduled visiting hours unless permission has been granted by the Chief Administrative Officer to visit during other hours.

b) Investigators, law students, or paralegals shall be required to present a written statement from a registered attorney indicating that they are working under the supervision of an attorney who is representing an offender and indicating the names of the offenders with whom they are authorized to visit.

c) Attorneys or those working under their supervision are requested to notify the Chief Administrative Officer of the designated time and date of the visit at least two days in advance of the visit in order to make special visiting room arrangements.

(Source: Amended at 27 Ill. Reg. 8039, effective July 1, 2003)

Section 525.50 Attorney Visitation – Juvenile Division (Court Agreement)

a) To assure that persons committed to the Juvenile Division may privately confer in person with attorneys of their choice or with attorneys retained by their parents or with attorneys appointed by courts, the following procedures are established:

1) Attorneys may routinely visit offenders between the hours of 9:00 a.m. and 5:00 p.m. daily, unless other arrangements have been made with the Chief Administrative Officer of the facility.

A) Except in emergencies, at least 24 hours before the visit, attorneys are requested to notify an employee of the facility designated by the Chief Administrative Officer to arrange visitations, the date and time at which they wish to confer with the offender.

B) The designated employee will immediately confirm or deny the arrangements.

2) The visiting attorneys may establish that they are attorneys registered with the Attorney Registration and Disciplinary Commission of the Supreme Court of Illinois (130 East Randolph, Suite 1500, Chicago, Illinois 60601) by exhibiting their Commission identification card.

A) If no card is available, the facility shall call the Commission (800/826-8625 or 312/565-2600) to determine if the attorneys are registered.

B) Visiting attorneys not listed with the Commission or those practicing out of state shall be approved by the Chief Administrative Officer only after it has been established that they are licensed to practice law.

3) Any time prior to any attorney-offender conference, the offender shall sign an authorization. The authorization shall be filed in the offender's master record file and shall be substantially in the following form:

I, (name of offender), hereby authorize (name of attorney), Attorney at Law, to represent me as my attorney and advocate.

_____   _____
Date   Signature

      A)   In the event that the offender's written authorization is not submitted for the attorney, the designated employee will immediately confer with the offender for the purpose of obtaining written authorization.

      B)   In lieu of the above authorization, any time prior to the visit, an attorney may present a copy of a court order appointing the attorney to represent the offender.

b)   The aforementioned shall apply also to law students, paralegals, or attorneys' agents to the extent that such persons present a written statement from registered attorneys indicating that the person is working under the supervision of an attorney.

c)   Before this Section of the Subpart may be modified, the Department legal staff shall be consulted. This Section was promulgated pursuant to the settlement of litigation by order of the court. It may not be modified without the approval of the court.

(Source: Amended at 27 Ill. Reg. 8039, effective July 1, 2003)

Section 525.60 Restriction of Visitors

a)   The Chief Administrative Officer may limit the frequency and duration of visits in accordance with the availability of space and staff.

b)   The Chief Administrative Officer may limit the number of persons allowed per visit in accordance with considerations of space, time, and security.

c)   Visiting privileges may be temporarily suspended by the Chief Administrative Officer during an institutional emergency or lockdown and for a reasonable time thereafter, upon the approval of the Director.

d)   Visitors and offenders shall not be permitted to exchange any item during a visit, except with prior approval of the Chief Administrative Officer.

e)   The Chief Administrative Officer may deny, suspend, or restrict visiting privileges based, among other matters, upon the following:

    1)   Security and safety requirements;
    2)   Space availability;
    3)   Disruptive conduct of the offender or visitor;
    4)   Abuse of the visiting privileges by the offender or visitor; or
    5)   Violation of State or federal laws or departmental rules by the offender or visitor.

f)   Any of the following actions on the part of a visitor may result in a temporary restriction of up to six months:

    1)   Disruptive conduct of a minor nature.
    2)   Disobeying an order or posted rule.
    3)   Refusal to submit to search.
    4)   Possession of drugs when the visitor has demonstrated there was no intent to conceal or introduce drugs into the facility.
    5)   Possession of alcohol when the visitor has demonstrated there was no intent to conceal or introduce alcohol into the facility.
    6)   Being under the influence of alcohol or drugs.
    7)   Possession of other contraband as defined under State, federal, or local laws or other departmental rules not specifically outlined in this Subpart.

g)   Any of the following actions on the part of a visitor may result in a permanent restriction:

    1)   Assaultive behavior on any individual.
    2)   Sexual misconduct.
    3)   Possession of weapons.
    4)   Possession of drugs or drug paraphernalia.
    5)   Unauthorized possession of money.
    6)   Possession of escape paraphernalia.
    7)   Possession of alcohol.
    8)   Providing false identification or information.
    9)   Disruptive conduct of a major nature.
    10)   Violation of State, federal, or local law during a visit, including arrest or conviction based on any action committed during a visit.
    11)   Any recurrence of an action that previously resulted in a temporary restriction.

h)   Employees who have been involved with offenders or former employees who have either resigned or have been terminated as a result of involvement with offenders may be permanently restricted from visits if it is determined they may be a threat to safety or security.

i)   If contraband is discovered in the possession of an offender either during or after a visit, it will be assumed that the contraband was introduced by the offender's visitor.

j)   Visits of offenders hospitalized in the community may be restricted to the immediate family and shall be subject to the general visiting policies of the hospital.

k)   Written notification of temporary or permanent restriction of visiting privileges shall be sent to the visitor and to the offender. Any person excluded from an offender's visiting list at one correctional facility shall be excluded at all facilities. The notice of temporary restriction shall state the exact length of the restriction.

l)   Notices of permanent restrictions shall inform visitors and offenders that they may request that the Chief Administrative Officer review the decision after a six month period. After the initial six month review, permanent restrictions shall be reviewed by the Chief Administrative Officer on an annual basis upon request of the offenders or their visitors. Written notification of the decision shall be sent to the visitor and to the offender.

m)   The Chief Administrative Officer may restore visiting privileges at any time.

(Source: Amended at 27 Ill. Reg. 8039, effective July 1, 2003)

SUBPART B: MAIL AND TELEPHONE CALLS
Section 525.100 Applicability

This Subpart applies to all correctional facilities within the Department of Corrections.

(Source: Amended at 27 Ill. Reg. 8039, effective July 1, 2003)

Section 525.110 Definitions

a)   "Assistant Director" means the second highest ranking official of the Department.
b)   "Chief" or "Deputy Director" means the highest ranking official of a district or division within the Department.
c)   "Chief Administrative Officer" means the highest ranking official of a correctional facility.
d)   "Department" means the Department of Corrections.
e)   "Director" means the Director of the Department.
f)   "Incoming privileged mail" means mail from the following:

    1) The Director;
    2) Assistant Director, Chiefs, and Deputy Directors of the Department;
    3) Department attorneys;
    4) Members of the Administrative Review Board;
    5) Members of the Prisoner Review Board;
    6) The Governor of Illinois;
    7) Federal or Illinois legislators;
    8) Chief Executive Officers of the Federal Bureau of Investigation, the Drug Enforcement Administration, the Criminal Division of the Department of Justice, the United States Customs Service, the Secret Service, the Illinois State Police, and Sheriff's Offices and Police Departments in the State of Illinois;
    9) Illinois Inspector General;
    10) John Howard Association; and
    11) Legal mail.

g)   "Outgoing privileged mail" means mail to the following:

    1) The Director;
    2) Assistant Director, Chiefs, and Deputy Directors of the Department;
    3) Department attorneys;
    4) Members of the Administrative Review Board;
    5) Members of the Prisoner Review Board;
    6) The Governor of Illinois;
    7) Federal or Illinois legislators;
    8) Chief Executive Officers of the Federal Bureau of Investigation, the Drug Enforcement Administration, the criminal Division of the Department of Justice, the United States Customs Service, the Secret Service, the Illinois State Police, and Sheriff's Offices and Police Departments in the State of Illinois;
    9) Illinois Inspector General;
    10) John Howard Association;
    11) Clerks of courts or of the Illinois Court of Claims; and
    12) Legal mail.

h)   "Legal mail" means mail to and from the following:

    1) Registered Attorneys who provide direct legal representation to offenders;
    2) State's Attorneys;
    3) The Illinois Attorney General;
    4) Judges or magistrates of any court or the Illinois Court of Claims Judges; and
    5) Any organization that provides direct legal representation to offenders, but not including organizations that

       provide referrals to attorneys, such as bar associations.
 i) "Offender" means a person committed to the Department or to the custody of the Department.

(Source: Amended at 35 Ill. Reg. 5400, effective April 1, 2011)

Section 525.115 Responsibilities

a) Unless otherwise specified, the Director or Chief Administrative Officer may delegate responsibilities stated in this Subpart to another person or persons or designate another person or persons to perform the duties specified.

b) No other individual may routinely perform duties whenever a Section in this Subpart specifically states the Director or Chief Administrative Officer shall personally perform the duties. However, the Director or Chief Administrative Officer may designate another person or persons to perform the duties during periods of his or her temporary absence or in an emergency.

(Source: Amended at 20 Ill. Reg. 15960, effective January 1, 1997)

Section 525.120 Processing of Mail

a) Mail shall be delivered and posted promptly.

b) Offenders may correspond with anyone in the free community in accordance with this Subpart without prior written approval of the Chief Administrative Officer, except with employees, former employees, or releases of the Department. Permission for committed persons to correspond between intra-state and inter-state correctional facilities shall require the approval of the Chief Administrative Officers of both facilities and shall be based on safety and security concerns.

c) Each facility shall establish procedures in cooperation with the local post office for processing certified or registered mail. To send certified or registered mail, offenders must have sufficient funds in their trust fund accounts and must attach to the envelopes signed money vouchers so that the proper postage may be applied and the amount deducted from their trust fund accounts.

d) Offenders shall not be permitted to open, read, or deliver another offender's mail without the person's permission. However, offenders may transport mail in sacks or other closed containers under the direct supervision of an employee.

e) No disciplinary restrictions shall be placed on an offender's mail privileges.

(Source: Amended at 27 Ill. Reg. 8039, effective July 1, 2003)

Section 525.130 Outgoing Mail

This Section applies to all correctional facilities within the Department.

a) Offenders shall be permitted to send privileged and non-privileged letters at their own expense. Offenders with insufficient money in their trust fund accounts to purchase postage shall be permitted to send reasonable amounts of legal mail and mail to clerks of any court or the Illinois Court of Claims, to certified court reporters, to the Administrative Review Board, and to the Prisoner Review Board at State expense if they attach signed money vouchers authorizing deductions of future funds to cover the cost of the postage. The offender's trust fund account shall be restricted for the cost of such postage until paid or the offender is released or discharged, whichever is soonest.

b) Offenders must clearly mark all outgoing mail with their name and in adult facilities with their institutional number. Mail that is not properly marked, including privileged mail, shall be opened and returned to the sender if the sender's identity can be determined. If the sender's identity cannot be determined, the mail shall be destroyed.

c) Outgoing privileged mail must be clearly marked as "privileged" and sealed by the offender. Outgoing mail which is clearly marked as privileged and addressed to a privileged party may not be opened for inspection except as provided in subsection (d) of this Section.

d) In adult facilities, outgoing privileged mail shall be examined for dangerous contraband, using an x-ray, fluoroscope, or other similar device. Such examination may be conducted in juvenile facilities. Outgoing privileged mail may be inspected for dangerous contraband by other means which do not damage the mail and which do not permit the mail to be read. Except in an emergency, outgoing privileged mail shall not be opened, unless there is reasonable suspicion that dangerous contraband is contained therein, legal services is consulted, and the mail is opened in the offender's presence.

e) With the exception of privileged mail, all mail shall be unsealed when collected or placed in housing unit mailboxes. Sealed mail that is not privileged will be opened and returned to the sender if the sender's identity can be determined. If the sender's identity cannot be determined, the mail shall be destroyed.

f) Each correctional facility shall establish procedures for the collection of outgoing mail. Collections shall be made daily, Monday through Friday, except on State holidays. Every effort shall be made to ensure that mail is delivered to the U.S. Postal Service on the same day.

g) Outgoing non-privileged mail shall be inspected for contraband. If a letter from an offender is confiscated because it contains contraband, the offender shall be notified promptly in writing.

h) Department employees may spot check and read outgoing non-privileged mail. Outgoing non-privileged mail or portions thereof may be reproduced or withheld from delivery if it presents a threat to security or safety, including the following:

1) The letter contains threats of physical harm against any person or threats of criminal activity;
2) The letter contains threats of blackmail or extortion;
3) The letter contains information regarding sending contraband into or out of the facility, plans to escape, or plans to engage in criminal activity;
4) The letter is in code and its contents cannot be understood by correctional staff;
5) The letter violates any departmental rules or contains plans to engage in activities in violation of departmental or institutional rules;
6) The letter solicits gifts, goods, or money from other than family members;
7) The letter contains information which, if communicated, might result in physical harm to another;
8) The letter contains unauthorized correspondence with another offender; or
9) The letter or contents thereof constitute a violation of State or federal law.

i) Any outgoing letter may be stopped and returned to the sender if the person to whom it is addressed (or a parent or guardian, if the addressee is a minor or incompetent) has notified the Chief Administrative Officer in writing that the person does not wish to receive mail from the offender. This rule shall not be construed to prevent offenders from corresponding with their children unless their parental rights have been terminated.

j) If an offender is prohibited from sending a letter or portions thereof, the offender shall be informed in writing of the decision.

k) Material from a letter which violates subsection (h) of this Section may be placed in an offender's master file.

l) Offenders may not send packages without approval of the Chief Administrative Officer, whose decision shall be based on administrative, safety, and security considerations.

(Source: Amended at 27 Ill. Reg. 8039, effective July 1, 2003)

Section 525.140 Incoming Mail

a) Incoming privileged mail must be clearly marked as "privileged" and be clearly marked with the name, title, and address of the sender.

b) Incoming privileged mail may be opened in the presence of the offender to whom it is addressed to inspect for contraband, to verify the identity of the sender, and to determine that nothing other than legal or official matter is enclosed.

c) Incoming privileged mail may contain communications only from the privileged correspondent whose name and address appear on the envelope. If non-privileged material or correspondence from a third party is found to be enclosed, such material shall be treated as non-privileged mail.

d) All incoming non-privileged mail, including mail from clerks of courts, shall be opened and inspected for contraband.

e) Cashier's checks, money orders, and business checks subject to the restrictions imposed by 20 Ill. Adm. Code 205 shall be deposited in the offender's trust fund account, with a record made of the sender's name, the amount received, and the date. For purposes of this Section a business check shall mean a check written on any agency's or firm's account and any check written on an employer's personal account for wages due a person assigned to a transition center. Offenders shall be notified of all monies received and deposited in their trust fund accounts. However, any checks or money orders which exceed the limitation on the amounts (20 Ill. Adm. Code 205) shall be returned to the sender, and the offender shall be notified.

f) Personal checks and cash shall be returned to the sender, and the sender shall be notified that funds cannot be received in that form.

g) Correctional officials may spot check and read incoming non-privileged mail. Incoming mail or portions thereof may be inspected, reproduced, or withheld from delivery for any of the reasons listed in Section 525.130(h) of this Subpart or in Subpart C of this part.

h) When an offender is prohibited from receiving a letter or portions thereof, the committed person and the sender shall be notified in writing of the decision.

i) If an offender has been transferred or released, first class mail shall be forwarded to the person if the address is known. If no forwarding address is available, the mail shall be returned to the sender.

j) If an offender has been absent from the facility on a furlough or pursuant to writ, the person's mail shall be held at the facility for a period of one month, unless the offender has made a written request to the Chief Administrative Officer to have the mail forwarded to another address. At the conclusion of the month, first class mail shall be forwarded to the offender's address, if known, or returned to the sender, unless alternative arrangements have been made.

k) Offenders may receive publications, including books, periodicals and catalogs, in accordance with Subpart C of this Part, and may receive typewriters ordered directly from a supplier through the commissary. Other packages may be received only as approved by the Chief Administrative Officer. All packages shall be opened and searched prior to delivery.

(Source: Amended at 27 Ill. Reg. 8039, effective July 1, 2003)

Section 525.150 Telephone Privileges

a) Telephone privileges shall be granted to offenders in accordance with their institutional status and provisions of this Section.
b) Collect calls may be made to persons where billable.
c) Offenders may not place telephone calls to:

1) Toll free area codes, including but not limited to 800 series area codes, or to area codes or prefixes for which a charge is assessed to the line from which the call was placed, including but not limited to 800 or 900 series area codes or 976 prefixes;
2) Emergency or directory assistance or to long distance carriers;
3) Persons or companies which have requested that a block be placed on their telephone numbers;
4) Numbers suspected of being used fraudulently or for fraudulent purposes;
5) Parolees, ex-offenders, former employees, or current employees absent the approval of the Chief Administrative Officer; or
6) Numbers or persons restricted for other legitimate penological reasons, including security and order.

d) A block may be placed on telephone calls to:

1) The local community except to the offender's friends, family, and others in the local community who request to receive calls from the offender.
2) A telephone number for which there is a large unpaid balance on the account, with the exception of telephone numbers of attorneys and law firms.
3) Any telephone numbers listed in subsection (c) of this Section.

e) Offenders may not engage in call forwarding or in conference calls.
f) In the case of valid emergencies, such as critical illness or death in an offender's immediate family, consideration shall be given to allowing a special telephone call, regardless of the individual's institutional status. Immediate family shall include parent or guardian, children, brother, sister, grandparent, whether step, adopted, half, or whole, and spouse.
g) Offenders who are the subject of a new criminal indictment, information, or complaint shall be permitted to make reasonable telephone calls to attorneys for the purpose of securing defense counsel, regardless of the individual's institutional status.
h) All offenders' telephone calls shall be subject to monitoring and recording at any time by departmental staff, unless prior special arrangements have been made to make or to receive confidential telephone calls to or from their attorneys.
i) Notices shall be posted at each telephone from which offenders are normally permitted to place calls and in the offenders' orientation manual. The notices shall state that offenders' telephone calls may be monitored or recorded or both.

(Source: Amended at 37 Ill. Reg. 1645, effective February 1, 2013)

SUBPART C: PUBLICATIONS

Section 525.200 Applicability

This Subpart applies to all correctional facilities within the Department of Corrections.

(Source: Amended at 27 Ill. Reg. 8039, effective July 1, 2003)

Section 525.202 Definitions

"Chief Administrative Officer" means the highest ranking official of a correctional facility.
"Department" means the Department of Corrections.
"Director" means the Director of the Department of Corrections.

"Obscene" means any material that the average person, applying contemporary adult community standards, would find that, taken as a whole, appeals to the prurient interest; and the average person, applying contemporary adult community standards, would find that it depicts or describes in a patently offensive way, ultimate sexual acts or sadomasochistic sexual acts, whether normal or perverted, actual or simulated, or masturbation, excretory functions or lewd exhibition of the genitals; and taken as a whole, it lacks serious literary, artistic, political, or scientific value [720 ILCS 5/11-20(b)].

"Offender" means a person committed to the Department or to the custody of the Department.
"Publication" means any book, booklet, magazine, newspaper, periodical, or similar materials.

(Source: Amended at 27 Ill. Reg. 8039, effective July 1, 2003)

Section 525.205 Responsibilities

a)   Unless otherwise specified, the Director or Chief Administrative Officer may delegate responsibilities stated in this Subpart to another person or persons or designate another person or persons to perform the duties specified.

b)   No other individual may routinely perform duties whenever a Section in this Subpart specifically states the Director or Chief Administrative Officer shall personally perform the duties. However, the Director or Chief Administrative Officer may designate another person or persons to perform the duties during periods of his temporary absence or in an emergency.

(Source: Added at 11 Ill. Reg. 16134, effective November 1, 1987)

Section 525.210 General Guidelines

a)   Each facility shall maintain a current approved list of publications.
b)   Offenders shall be informed of the procedures governing publications during orientation and this Subpart shall be available to offenders.
c)   Each offender may subscribe to, solicit free copies of, or buy copies of newspapers, magazines, books and other publications for delivery to the facility in accordance with this Subpart. A member of the individual's family or a friend may also order, solicit or bring approved publications to the facility. However, publications shall be limited to a maximum of 5 per visit and shall not packaged, wrapped, or otherwise contained in any way.
d)   All publications shall be delivered promptly after necessary inspection for contraband. If it appears to violate the standards set forth in Section 525.230, the publication shall first be referred to the Publication Review Officer for review and determination.
e)   Publications determined to be unacceptable shall be disposed of as contraband in accordance with 20 Ill. Adm. Code 501: Subpart C.

(Source: Amended at 27 Ill. Reg. 8039, effective July 1, 2003)

Section 525.220 Publications Review Officer

The Chief Administrative Officer shall appoint at least 2 employees to serve as Publication Review Officers to review publications. At least one individual shall be from program staff and at least one individual shall be from security staff.

(Source: Amended at 27 Ill. Reg. 8039, effective July 1, 2003)

Section 525.230 Procedure for Review of Publications

a)   A Publication Review Officer, hereafter referred to as Officer, shall review publications to determine whether to recommend prohibiting acceptance of any publications that he or she finds to contain material determined to be:

   1)   Obscene;
   2)   Detrimental to security, good order, rehabilitation, or discipline or if it might facilitate criminal activity, or be detrimental to mental health needs of an offender as determined by a mental health professional.

b)   A publication may not be rejected solely because its content is religious, philosophical, political, social, or sexual or because its contents are unpopular or repugnant. A publication that may be rejected includes, but is not limited to, a publication or portion thereof that meets one of the following criteria:

   1)   It is obscene;
   2)   It is written in code or facilitates communication between offenders;
   3)   It depicts, describes, or encourages activities that may lead to the use of physical violence or group disruption or it facilitates organizational activity without approval of the Chief Administrative Officer;
   4)   It advocates or encourages violence, hatred, or group disruption or it poses an intolerable risk of violence or disruption;
   5)   It encourages or instructs in the commission of criminal activity;
   6)   It includes sexually explicit material that by its nature or content poses a threat to security, good order, or discipline or it facilitates criminal activity;
   7)   It is otherwise detrimental to security, good order, rehabilitation, or discipline or it might facilitate criminal activity or be detrimental to mental health.

c)   If a review is initiated, the offender shall be notified in writing that the publication is under review and the notice shall include an explanation why the publication is deemed to contain unacceptable material in accordance with the standards set forth in this Section. If the publication was mailed directly from the publisher, a copy of the notice shall be sent to the publisher. The written notice shall be sent to the offender and the publisher, if applicable, no later than 30 days from the date the correctional facility receives the publication. The written notice shall indicate that:

   1)   The offender may submit a written supportive statement or other documentation within seven days after the date of the notice that the publication is under review. An extension will be granted if in the opinion of the Officer there is a legitimate reason why relevant information could not be submitted timely.
   2)   The publisher shall be allowed 21 days from the date of the notice to file an objection and to submit a written supportive statement or other documentation.
   3)   The offender may request to appear before the Officer. The appearance will be allowed if the Officer

determines that the appearance is necessary for an appropriate review.

4) The offender may ask for assistance or information regarding the publication review procedure.

5) If the publication is approved, it will be forwarded to the offender upon completion of the review. If the publication is not provided to the offender within 60 days after the date of the written notice, the publication shall be deemed disapproved and the offender may file a grievance in accordance with 20 Ill. Adm. Code 504: Subpart F.

d) Any recommendation for denial shall be forwarded to the Chief Administrative Officer with an explanation. If the Chief Administrative Officer concurs with the recommendation to deny the publication, the publication shall be disapproved.

e) The Publication Review Officer shall maintain copies of decisions in a designated area for at least three years.

f) If after six consecutive issues of a publication have been denied and it is determined unlikely that future issues of the publication will be approved, the publication may be banned.

g) If the characteristic content of a banned publication significantly changes to no longer warrant denial of the publication in accordance with this Section, an offender may request another review of the publication by the Officer. A previously banned publication shall be subject to review no more frequently than every four months. If a review is to be initiated, the offender shall be advised to arrange for one or more issues of the publication to be submitted to the Officer at the offender's expense.

1) The review shall be conducted in the same manner as the initial review of the publication.

2) If an issue of a previously banned publication is approved, an offender may request subsequent issues to be reviewed notwithstanding the four month review period.

3) The Officer may recommend that a previously banned publication be approved.

h) The Director may establish a Central Publication Review Committee to periodically review and make recommendations regarding facility determinations or recommendations to the Director who may approve or disapprove the recommendations based on the standards set forth in this Section. If a Committee is appointed:

1) Committee members shall consist of at least one representative each from administrative and operational staff.

2) Reviews need only be conducted by one member of the Committee.

3) The facility and the offender shall be notified of any decision made by the Director.

(Source: Amended at 30 Ill. Reg. 14843, effective September 1, 2006)

SUBPART D: MARRIAGE OF OFFENDERS

Section 525.300 Applicability

This Subpart applies to all correctional facilities within the Department of Corrections.

(Source: Amended at 27 Ill. Reg. 8039, effective July 1, 2003)

Section 525.302 Definitions

"Chief Administrative Officer" means the highest ranking official of a correctional facility.
"Department" means the Department of Corrections.
"Director" means the Director of the Department.
"Offender" means a person committed to the Department or to the custody of the Department.

(Source: Amended at 27 Ill. Reg. 8039, effective July 1, 2003)

Section 525.305 Responsibilities

a) Unless otherwise specified, the Director or Chief Administrative Officer may delegate responsibilities stated in this Subpart to another person or persons or designate another person or persons to perform the duties specified.

b) No other individual may routinely perform duties whenever a Section in this Subpart specifically states the Director or Chief Administrative Officer shall personally perform the duties. However, the Director or Chief Administrative Officer may designate another person or persons to perform the duties during periods of his or her temporary absence or in an emergency.

(Source: Amended at 20 Ill. Reg. 15960, effective January 1, 1997)

Section 525.310 Request for Permission to Marry

a) Marriage between two offenders confined in Department facilities shall be prohibited.

b) An offender who wishes to become married shall submit a written request to the Chief Administrative Officer a minimum of 30 days in advance of the date requested for the marriage ceremony.

1) The notice shall include the name and address of the intended spouse and a description of any actions which

have been taken in obtaining a marriage license and in complying with applicable provisions of the law.

    2)   All financial obligations shall be the responsibility of the offended or the intended spouse.

    3)   A request for a transition center leave may be submitted at the same time as the request to marry. The request shall be reviewed in accordance with 20 Ill. Adm. Code 530: Subpart D.

c)   The facility chaplain or an individual designated by the Chief Administrative Officer shall conduct a pre-marital counseling session with the offender or the intended spouse or both.

d)   The Chief Administrative Officer shall review the request to marry and shall approve or deny the request based on security concerns, the best interest of the offender, or other legitimate penological interests. The Chief Administrative Officer's decision regarding the request to marry and, if applicable, the leave request, shall be made in writing. A copy of the written decision shall be provided to the offender.

e)   Except as provided in Section 525.310(f), the facility shall make its chapel or another suitable location available for the performance of the approved marriage ceremony.

    1)   The facility's chaplain shall review the type of ceremony that is requested and refer a description of the proposed ceremony to the Chief Administrative Officer for approval.

    2)   Witnesses and guests shall not exceed 6 in number, excluding the officiating clergyman. Witnesses and guests must be on the offender's approved visiting list, except as otherwise approved by the Chief Administrative Officer.

    3)   Facilities for the consummation of marriages or for a reception shall not be provided.

f)   The marriage ceremony and reception, if any, of an offender housed at a transition center shall be at the offender's or intended spouse's expense and at a suitable location in the free community as approved by the Chief Administrative Officer.

(Source: Amended at 27 Ill. Reg. 8039, effective July 1, 2003)

AUTHORITY: Implementing Sections 3-2-2, 3-7-1, 3-7-2, 3-8-7, 3-8-8, 3-10-8, and 3-10-9 of the Unified Code of Corrections [730 ILCS 5/3-2-2, 3-7-1, 3-7-2, 3-8-7, 3-8-8, 3-10-8, and 3-10-9] and Section 1-3 of the Juvenile Court Act of 1987 [705 ILCS 405/1-3] and authorized by Sections 3-2-2 and 3-7-1 of the Unified Code of Corrections [730 ILCS 5/3-2-2 and 3-7-1]. Subpart A is also implementing a Consent Decree (Tillman vs. Rowe, #77 C 1008, N.D. Ill., 1977). Subpart C is also implementing a Court Agreement (Ryan vs. Walker, #04 C 4635, N.D. Ill., 2006).

SOURCE: Adopted at 8 Ill. Reg. 14598, effective August 1, 1984; amended at 9 Ill. Reg. 10728, effective August 1, 1985; amended at 11 Ill. Reg. 16134, effective November 1, 1987; amended at 12 Ill. Reg. 9664, effective July 1, 1988; amended at 14 Ill. Reg. 5114, effective April 1, 1990; amended at 14 Ill. Reg. 19875, effective December 1, 1990; emergency amendment at 16 Ill. Reg. 3583, effective February 20, 1992, for a maximum of 150 days; amended at 16 Ill. Reg. 10439, effective July 1, 1992; peremptory amendment at 17 Ill. Reg. 1666, effective January 22, 1993; expedited correction at 17 Ill. Reg. 11903, effective January 22, 1993; peremptory amendment at 17 Ill. Reg. 8069, effective May 27, 1993; amended at 20 Ill. Reg. 15960, effective January 1, 1997; emergency amendment at 21 Ill. Reg. 641, effective January 1, 1997, for a maximum of 150 days; amended at 21 Ill. Reg. 7139, effective May 31, 1997; amended at 27 Ill. Reg. 8039, effective July 1, 2003; amended at 30 Ill. Reg. 14843, effective September 1, 2006; amended at 35 Ill. Reg. 5400, effective April 1, 2011; amended at 37 Ill. Reg. 1645, effective February 1, 2013.

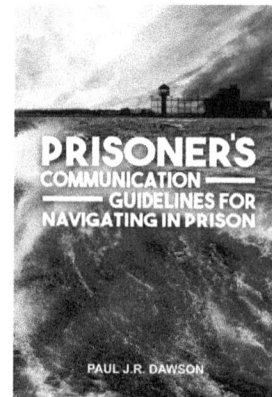

Chapter 21

Becoming the System

"The idea that it takes money to make money has been contradicted countless times by modern business alchemists who've spun lead into gold." -Jim Motavalli

I'm not going to sugar coat it, most of you reading this book are hoping to come-up with a pen pal to help out with money. I understand. But trying to find money in pen pals is hard. There's an easier way to make money in the pen pal game. How? By becoming the system itself. Let me show you how I did it and how you can too.

You can make money in the pen pal game by doing one of the following (or all of them):

- Sell pen pal lists of names and addresses.

- Sell special reports based on your pen pal experiences.

- Sell a book (like this one) on how-to get pen pals.

- Start your own pen pal website.

- Help prisoners post their online profiles.

Let's look at these five areas more in-depth.

Selling Pen Pal Lists

My info-cellpreneur comrade, George Kayer, is doing this now. His company, Girls and Mags, gets 200 names and addresses (some with photos) off online pen pal websites and sends them to prisoners for $19.98. He promises that no two lists will be the same. Great Business.

For those of you who know my story, know that I started out selling pen pal lists. 100 names and addresses for $10. My lists were not as good as George's because mine didn't have photos and I was selling the same lists to other prisoners. But this market is still wide open to anyone who can get the most up-to-date and accurate lists. There are numerous prisoners who will buy them no matter what I write about them. Here's a strategy that I first put in a special report and sold. Then I included it in my book, *The Millionaire Prisoner*. Still, I haven't found someone using it yet.

How to Get Pen Pals to Contact You First… and Make Money at the Same Time

Step 1. Place an ad on FREE classified websites like Craigslist.com, MetroDate.com, and BackPage.com. There are more (7,000 places where you can place a free ad), but you'll have to check out www.buysellbid.com and www.freeclassifiedlinks.com. For $29.95 you can get a listing of all the free classified sites online from www.classifiedclub.com. Your ad could be like this:

FREE PEN PAL ADS

For women who'll write prisoners send info, bio & photo to:

Name

Address

City, State, Zip Code

Email Address

Here's why you word it like that. Not every woman is open to writing prisoners. It just isn't so. We wish. But if you put the above ad up, only women who want to write prisoners would respond! Once women submit their ads, sort through them and write to the ones you like. The ones you aren't going to write to, are the ones you can make money from by selling their ad to others.

Step 2. Typeset your ads into an ad sheet and sell it. Specialized lists like this have sold for $6 for only 20 addresses. So the more ads you have, the more money you can make. Once you have your ad-sheets developed, you need to move to the next step.

Step 3. Place your ad in *Prison Legal News* and other prison-based publications. Your ad could look like this:

Women Who Write Prisoners

$6 or 14 "Forever" Stamps to:

Name

Address

City, State, Zip Code

Step 4. As you get orders and more money, you could buy more ads online using Google AdWords and Facebook ads and expand to other magazines and periodicals. You could do well for yourself, as long as you keep up-dating your lists.

Do you think this system is improbable? It's not. Gordon "Limo" Emond was an Arizona prisoner who teamed up with Specialty Publications and produced a variety of lists for $6. He also offered to write a 300-word introductory letter to your pen pal for $8. Brilliant! He would get first crack at possible pen pals and make money at the same time. Learn from him.

Special Reports about the Pen Pal Game

I've made a few thousand dollars off special reports. My most famous was the *How to Get FREE Pen Pals* manual. It was only a 20-page booklet/special report that we sold for $9.95. Later I raised the price to $17.95. I just wrote it based on my experiences in the pen pal game. Most of that report is the basis behind chapter 4. That's the great thing about these reports, you can reuse them in *any way* you see fit. The special report that starts on the next page is only seven pages long, but we sold it for $7. We also give it away as a free bonus for those who bought the *How to Get FREE Pen Pals* booklet. Think about some pen pal game that you know, that I haven't included in this book. Got some? You could put it into a special report and sell it. And then you could be an info-cellpreneur, like me, or you could become a *Millionaire Prisoner*™ and get listed in the Hall of Fame? But you'll never know unless you try. Check out this special report just to see how easy it is to write one

---

Resource Box

If you are interested in learning more about writing special reports and self-publishing, here are some resources to check out:

- *How to Write & Sell Simple Information for Fun and Profit* by Robert W. Bly with Fred Gleeck

- *How to Make a Whole Lot More Than $1,000,000 Writing, Commissioning, Publishing and Selling "How-To" Information* by Dr. Jeffrey Lant

- Information Marketing Association at www.infomarketing.com

How To Effectively Use Online Pen pal Sites: 10 Secrets Every Prisoner Should Know!

Every time you pay to place an online pen pal ad it costs you money that you may not get back. Are you confident you're getting the best results for every ad that you pay for? After reading this special report you'll know 10 ways to make your investment in online pen- pal ads produce better results. But first, let me tell you who I am and what I've learned.

My Experience with Prison Pen pal Websites

My name is Joshua Kruger and I'm a prisoner in Illinois serving a life sentence for a 1999 murder. If you've read some of my other special reports or booklets then you already know that I love to write letters to pen pals. Over the years I've developed some strategies that help me have success in the pen pal game. The secrets in this report are to be used on services where you pay to place your profile online. (If you want tips and strategies for getting free pen pals then see my booklet "How to Get Free Pen Pals!" for my special report "How to Get Pen Pals to Contact You First ... and Make Money at the Same Time!"

In 2003 I began using online websites to get pen pals. My journey started with the now defunct website: The *Pampered Prisoner*, and a small personal ad on: Prison Talk Online (PTO). A few years ago I went on: *Friends Beyond The Wall* (FBTW). I've also been on: Lostvault.com and: Jailmail.net. In research for my book, The *Millionaire Prisoner*, I put up profiles on: WriteAPrisoner.com, FriendsWithPens.org, and PrisonInmates.com. Did I get responses? I got two from *The Pampered Prisoner*, three from FBTW, and I got flooded with mail from my ad on PTO.

But PTO is not a pen pal site per se. It's an online forum and network for people interested in talking about prisons and prisoners. PTO has changed its format since I was on there on 2003, but if you can still post your contact information on PTO, I would highly suggest that you do so. I have gotten 5 pen pals from *Write A Prisoner*, one from PrisonInmates.com, and nothing from *Friends With Pens*. Before I make any recommendations about what you should do, let me offer you some of the research that I've found. These strategies will help you understand why some sites are good and some aren't.

Why Use Online Pen pal Sites?

Why, because you cannot get access to millions of possible pen pals in any other forum. Let's look at the facts. There are over 90 million single people in America. A lot of them will try online dating to find love. (In 2011, 40 million people tried it.) In his book *Microtrends*, Mark Penn said that one in five Americans in their twenties, are using online dating. Its one in ten for people 30 and over. Some of these people will try online prison pen pal websites. Why? Either they saw an ad for the site somewhere; a friend recommended it because they found love using it; or they saw it mentioned on CNN, Dr. Phil, or another television show. The great thing about using online pen pal sites is that they work for you 24/7, even while you sleep.

One reason that I like online prison websites is that anyone who logs onto it is more inclined to writing a prisoner. You don't have to sell them on the fact of your confinement. Some people find the fact that you're in prison a bonus. Women who love bad boys like it. Some men look at women behind bars like pieces of forbidden fruit and seek them out. I've had other women tell me that they know prisoners will not leave them or cheat on them (at least physically). Dr. Phil may not like the idea of women starting a relationship with prisoners, but the fact is, they do, and it will continue to happen. If you aren't online then you might miss out on finding love. But, not all prison pen pal websites are created equal.

Which Website is the Best?

That is the million-dollar question isn't it? In December 2010, prisoner-service company: *Help From Beyond The Walls* used www.statbrain.com to compile stats about the number of people who view prison pen pal sites each day. The site with the most average page views was: WriteAPrisoner.com, with over 5,000 page views a day. Second was: Meet- an-Inmate.com, with over 4,000 page views. The only other site that got over a thousand page views was: Cellpalls.com. Why did these sites get the most page views; because they have the most Google links! Since Google is the largest (and most used) search engine in the world, when anyone does a search for "prison pen pals" on Google, they'll get directed to one of these websites. I had my personal assistant do a Google search in 2012 and the first site listed was: WriteAPrisoner.com. Don't be fooled by other websites that say they get high traffic, they don't.

One last thing about "hit counters" and "page views". In the first four months I was on WriteAPrisoner.com, my profile received 1500 plus page views. This averages out to about 375 page views a month. But that doesn't necessarily mean that 375 different people are seeing my profile page each month. It could be one person going from profile to profile and then coming back to mine that drives up the page views? I do know that I've kept my profile on the front pages of WriteAPrisoner.com by adding blogs, poetry, and new text... and still have only been seen by a few hundred people each month. Keep this in mind when deciding what you're going to do.

Total Pageviews

1 0 0 0 0 0 0

A small disclosure is warranted: I know prisoners who have met their wives on WriteAPrisoner.com. I also know prisoners who've met wonderful people on PrisonInmates.com and Lostvault.com. My advice is that if you're going to pay to go on a prison pay pen pal website, you should look at *Write A Prisoner* first. But no matter what service you choose, there are some secrets you need to know.

10 Secrets Every Prisoner Should Know

Secret #1: You must have a clear, up-to-date, smiling photo! This is what prospective pen pals see first. Yes, some prisoners have gotten hits without posting a photo, but not as many as the prisoner who has a good smiling one. Other photos that are good to use are ones showing you doing something active, like playing a sport or swimming. I know one prisoner who put up his baby picture and got more hits afterward. So be unique in your photo selection, but make sure you have a good smiling photo to put on your profile page.

Secret #2: You should use a great opening line or headline. The headline is the ad for your ad. It should induce the prospective pen pal to read further. It should be set in bold and capital letters if you can. It could ask a question or it could be funny. But if you choose to use humor, be careful lest your joke fall flat or attract the wrong people. One prisoner used "Plus-size women really turn me on!" as his headline. That's exactly what he got... and he got more than one! Your headline, whatever it is, should reveal your personality. Make it stand out, make it bold, make it urgent, and make it memorable. If you can do that you have a great headline.

Secret #3: Sell yourself, but do it softly, using words that stimulate the imagination. Use stories and anecdotes to paint word pictures. And always check spelling and grammar before sending off your profile text.

Secret #4: Be honest, positive, and exciting in your profile text. Never complain in your ad and don't put yourself down. Hoping for sympathy is not the way to attract people.

Secret #5: Say what you're looking for. If you're looking for a friend then say that. Is it marriage? Say that! If kids are important to you then say it. Same thing for animals or whatever. It's better to reveal what you truly want so you can get it, instead of getting frustrated trying to make someone into something they're not.

Secret #6: Don't put too many limitations on your prospective pen pals. You don't want to close-out people just because they have blond hair or are 5 foot tall. That would be superficial. But it is perfectly okay to say that you prefer a Christian or non-smoker, if that's really important to you.

Secret #7: Tell the best possible story you can about yourself in the least amount of words. My rule has been

40/40/20. That's 40 of the profile should be about me, 40 about what I'm looking for, and 20 on what I want them to do, i.e. call, write, email, etc. Most websites have a word limit for your profile text. Do the math and use the 40/40/20 rule.

Secret #8: Try to write something no one else will write. Be unique or funny. Create an image of what it's going to be like to be around you. People will write you if they see that you are different. Just remember to make sure what you write fits your personality. And never use: "Candlelight dinners" and "Walks on the beach." Never, ever!

Secret #9: Be specific when describing your interests. Not: "I like listening to music, watching movies, and playing sports." Instead say: "I like listening to Led Zeppelin, watching Adam Sandler comedies, and playing softball." Show what you like with specifics.

Secret #10: Don't allow your ad to be shuffled into the pile. That means you must keep your profile page on the front pages of the site. If you have to pay to do so, do it! What good is a profile page if no one sees it? Do what you got to do, and you'll get some hits.

Bonus Secret: Do not talk about money in your ad. I read a USA Today article about how prisoner Jerry Lee Beatty put up a profile on Voice for Inmates.com and said: "I need finances for attorneys, art supplies, and some everyday essentials." Don't do that. Build friendships first, then, seek help. It's okay to check the "Seeking Donations" box if the site offers it, but don't ever talk about money or finances in your ad.

There you have it. Ten secrets that every prisoner should know and use before posting an online pen pal profile.

Selected Bibliography

If you would like to learn more about writing great personal ads, here are some books you may want to read. A lot of them are out of print, but you can find used copies online. Utilize Bookfinder4U.com to find the best price. *25 Words or less: How to Write Like a Pro to Find That Special Someone, Through Personal Ads* - by Emily Calvo & Lawrence Minsky

Dot.com Dating: Finding Your Right Someone Online - by Drs. Les & Leslie Parrott
Love By Mail: The International Guide to Personal Advertising - by Richard Cote
How to Be OUTRAGEOUSLY Successful with the Opposite Sex - by Paul Hartunian
Love Bytes: The On-Line Dating Handbook - by David Fox
Plain Fat Chick Seeks Guy Who Likes Broccoli - by Kathy Hinckley & Peter Hesse
Women Who Love Men Who Kill - by Sheila Isenberg
Advertising for Love: How to Play the Personals... - Author Unknown

Online Pen pal Website Directory

The addresses listed here were accurate as of publication. But websites come and go, and this list is by no means comprehensive. Always send a LSASE when requesting their brochures and services.

CellPals.com

PO Box 1594

Montgomery, TX 77356

1 (855) PEN-PALS (736-7257)

Lost Vault.com

PO Box 261

Washburn, TN 37888

email: penpals@lostvault.com

Friends Beyond The Wall

2600 South Road, Suite 44-244

Poughkeepsie, NY 12601-7003

email: info@friendsbeyondthewall.com

Inmate Connections.com

465 NE 181st, #308

Portland, OR 97230

Inmate Classified

PO Box 3311

Granada Hills, CA 91394

Prison Pen Pals

PO Box 235

East Berlin, PA 17316

email: info@prisonpenpals.com

Prison Inmates Online

8033 W. Sunset Blvd. #700

Los Angeles, CA 90046

email: info@prisoninmates.com

Another Online Avenue

For $20, EPS will post your photo and profile on 2 online pen pal websites: *Global Pen Pals* and *Pen Pals NOW*. These sites are for regular free world people, but are worth a try because they have thousands of pen pals on their sites. Send EPS a LSASE and request more information about their pen pal services. You can reach them at:

Elite Prisoner Services (EPS)

PO Box 2131

Appleton, WI 54912-2131

A Parting Shot

Once you're in the pen pal game, it's simply a matter of using the proven strategies over and over again to get the results you desire. Throw in the power of the internet to greatly multiply your efforts and you can succeed beyond your wildest dreams. Follow the secrets in this special report and you can get the results you want. Always remember that one great pen pal is better than ten bad ones. Quality is always better than quantity.

As I do in all my work, I invite you to stay in touch with me. Let me know how you do. Share your success. Tell me what you learned along the way. Who knows, I might just immortalize you in one of my future books or reports?

No matter what, be blessed!

Yours for *Pen Pal Success,*

Josh Kruger

A Pen Pal Authorpreneur

Resource Box

To learn how to get pen pals for FREE, get a copy of Josh Kruger's booklet: "How to Get FREE Pen Pals" ($9.95 postpaid or 22 FCS stamps from Superior Enterprises, Dept. JK, 661 Hazel St. , Akron, OH 44305-3340).

Check out the Millionaire Prisoner Blog at: millionaire prisoner.blogspot.com

To get more information about the services of Mr. Kruger, be sure to email him at: millionaireprisoner@gmail.com

If you're a prisoner who doesn't have access to email, then you must have a third party send a note to him at: Josh Kruger Joliet, IL

If you want to add some extra money to your pocketbook during football season, be sure to get a copy of Mr. Kruger's new booklet: "How to Win Your Football Pool" ($9.95 postpaid or 22 FCS stamps from Superior Enterprises).

If you order both the "How to Get FREE Pen Pals" and "How To Win Your Football Pool" booklets ($19.90 postpaid or 44 FCS stamps from Superior Enterprises) you'll get a FREE Bonus special report: How to Get Pen Pals to Contact You First ... and Make Money at the Same Time! (A $7.00 value FREE!)

When you have prison problems, the Millionaire Prisoner can solve them.

Freedom Jones wrote *How to Get Girls While in Prison* with his own perspective on the prison pen pal game. My comrade Mike Enemigo wrote *The Art & Power of Letter Writing for Prisoners*. George Kayer did his own *Pen Pal Catalog for Prisoners*. Why not you? Yes, I've written this book, but there's always room for more. Nothing is stopping you but you. Use your imagination. You don't have to write the same one we've wrote. How about a book of a bunch of sample pen pal letters? Or a novel? Raven Skye did one called *The Pen Pal*. Even John Grisham has one about some prisoners using the game to blackmail people who place homosexual personal ads in *The Brethren*. I look forward to reading your pen pal book. (FYI: if you do write a book, you automatically raise your status in the eyes of all the possible pen pals out there. Trust me, it's what Neil Strauss described in *The Game* when he talked about "creating the lifestyle".)

Your Own Pen Pal Website

There's always room for more legit pen pal websites. But you have to come with something original. The key would be getting women to respond to the ads your customers placed. If you could make that happen, your prisoner-customers would tell all their friends and you'd have an unlimited supply of new clients. The key would be to place Google and Facebook Ads, so you climb up the search rankings and get people to come to your website. This is something you might think about it.

Help Prisoners Post Their Online Pen Pal Profiles

Let me tell you something. If I was in the free-world, I'd do all of the above things. But this strategy would be the one I would use to get rich. I'd set up a system where I put prisoners on twenty different FREE sites like Pen Pals Now, InterPals.net, and Passions.com. I'd charge them $100 for 20 sites. Then I'd offer to monitor their pages for them, for a monthly fee in different membership plans. Prisoners would gladly pay these fees if they could get a steady stream of pen pals. Wouldn't you? I would. There are companies out there saying that they'll do this for you, but I haven't found one that can do it in a timely manner and guarantee responses. I would do both. If you can find someone to help you do this, then you both could make a lot of money. The game is to be sold, not told!

How to Start a Pen Pal Newsletter

They're very easy to start, and can provide extra income for the business-minded prisoner. You can use a simple one page, typewritten sheet to get started. It could be a quick run-down on what your members are up to, i.e., "Mark C. is planning to start a college correspondence course next month; Janelle S. is attending night classes for a beautician's license; John K. is selling his mail-order business; Brad L. is setting up his own pen pal website; Dave A. is transferring to the Feds."

This kind of membership involvement will get your "Newsletter" off to a running start, and keep your readers loyal to you because of the "gossip" you pass along in each issue. Follow up your gossip column with either a question and answer section, or letters from readers, ala Ann Landers or Dear Abby. Complete the newsletter with a short story on how to meet men or women, what to say and how to develop a friendship. The back page, or extra page, is then a listing of men and women - including a short description of each, and their addresses - wanting to correspond with or meet people with similar tastes.

You'll need a typewriter, paper, and names of people interested in writing and receiving Pen Pal letters. You can quickly secure your own mailing list by getting names and addresses from the ads placed in pen pal publications, and other singles magazines that carry ads. It wouldn't take long to get a basic "100" to begin your operation.

You should have a letterhead and imprinted mailing envelopes and return envelopes. You can normally get 1000 of each for $100. Next, make up a sample copy of your newsletter, and an application sales letter that will explain your membership fee of about $20 per year for the newsletter, plus $2 per month each time you carry a member's name and address in your "pen pals wanted" section. Be sure to ask for reports on what members are doing and encourage them to bring you up-to-date from time to time-this keeps the "personal touch" gossip supplied.

After you have your newsletter made up, you should send out sample copies, with your sales letter/membership application, to your list of names that you have- your basic "100." At the same time you do this, you should run an advertisement in as many small, mail-order and pen pal publications that you can afford. Your ad could read something like this:

Pen pal Listings! Nationwide Circulation!

$2 or 5 FCS stamps to:

Company Name, Dept. DF

City/Town, ST 99999

Or

Josh's Monthly Pen Pal Newsletter!

Club news and membership listings. $2 or 5 FCS stamps to:

Company Name, Dept. DF

City/Town, ST 99999

Of course, you'll want to keep records on all your members, and continue to update the listings you carry, but basically that is all there is to getting started. You could even run ads of the above kind in your local newspapers and expect a good response. I definitely recommend that you send for sample copies of other pen pal magazines and newsletters to see how they operate and what ideas of theirs you can adapt for use in your newsletter. Become a "browser" and look through all the magazines related to pen pals and mail order introductions every time you see them. Order sample copies of any new publication that you don't have or have never seen. Learn from them.

Be sure to get your newsletters out regularly, and don't stop advertising. Keep up your efforts to sell as many issues of each publication as you can, expand your membership list, and get as many new listings for each issue as you possibly can.

Something else that you may want to consider is to offer 3 back issues of your publication for $5, or as a free bonus to all new subscribers. You could carry this idea as a free bonus in your advertisements, and as a special offer in your newsletter.

You should also expand your income potential by offering booklets, books, CDs, MP3s, and other motivational and information products. Make sure the How-To information that you offer for sale is in line with what your subscribers would want to read. You don't even have to have the products in stock, but could become an affiliate of another service and just get a fee from each sale you make.

By keeping good records of all the mail you receive, you can also sell or rent name lists of people who have responded to your offerings. Real opportunities exist for sales of this type, especially when it comes to email databases. These opportunities are only limited by your imagination. And of course, since you're the publisher, you'd get first crack at any new pen pals that advertise in your newsletter.

The prison market is ripe for this type of newsletter. If your newsletter adds value to your reader's life they will continue to subscribe. Here are some tips to help you deliver that value.

1. Provide the contact information for companies and services that will help your readers solve their problems. For our discussion, this means "getting pen pals, finding love, etc."

2. Give your readers tips and have monthly columns. For instance, you could have a section in your January issue called: "The Top 10 Tips for The New Year." Or in your February issue: "Valentine's Day Tips & tricks."

3. Have contests and give out free products. These products could be booklets, special reports, books, and/or other stuff your readers would love.

4. Provide sample letters and personal ads and templates that your readers can use verbatim.

5. Always show your readers how to save time and money in getting the results they need and want. They'll love you for it.

6. Stick to one main theme, i.e., pen pals. Make sure all of your newsletters articles, how-to information, and the companies that you list, pertain to that one, central them.

Your niche could be prisoners who want pen pals, and the free-world people who'll write them. If you allow other companies to advertise in your newsletter you could expand your income streams immensely. This is just one more way for you to make money from inside prison.

But your newsletter doesn't have to be about pen pals. It could be about anything you're an expert on. Chris Zoukis started his *Education Behind Bars Newsletter*. *Prison Legal News* started out as a 10-page typed newsletter while Paul Wright was in prison. Dave "Razor" Babb is the creator and original editor of the *Corcoran Sun* newsletter and award winning author of two memoirs and three novels. He does it all from his cell with just his mind and typewriter. You can do it too. All you need is someone on the outside to help you with monthly mailings and to check the mailbox for incoming mail. The sky is the limit.

Offering a free newsletter is a great way to build a list of contacts who'll buy your stuff. Tim Twitty is a prisoner who used his free *Secrets to Instant Wealth* newsletter to sell other products. Chris Zoukis used his to establish his expertise on prison education and market his book. If you have products to sell, think about using a free newsletter to get the word out.

Here are some rules to remember if you start a FREE newsletter:

- A free newsletter is not an "information provider" per se. It can't be because you're providing it for FREE. You must turn it into a newsletter that sells your products or brings in more business.

- Because a free newsletter is a marketing tool, you must provide articles about the type of success your target audience needs or wants. This keeps them coming back to you as the go-to-source.

- You must explain in vivid detail the problems your target audience faces and how your products or services solve them.

- You must provide your contact information and show how easily you can be reached.

- When writing your newsletter, talk to your target audience like they're your friends. Who do you trust more, your friend or a salesman? Exactly. People buy things from people they trust. So become the trusted voice they come to.

Following all of the above tips and tactics will help you out. But if you're really interested in starting your own newsletter, I recommend you get the following books and study them:

How to Make Newsletters, Brochures & Other Good Stuff without a Computer System by Helen Gregory. This book is outdated and out-of-print, but still available online. It will help you create a newsletter by hand if you have to do it from your cell.

Make Money Writing Newsletters & *Marketing With Newsletters*, both by Elaine Floyd. The titles speak for themselves. You need to read them if you're going into the newsletter game.

Publishing Newsletters: A Complete Guide to Markets, Editorial Content, Design, Printing, Subscriptions, and Management by Howard Penn Hudson. If you can only get one book on newsletters, get this one. You'll constantly refer back to it.

If you do decide to start your own newsletter, make sure you send me a sample copy and I'll review it for you for free.

Upgrading Your Newsletter to a Free E-zine

An online newsletter or electronic magazine (E-Zine) is a great way to build your list of contacts and make extra money. Of course you'll need to enlist the internet-savvy person in your network, but it'll be worth it. Your e-zine is sent to your subscribers email address. Most online information marketers offer a free e-zine with the ability to upgrade to a subscription paid e-zine that offers more in-depth information. If your target audience has access to email, then you should have an e-zine. Here are some of the benefits to starting your own free email newsletter:

1. You can publish it at little or no cost using available free web tools

2. It's a free way to build a mailing list (the most important item for any business.

3. Businesses will pay to advertise in your newsletter. See *How to Make Money with E-Zine Advertising* by Charlie Page for more information.

4. You'll be seen as an expert on your topic.

5. You can sell your products and services in each newsletter.

6. You could offer other products from affiliates that you get a commission on when one of your subscribers makes a buy.

You may be thinking that it would be hard to set up or write? But it isn't. Anyone who has Microsoft Word can design a text-based e-zine. Keep it simple, it doesn't have to be fancy. A lot of people read emails with graphics off anyway. And you don't even have to write the articles you include in your e-zine. You could hire a ghostwriter, or list your e-zine in appropriate directories and request article submissions. There's all kinds of people who might submit articles as long as you give them credit for writing it. Who knows, a free e-zine could be your ticket to fame.

Hopefully this chapter now got your imagination running with the possibilities of becoming the system and making money legitimately. You don't have to run game to make money in the pen pal world. I don't and you shouldn't. Do things the right way and you can have true Pen Pal Success! See you at the top.

"A prison is indeed one of the best workshops." -Sidonie Gabrielle Colette

Chapter 22
LGBTQ Pen Pals

"In the free-world, all things LGBTQ are in. But inside the pen all we want is to get out. Who cares about 'coming out'!." -Kim, LGBTQ Prisoner

All things LGBTQ are in. President Trump tweets about transgender people in the military. LGBTQ "Pride" month is celebrated online and in National media. Playboy recently showcased a transgender model in a pictorial. Hit TV shows like FX's Pose, VH1's Rupaul's Drag Race, and TLC's All About Jazz push all things LGBTQ. Even Publisher's Weekly did a huge section on the rise of LGBTQ books. I've been doing time since I was 14 years old so I'm not new to LGBTQ prisoners. As a former member of a nationally recognized street gang it was taboo for me to associate with gay or transgender prisoners. It wasn't until I dropped out of the gang to pursue my book publishing dreams that I began to see the power of LGBTQ pen pals.

After I released my first set of books I was transferred to a new prison. Because I had read that Publisher's Weekly section of LGBTQ articles I was looking for a prisoner to collaborate with on a book of my own. I found a transgender prisoner named Janiyah who was an aspiring writer. We began preliminarily discussing a "tell-all" book based on her expereinces called, "Prison Bitch." That fell through as Janiyah was not focused enough on the project. But the Universe has a funny way of working things out. Janiyah had a transgender girlfriend named Skylar. We became great friends and discussed a lot of business ideas. Skylar eventually went to segregation because a lesbian guard hated on her. While in seg, a friend of hers named Jon Jon who had bought the first edition of this book, let her read it. After she got out of seg, Skylar let me know that she had read Pen Pal Success, and we discussed more business ideas. I ended up getting moved to another gallery in another cellhouse so I couldn't collaborate more with her. But that wasn't the end of our mastermind relationship.

Over the weeks that followed I kept hearing how Skylar was helping other prisoners get pen pals. Some of those guys had claimed to me that they didn't need this book. Yet, there they were getting her help. Secretly, I think they really wanted to get with her! LOL. But the truth was that she was getting results! Two of the guys that she wrote profiles for really came up. I've been on visits with one of them whose girl travels all the way from Illinois from Florida to see him. That's Skylar's work. When I saw her I made sure to tell her to stop doing it for free. Because we all know "that the game is to be sold, not told."

Eventually I was moved back to the same cellhouse as Skylar. This was 2019 and I was writing full-time. I wasn't looking for any new pen pals. But Skylar kept telling me I had a talent and needed to go back online to get pen pals. I didn't feel like it, not when I was already making thousands of dollars a year off my books. But Skylar Doll is a force of nature and convinced me to go back online. I only did it because she sold me by saying she would write my profile and write any pen pals that I got. That way I could spend most of my time working on my legal stuff and book projects. I couldn't beat that deal so I took her up on her offer. She wrote up my profile and I made a few minor tweaks to it. Then I put it up on WriteAPrisoner.com. Here's the ad text:

> Hi! My name is Josh. My friends describe me as smart, self-motivated, loyal, a good friend, comical at times, polite, generous, kind hearted and humble.
>
> I really enjoy the arts. I personally am an artist who loves to create with words, or you can simply say I'm an accomplished author and poet. I enjoy other types of art as well, especially music. My taste in music is very diverse and eclectic. I enjoy eating, not so much cooking. Although I can make the best peanut butter and jelly. LOL.
>
> While here I plan on getting my education finished. I also plan on continuing to find ways to build a better society with my cellpreneurial skill-set. Also, I'm focused on getting back into court to overturn my case or to get an early release date.
>
> I look forward to meeting people from all walks of life. I believe diversity is the color that paints the canvas of one bright, beautiful world. I'm willing to correspond for however short or however long, as long as we both have a positive impact on each other because I know the power of a smile or a simple hello.

Josh Kruger

Well, I look forward to hearing from you if you made it this far! Here's to a future filled with a lot of laughs and long, beautiful days and star-filled nights. I hope to see a letter that your had has graced soon. Until then may you be blessed! Respect.

I put that up and put down "Bisexual" as my sexual orientation. I did that for two reasons. The main one was because Skylar said she would write any pen pals I got. The other reason was that I wanted to test out theory that I heard. Another prisoner told me if you put "Bisexual" you'll get more hits on your profile? I was about to find out if that was true?

Of course I know you want to know about my results? My ad worked because I got numerous hits. Some I do not write anymore. Some I do. Most of the people who responded to this ad were either artists, or had an interest in art. My best pen pal is from Chicago and he does arts and crafts. For my birthday, he sent me two books to help me complete another book I was working on. Another response I got was from Rebecca. She's a beautiful 19-year old college student, who is majoring in Art Therapy. So the ad worked. i got the responses I should have. But there were some problems also.

First, one girl just wanted to get married so we could go on Love After Lockup. And she already had a husband that she was separated from! She lived at home with her mom and didn't have a job. We were not a good fit. A bunch of other hits I got were just cards from pen pals wishing me well. Once I wrote them back thanking them and asking more about them I never heard anything else.

The second problem was that after almost six months my profile had only been viewed 1,304 times. That equals out to about 217 visitors a month. The cost of my ad was $40, and I paid $10 to add another photo. So for $50 I got 1,304 page views, or about 4¢ a view. I got seven hits (or responses) on a $50 profile. That equals out to about $7 a hit. To be fair to those numbers, you have to look at the statistics and demographics behind the pen pal game. I'm a lifer, and it says so on my profile page. That brings my response rate down. If I had an outdate that was only a few years away I would get more responses. Did it hurt? I don't know? What I do know is that there is a better way to get pen pals than using outdated strategies. For more on this, see Chapter ???

Because Skylar said she would write the penpals I also went on prisonpenfriends.com. On the next two pages are my profile from their site. Notice how I said "transgender" in my profile text. I was trying to get some tgirls to contact so I could turn them over to Skylar. No tgirls contacted me, but I did get some LGBTQ hits. One was from an accountant in a law firm in New York. I thought he might be someone I could netowrk with? But he only wanted to write emails about his foot fetish. For real, I can't make this stuff up. His fantasy was for him to lay on the ground and for me to walk all over him with my size 13, bare feet. He said he wanted to go so far as to put my feet over his mouth and nose to suffocate him! I let Skylar email him. After she got transferred I cut him off. I'm straight, he's definitely not my cup of tea. He did say he had other prisoners he emailed. Hey, whatever floats your boat. All of us have certain preferences. i'm not passing judgment on anyone. He just wasn't what I was looking for.

I ended up meeting Skylar's friend Jon Jon later. He heard me and Skylar talking over the gallery and said, "Hey Josh, how come you didn't put thisstuff in your book?" Everyone laughed, and it was then that I knew I had to put a LGBTQ Pen Pal chapter in an updated version of this book. It has always been my strategy to do what is FREE first before I pay money for services. Here are some addresses of places you could write to get a LGBTQ pen pal. Please be forewarned. They have a long waiting list and it could be some time before you hear back from them.

Black & Pink
6223 Maple St. #4600
Omaha, NE 68104

Midwest Trans Prisoner Pen Pal Project
c/o Boneshaker Books
2022 23rd Avenue South
Minneapolis, MN 55404

Prisoner Correspondance Project
QPIRG Concordia
Concordia University
1455 de Maisonneuve O
Montreal, QC H3G 1MB

Why not have the mastermind herself, Skylar Doll, write the rest of this chapter? Devin "Skylar" Mottley is The Millionaire Prisoner's "go-to-girl" on all things LGBTQIA, and, beyond that, an expert on new-age pen pal strategies. She's a dynamic cellpreneur who lives by the philosophy that there are no rules except for the servants who are ruled by the masters. You can meet her by reading the rest of this chapter.

#LGBTQIA Prison Lives Matter
by Devin "Skylar" Mottley

As media expert Ryan Holiday likes to point out, there's a now famous line from the hit TV show Sex and the City: "First come the gays. Then the girls. Then...the industry." Lady Gaga actually followed that strategy to get famous. She started performing in gay clubs and burlesque shows in New York and San Francisco. Then she went to dance clubs and the fasion crowd. Eventually she seduced the mainstream masses. She even got Josh! Don't tell him I told you this, but he loves Lady Gaga and has a lot of her songs in one of his playlists on his tablet. LOL. For more on how she did this you'll want to read Monser Loyalty: How Lady Gaga Turns Followers into Fanatics by Jackie Huba. In the rest of this chapter I'll show you how you can get the gays and the girls. The rest of the Pen Pal Success system can give you some ideas about how to conquer the whole industry.

So, my name is Skylar and I'm a transgender woman currently incarcerated in the Illinois Department of Corrections. I don't have a weird sex case or anything like that but I do have a case that people seeking relationships tend to shy away from which is an aggravated domestic with strangulation. For that crime I was sentenced to 13 years at 85% which is 11 years behind bars in total.

I'm telling you all of these things not to boast or to brag but, to instead paint the picture of my initial impression to society and most importantly potential pen pals. With all that I told you it's safe to assume that I might have had minimal success, right?

Well I'm here to tell you that, that safe assumption is wrong. I'm also here to tell you how me, someone so unlikely gained extrordinary pen pal success.

So like most of you, I began to feel lonely during my bid. That lonliness turned into frustration. That frustration turned to anger. That anger turned into a short 10 momth segregation trip. Durring that segregation stint my lonliness was amplified by my single cell status, constant harrassment from guards, being ostracized by the non LGBTQ inmate population and the lack of consistant communication with friends and family form the outside.

So one day I was sitting on my bed in my cell listening to the other segregation inmates talk back and forth which had become one of my main sources of entertainment. This time the conversation had a serious tone to it which is out of the norm. So I began to listen closely to the conversation that was taking place.

The conversation was between several hetorosexual inmates talking about a pen pall site called Writeaprisoner.com They were boasting about all of the women that were writing them from the site. Of course the conversation turned after one of those inmates mentioned the downside of the site which was all of the "fags" that wrote him from the site.

My ears perked up at what he considered a downside. To my utter amazement he wasn't the exception, all of the people who were talking began conversing about their unwanted mail from all types of LGBTQ pen pals. I immediately wanted in.

I talked to my neighbor and asked him for a Writeaprisoner brochure. Not only did he give me a brochure but he gave me several other brochures to different sites, his print out for his profile, and a quick note saying that I shouldn't waste my time because he's been on that site for almst a year with only two responses. I can't lie, doubt began to creep into my mind about what would happen to me.

I opened his profile print out and it was very simple. The jist of it was "Hey beautiful women of the world this is me seeking you. I don't have much time left and I'm looking to find that special someone, is it you"?" Reading that gave me a sigh of relief. I could see that he didn't sell himself and he was very specific in what he was looking for which was women.

When I made the decision to pay for a pen pal site I was new to transitioning. I wasn't on hormone replacement therabpy, and my at the time baby dreadlocks were going through the ugly stages of locking. So to say the least, I wouldn't be getting hits off of looks alone!

Though I was new to transitioning I wasn't new to our community. I was a Boys Town/Belmont and hustled regular which for those of you that don't know what or where that is, its the LGBTQ area of Chicago, IL. With that being said, I've known first hand about the colorul individuality that we all have and we pride ourselves on. I knew that if I were to have any pen pal success I'd have to ensure that my vibrant personality wouldn't repel all of the other colorful personaility that I was trying to attract.

So I grabbed my pen and a few sheets of paper. I began thinking about all of the good qualities that friends, loved ones, and a few guards said that I possessed. My list was very simplistic. I had basic words describing my colorful personality. The words that I had describing me were words like smart, funny, ok to be around, sarcastic, focused, can talk to all types of people, willing to go above and beyond and friendly.

Those words describe a good person, but it doesn't add flare to a person. So I did what I always do when I want to add flare to my basic vocabulary...I grabbed my dictionary and thesaurus. For words that i couldn't think of anything better to express them with I used my thesaurus to find similar words. Smart became intelligent, funny became comedic or humorous, okay to be around became chill and down to earth, focused became goal oriented, sarcastic became witty, can talk to all types of people became cultured, willing to go above and beyond became outgoing, and finally friendly became amicable. Intelligent, comedic, humorous, down to earth, goal oriented, witty, cultured, outgoing, and amicable sound way more pleasant to the ear than the drab words wwe used before.

Now it's your turn, grab your pen and your paper and write down all of the words people have used to describe you. If the words sound plain jane use your thesaurus to find similar words that will add some flare to that list. Remember you are selling yourself and your personality in order to get hits so use the best words to paint an image of yourself.

Now I can't lie of course I wanted to find a lover/partner from one of these sites...hmm don't we all? LOL. At the same time i had to keep the main thing the main thing. Meaning I was getting on a pen pal site to fight my loneliness with friendships too.

My profile reflected that. My profile mentioned that I was looking for friends and whatever else might transpire. I mentioned friendship first though not because friendship was the most important but because I didn't want to disway people who were looking specifically for friends by saying looking for potential lovers/ partners and friends. If potential friends are reading your profile and they see seeking lovers/partners they might stop reading right there and move on to someone new. If a potential partner/lover sees friend first they have a better chance at continuing to read your profile.

We all know how fast life is and majority of us in the LGBTQ community live an even faster life due to the experience a lot of us endure at younger ages. A lot of us (not all of us) are even a little more promiscuous. So looking specifically for a relationship can be a turn off. The more plausible way for a relationship is to find a friend and take it from there by being genuine and creating a mental and emotional bond. Even outside of prison people are lonely and looking for a genuine friend. Sometimes those genuine friendships transcend into a full on romatic relationship.

I was now pacing in my cell trying to figure out what made me –Skyar– different others when it came to my hobbies and experiences. Not only did I need to figure that out but I also needed to figure out how I was going to word it and leave it open ended to encourage potential pen pals to inquire about my hobbies and experiences.

I grabbed my pen and paper once again and I jotted down quick things that I loved to do and unique experiences to me. Afterwards I had a list that read like this: I lived in Washington state, Illinois, Indiana and a short time in California. I've traveled to 16 states. I love reading non-fiction business buooks and fantasy books, I listen to screamo, metal, punjk, hardcore, edm, pop, country, r&b, new wave and a little hip hop, and I love to bake and make breakfast meals.

With all of that I had to figure out a way to dull all of that down in order to make people want to ask me questions. i want to be an open book but a book never tells you the end in the beginning. By dulling out my hobbies and experiences I leave open ended dialogues for a few months worth of letters, while still giving potential pen pals a feel of who I am and what I'm about.

All of the forementioned hobbies and experience turned into something similar to this: I've lived in several states and I possess quite a few traits that are associated with each one of those states. I love traveling in which I've done a lot of. I also have plans of possibly living abroad. I love music and I listen to a wide variety of music. I enjoy reading while drinking a nice glass of wine. I enjoy simple thngs to like trying new foods and cooking.

By dulling that down there are numerous questions a potential pen pal could ask. What states did you live in? Where were you born? What traits do you feel are specific to each state? What traits did you keep? Where have you traveled? How did you travel (ie. train, plane, boat, automobile)? Where is your favortite place? Do you have any future plans for vacationing? What genres of music do you listen to? Do you have a favorite genre/artist/or band? What kind of books do you read? Do you have any favorite authors? What was the last book that you read? Wow, what type of wine do you drink? Do you like any other types of alcohol? What type of foods have you tried? Do you have a favorite dish or meal time? What do you like to cook? What's the best dish you make? Who taught you how to cook? These are just a few questions that come to my mind. By leaving room for questions like these you make it easier for a potential pen pal to find different things to ask about while aso giving them room to relate to you.

After I was done with that I began looking over my notes. I realized that my notes seemed to sound upbeat, sophisticated and not the stigmitisms of a typical inmate. I saw that most profiles focused on an individual trying to flirt. This brought me back to thinking about my boys town days. i thought about the dating scene, how judgemental our community could be and how money orientated a lot of my LGBTQ friends could be. Which got me thinking about what I could offer my potential pen pals besides an emotional connection. Especially since I did flirt with the possibility of finding a partner/lover.

If you are like me you might have enough money to go to store and that comes from the kindness of family and friends. Even if I did have a steady source of income and enough money to offer someone in the world I wouldn't adbvertise it for fear of becoming a stain/mark to someone. So I had to figure out what I had to offer. That answer took me several hours to come up with but the answer was quite simple. The answer was potential. I have the potential of being more than just an inmate or a number. Finding your potential is something very specific to you!

My potential was my eagerness to learn. How quick I was at learning things. My will to change. Me having endless possibilities at physically changing. Finally me doing things already to bring forth some of those changes. I was trying to show that I was a diamond in the rough like so many of us are! I began jotting down my accomplishments and what things I wanted to achieve in the near future.

That part of my profile went a little like this: During my incarceration I've focused on bettering myself through informal education. I recently began learning some American Sign Language. I've started sharpening my skills at writing poetry. I'm hoping to eventually enroll into a correspondence college for business management. I have plans on starting hormone replacement therapy as well as getting the surgeries needed to complete the image, I have of myself in my head.

Writing that not only showed my potential but it left room for questions. Why did you decide to learn

American Sign Language? What type of poetry do you like? Do you have a favorite poet? Why do you want to take business management? Does your facility offer schooling? Why aren't you on HRT yet? Does your facility offer hormones? Are there other trans inmates on hormone therapy? What surgeries do you want? How do you plan to afford those surgeries?

Now I got to my favorite part which is describing myself. I know that sounds conceited but aren't we all at some point LOL! I was in seg so I didn't have the luxury of paying to take photos of myself from commissary. I was going to have to use a mugshot photo of myself that was taken on a segregation-to-segregation transfer from Lawrence C.C. to Pontiac C.C. which did me no justice. So, what the picture didn't show was going to have to get some make-up with the words I used to describe myself.

If I were to use basic descriptive words to describe myself, I would say: light skinned, medium height, medium build, a lot of tattoos, freckles, and short dreads. As you probably can figure out basic doesn't work and I'm not a basic woman! So, I had to figure out how to describe myself in a way that made it sound like all of these intricate ingredients were mixed together to create this fancy 5-star dish named Skylar.

I turned those basic descriptive words into this:

I'm a light mocha complected trans woman. I have a petite yet curvy frame that stands at 5'6 ½ ". I have very tasteful and intricately placed tattoos, I have a gentle splash of freckles on my face along with shoulder length dreadlocks.

If finding ways to describe yourself in this manner is hard, try separating your body into sections and focus on your best features. If that doesn't work ask a close friend to describe your best features as if you were food, art, or a scenery (ie: chocolate colored almond shaped eyes). The more descriptive you can get the better. Don't be shy, give yourself a glorious description! If you can't who else will? This is the best time to exude your confidence!

Now when it comes to the people that I as trying to meet I kept it very simple. I was defiantly interested in finding friends and I was definitely excited at the possibility of finding a partner, but I'm pansexual so I didn't need a specific gender, so I didn't exclude anyone. Honestly though some of you are looking specifically for a man or woman (both cisgender and transgender). I wouldn't outright say that. The reason I say that is because you don't want to close yourself off from the countless possibilities of encounters. If someone writes you that you wouldn't typically date it is easier to keep that person in the friend zone than to make up for missed opportunities that would be excluded due to your excluding your interest in other genders or sexual orientations.

That portion of my profile was very short and simple it went something like this:

I'm looking for open minded people from all walks of life that are okay with me being me.

Lastly this is for all the transgender, nonbinary gender, non-conforming, and whatever else there is out there where pronouns are an issue to someone who doesn't know you.

Specify in your preferred pronouns in your profile along with your preferred name if you have one. Also, be sure to instruct potential pen pals on your institutions policies on addressing your mail. For instance, at my institution, I can only have my assigned name on the envelopes, but my pen pals can head my letters with my preferred name, Skylar A. Peterson.

As far as sites go, I've been on numerous sites including writeaprisoner.com, friensbeyondthewall.com, writeaninmate.com, and prisonpenpals.com. I got the majority of my hits from writeaprisoner.com. I've been on that site for about a year and a half, and I've gotten 68 hits and counting. Out of those 68 hits I have consistent communication with 15 people, and I've been in 3 short but filling relationships. I also consistently communicate with three of them via phone and 10 of them via email. I've met people from all walks of life and from all over the world. I've received tons of emotional and mental support, educational opportunities, future job opportunities, help with getting my poetry out there, numerous books, and even the occasional financial help. This all helped me realize that the world isn't as dark as a lot of prisoners tend to think it is or as the media portrays it. Though I am open to a relationship with pen pals I now use these sites mainly for networking. Networking has opened doors for me that were once never open. I went from loneliness to at times overwhelmed with the amo0unt of mail I was getting in.

By us being. Avery small community in prison pay stuff forward. If you have a pen pal that you really aren't feeling, ask them is it okay if you send them one of your LGBTQ friends info that's incarcerated with you that might be a better fit. Some might not be as fortunate as others and any chance to talk or write to someone outside of prison is an escape from our harsh reality. Use these nonverbal ways of communicating as an opportunity to learn and use new words.

I am including two of my profiles that got me my most hits. I hope that you have as much pen pal success as me. I leave you all in peace, love, light, warmth, and solidarity, all underneath the rainbow.

Profile Alert! This profile was updated on 1/20/2020

Devin Mottley #M17551

(/inmates/devin-mottley-m17551/photos)
Picture 1 of 4

(/inmates/devin-mottley-m17551/photos)
Picture 2 of 4

Hello, my assigned name is Devin Mottley, but my preferred name is Skylar. I'm a transgender woman and I'm just starting my physical transitioning. I'm a very bright and energetic person. I enjoy traveling, listening to numerous genres of music, writing my own music and poetry, being outdoors, and bonding with family and friends. I love animals, especially dogs, reptiles, and amphibians. I've owned four snakes, iguanas, and countless dogs.

I was raised in three different states which were Illinois, Indiana, and Washington. I possess traits from them stigmatisms associated with the people from each one of those states.

I have plans on doing schooling through a correspondence course to get a business degree and some accounting classes. I want to pursue getting a real estate license as well. I'm also wanting to aggressively pursue starting my own business. I'm going to do a lot more traveling and I'm very open to the idea of living abroad. I'm also going to get the surgeries I need to obtain the perfect body image that fully represents myself and my femininity.

I'm 5'7 and about 130 pounds, very light complexion with a gentle splash of freckles on my nose and cheeks. I have numerous tasteful tattoos on different parts of my body excluding my head and my face. I have dreadlocks that now reach my eyes, but I will only let them grow to my hips.

I'm looking for like-minded people who will accept me for the unique individual that I am. I prefer someone who's down to earth, friendly, genuine, secure, adventurous, and willing to take the time needed to build a solid foundation in whatever type of friendship that begins to bud. To have someone who has one or two things in common would be well welcomed, but to meet someone with numerous things in common would be amazing, to say the least!

I thank you for taking the time to read my profile. I hope your day continues to be vibrant and full of sunshine. I can't wait to hear from you!

P.S. You have to address the envelope with my assigned name, but please head the letter with Skylar.

Chapter 23

Putting It Alll Together

"Your highest paid, most important skill is your ability to think, both before you act and while you are acting. It is your ability to choose what is more important and what is less important." -Brian Tracy

After you start getting pen pals you may want more? Most guys that I talk to say that you can never have enough pen pals? In my 20+ years inside and in the pen pal game I've noticed that all relationships go stale. Pen pals come and go. Baby mamas leave and come back. Especially when we are serving long-term sentences in the American gulag. This is just a fact of life. Once you accept this as fact you can do something about it. Putting what you've found in this book to work into your life is a first step. The question is are you going to work the hell out of it? Or are you going to be a part timer? That really depends on your goals? Only you can answer that. For those of you who want to go to the next level I want to share with you what I've learned since I last updated this book in 2017.

In the previous chapter I shared my experiences with Skylar Doll. After she got me back into the game it made me start thinking about updating this book. Because I'm a subscriber to *Prison Legal News* I constantly see new pen pal companies advertising their services in *PLN's* pages. And because it's my job to keep up to date with new pen pal companies. I always send my SASE's for any company advertising their services. Once I get their brochures and other paperwork, I review it. I'm looking for new ways of attracting pen-pals. So, if a new company is just redoing the same old 2000's method of getting pen pals I will not try their service.

A low price point usually means the services will be limited. That doesn't mean you can't come up off of free services. I have. And I know other prisoners who have. But you'll need someone to put you on those free pen pal websites and monitor them for hits. Here are the two main services I look for now:

- The company allows your new possible pen pal to send their first contact by email, which they process and forward to you.
- The company uses social media to help promote and get new pen pals for its members and clients. If a company does not offer these services, I will not use them. Since we are only as good as our information, I want to show you why these are now my rules. Some of what I say may sound repetitive from previous chapters, but I promise to tie it all together.

COVID-19 PEN PAL RESEARCH

In the early part of 2020 I was transferred from Pontiac Correctional Center to Menard Correctional Center in Southern Illinois. The week after I got to Menard the COVID-19 pandemic hit the prison system and we have been on quarantine lockdown ever since. Due to being stuck in my cell all day I decided to go on a research trip to get more pen pals and update this book. I was already back on WriteAPrisoner.com because of Skylar Doll's pushing me back into it. But I wanted to try out a couple other sites that weren't around when I first started this book. What I found has led me to a whole new system. But I'm getting ahead of myself. Let me give you the back story first.

Prison Social Network

One of the companies I contacted was Prison Social Network. PSN was started by Brian Rooney. He served 11 ½ years in the Michigan prison system. While he was inside he used to read all of the prisoner publications and built his stable to over 38 pen pals at once. Not bad at all. Once he got out he started PSN to help prisoners not just only make connections, but build a platform for their release. I liked where he was going so I signed up for his service and we started emailing back and forth. My PSN profile is on the next page. During our letters and emails, I was trying to pry from Brian some of his secrets. For instance, he told me he was involved with over 400 social media prisoner support groups. He told me he had two huge computer screens set up with another computer on the side that he monitors, like a stock trader does for stock prices and charts. Except he was monitoring for when someone liked one of his clients' profiles. Then he would hit them up to make sure they wrote the prisoner. It all sounded good. But because of my experience with Facebook, I knew that to be really successful I would have to incorporate social media in my system. That thought led me to ask Brian about using Facebook ads to point people to my profile. His answer may change your idea about this whole process.

He told me that he had a girl on his site that was using Facebook ads to generate 3-4K (thousand) views to her page. He said she paid $3 a day (or about $90 a month) and she was getting hundreds of hits to her profile. He said he couldn't understand why she kept doing it after all those hits? Well, we know don't we. Pen pals are her hustle so she can never have enough. Or that a lot of the people who contact her were not who she was looking for? Either way, I felt she was on to something and I asked for her name so I could interview her. Brian wouldn't give me her information due to the client confidentiality Rules. So, I had to try it out for myself. I sent Brian $200 with instructions to place some Facebook ads for my profile. Here's what happened.

Nothing. I didn't hear another word. Months went by and my emails weren't answered. But I knew something was wrong because my $200 check had not been cashed. I saw that the state of Michigan was hit hard by COVID and I instantly thought of Brian. Damn, did he get sick? Did he get locked back up? What happened? I don't know. I was able to cancel my check and get my money back, so no harm was done. He didn't steal my money. He just disappeared on me and his clients. That sucked. Lucky for me I had a backup plan to try out the Facebook ad theory.

Caged Kingdom Facebook Boost

At the same time, I began corresponding with Brian Rooney at PSN I saw an ad for a service celled Caged Kingdom. I sent in for their information and I liked that they had a service where you could do a Facebook boost of your profile. After Brian at PSN went ghost on me I signed up for Caged Kingdom's pen pal service. On the next page is my profile. The only thing I didn't like was that they charged people a $2.45 fee to send me a photo and email. Ouch! That isn't good for us. But I had to remember that my goal was to test out the Facebook boost service. So I paid Caged Kingdom to boost my ad on Facebook. They did a Facebook Insights boost (seen on the following page.) It was seen by 213 people, shared by 3 people, and engaged by 13 people. I ended up getting 2 new pen pals off that Facebook boost. So it worked. And I learned a lot from it. Because of that Facebook boost I decided to dive deeper into online ad metrics and the so-called "hit" counters.

Hit Counters & Response Rates

When pen pal websites first started there was a bunch of hoopla about "hit counters". These companies would tell you that your page was hit by thousands of people. But that was misleading. Just because someone sees your profile doesn't count as a "hit". A hit is a response. That's the only thing that should matter to you. I'll say it again. The only thing that matters is how many pen pals respond to your profile! In *Advertising With Small Budgets for Big Results*, Linda Carlson says that banner ads on websites pull at a rate of .01 percent. Google Adwords expert Perry Marshall says that a 2% Click Through Rate (CTR) is good. Marketing experts try to break even at a .5% response rate. Those are some basic numbers to go by. Here's how you do the math. My 2019 WriteAPrisoner profile got 1,304 views and 7 responses in six months. That is .005%. Not good. Using Linda Carlson's .01% rate I should have got at least 14 hits. I was close to any of the above CTR or marketing numbers.

$$\text{Total Hits / Page Views} = \%$$

Remember this above formula when computing the successfulness of your profiles.

Social Media Likes & Engagement

In the *Ultimate Guide to Facebook Advertising* Keith Krance does a great job of explaining "engagement":

"Remember, the objective in these types of ads is not necessarily a conversion or a click to your

Photos

Prison Picasso

Member since	Jul 2020
From	Danville ILLINOIS

Basic   Standard   Premium

SINGLE PHOTO $2.45

This package includes one 5*7 photo and a message up to 2500 characters in length. (Spaces are counted as characters) Shipping included

Send Mail Now ($2.45)

Additional Info

Birth Date
06/13/1978

Astrology
Gemini

Eyes
Blue

Hair
Brown

Race
Caucasian

Religion
Christian

Marital Status
Single

Incarcerated Since
01/1996

Earliest Release Date

Latest Release Date

Email Type
other

Crime Type
Murder

About Me

Words are powerful. Words can be a new beginning. Hopefully these words can be the start of something new and Powerful for us?

Hi I'm Josh. I'm tall, (6'4) slim (205), witty, and determined guy. I use my time to read and write and I have published several books. In my spare time I like to watch sports or movies. I love to eat not so much as cook. Although I can make the best peanut butter and jelly lol

I believe that friendships should be built on respect, compassion, and companionship which will eventually lead to love and loyalty. If this is something you would like to build upon feel free to drop me a letter. No matter what you choose to do please stay safe out there and be blessed.

Education & Military

Education: A.A

Military: No

website (although it can be as a side benefit). The primary objective here in a page post engagement ad is to engage.

In Facebook terms, 'engagement' can include clicking the image, playing the video, igniting the post, sharing the post, clicking the link in the post to your website-any number of actions that increase engagement with your audience."

If you look at the Facebook boost that Caged Kingdom did for my profile you'll see that it was "engaged" by 213 people. Those 13 engagements on 213 people is .06%. That is a lot better than my hit rate on WriteAPrisoner. But there's still a problem with the way Caged Kingdom is doing it. For those people who wanted to write me off this Facebook post they would have to either go to Caged Kingdom's website and pay $2.45 to do it through their app. Or they would have to physically do it on their own with pen and paper. That's too much work. You have to make it as easy as you can on your possible pen pals to contact you at first. Which leads me back to my original rule for a prison pen pal company: first contacts must be free!

But how much do Facebook ads really cost? Caged Kingdom charged me $7 to reach out to 213 people. That's not bad when you do the actual math. It's a little over 30¢ per person. Cheaper than me handwriting

213 letters and sending them out, which would cost over $127 in postage and envelope costs alone. Remember my 2019 WriteAPriosner profile? I paid $50 and my profile was seen by 1,304 people in six months. That's better than Caged Kingdom's numbers. But it's not really good, I'll tell you why. According to the fantastic book, *Ultimate Guide to Facebook Advertising*, I could reach at least 41,000 people and up to 110,000 people, depending on my targeted metrics. So for $50 I could reach 41,000 people. Wow! Using WriteAPrisoner's metrics I would have to spend $1,572! (41,000 / 1,304 = 31.44 x $50 = $1,572). The real key to this would be that any Facebook promotion you could do should be targeted to that specific people of a certain age, location, likes, etc. That target metric is your pen pal avatar.

Your Pen Pal Avatar

Who is your perfect pen pal? What types of magazines do they read? What TV shows do they watch? What beliefs do they have? What fetishes do they have? What hobbies do they have? What websites do they visit? You ask these questions so you can target your perfect pen pals online. You'll get more hits for your money this way. And be happier with the this that you get. For instance, here's my pen pal avatar:

> "My best pen pal is a single, lonely woman, 30+, college graduate, who reads Inc., Entrepreneur, and Prison Legal News (or believes in prisoner rights). She watches Love After Lockup, Shark Tank, The Profit, and ABC's For Life.

If I wanted to do one for college students, it would be:

> "My best young pen pal is a college student who is majoring in criminal justice, reads Prison Legal News, and watches Love After Lockup, ABC's For Life, and prison documentaries."

So how could I find these women? By using Facebook and other social media websites. I could start with the following searches:

> "Pages liked by people who like Prison Legal News"
> "Pages liked by people who like ABC's For Life."
> "Pages liked by people who like Love After Lockup."
> "Pages liked by people who like prison pen pals."
> "Pages liked by people who like prisoner rights."
> "Pages liked by people who like prison reform."

Once I found all of those pages, I would like them also. Then I would do searches for the following:

> "People who like Prison Legal News."
> "People who like ABC's For Life."
> "People who like Love After Lockup."
> "People who like prison pen pals."
> "People who like prisoner rights."
> "People who like prison reform."

Then I would go to Google and search for "prison pen pal forums" and "prisoner rights forums." You do searches like this and you'll find some websites and network opportunities that you've never heard of. These will be opportunities for you to connect with people who are empathetic to the prisoner's journey. And also, a place to put your pen pal ad boosts on.

> "If you have less money in the bank than you have followers on Instagram, you need to get a new group of friends."
> -Billionaire P.A.

Millionaire Prisoner Pen Pal Attraction System

With all of this in mind I wanted to come up with a system that would get you the most bang for your bucks spent. Because my best results have come from using Facebook I had to incorporate that platform into the system. What's the system? It's a process that works time after time to deliver pen pal hits to your tablet or mailbox. It allows you to get these hits with minimal effort on your part. For this system to be most effective you need to write out who your perfect pen pal really is. That way you can target (boost) your posts to those people who fit that specific target audience. If you've done that, heres how you set up the system.

Step 1: If you don't already have a Facebook page, have one set up for you.

Step 2: Setup a profile on a prison pen pal website. You need one on a website that offers your first contact for free. Penacon does. WriteAPrisoner also. I prefer Penacon because I can pay $65 for a lifetime profile instead of $40-$50 a year.

Step 3: Once you have these pages/profiles setup you're ready to do ads/boosts. Post on Facebook anhd then "boost" those posts to your targeted pen pal demographic. Or do Facebook ads directing the target audience to your profile page.

Step 4: Measure your results and tweak the metrics to try and get a better response rate if you didn't get what you wanted.

The key to this system is to post with questions that make your target audience want to respond. For instance, if I wanted to do a post on Facebook that I boosted I'd do it like this:

Does "Love After Lockup" hurt lifers?

Most of us inside think so. Why? Because threre are no lifers on the show. So women who watch it are overlooking us. They want a short-timer who'll come home and be their prince charming. Nothing wrong with that. But lifers need love too. And if given a chance, we might be better?

Yes, I'm a lifer. And in my book *Pen Pal Success*, I show prisoners how to get pen pals. When I wrote that book there was no *"Love After Lockup"* TV show. So I'm curious. What's the women's side of the debate? What does a lifer have to do to find his dream girl? I'd love to hear your thoughts. Maybe I'll put you in my next book?

You can learn more by clicking on the below link:

Then under that I'd put the link to my pen pal profile. Or you can use your email address also? You want it set up so that when they respond to your post it is automatically forwarded to you.

Remember that this is the same system that Brian Rooney of Prison Social Network used when that girl was getting 3,000 views and hundreds of pen pal responses. I can tell you from experience that you will not be able to successfully manage over a 100 penpals if they are writing to you regularly. You'll have to choose who is most important to you and devote your time to them. The great thing about this system is that you could use any time you want to get a bunch of hits. I hope it works as well for you as it has for me.

Disclaimer: I pay for my own ads and profiles. No company pays me to hype their service. I write from experience of my own results. You may have different results? If you have a short prison sentence you should do better than me. Especially with those lovely women who watch Love After Lockup. Target your ads and posts accordingly.

Recommended Reading
For more about this type of strategic marketing I suggest you read all of the following books:

New Rules For Marketing and PR by David Meerman Scott
Ultimate Guide to Facebook Advertising, Second Edition by Perry Marshall, Keith Krance, and Thomas Meloche
Ultimate Guide to Google Adwords, Fourth Edition by Perry Marshall, Mike Rhodes, and Bryan Todd
80/20 Sales and Marketing by Perry Marshall
Advanced Google Adwords by Brad Geddes
Facebook Marketing: An Hour a Day by Mari Smith

PRISON SOCIAL NETWORK

www.prisonsocialnetwork.com

Contact someone today and make a difference !

Home   About   WOMEN'S Profiles   MEN'S profiles   LGBT+   Death Row/Lifers   List A Profile   Contact   FAQ   Blog   Links

Joshua Kruger # K50216
42, Illinois

Email: ConnectNetwork.com (link provided)
Gender: Male
Sexual Orientation: Straight (Trans Inclusive)
Race: White
DOB: June 13th, 1978
Release Date: N/A Life
Wants To Connect With: Friends

Brown hair, Blue eyes, 6'4", 205 lbs.

ABOUT JOSHUA

Hi,
I hope you are staying safe out there. I am looking to expand my
outlook in life by meeting new people from outside these walls.

I'm a published author and poet. In my free time I like to watch
sports and movies. Yeah, I know, just like the typical guy, huh? Lol. I
love to eat good food...not so much as cook it, because I am not that
good of a cook. Although I can make a mean peanut butter and jelly
sandwich...(smiling).

I love music especially Lady gaga, Joyner Lucas, NF, and old Classic
rock. It all depends on my mood at the time.

I would love to meet you and get to know you better. If you want (or
need) a friend, I will not judge you, but accept you as you are, then
I'm your guy. Feel free to hit me up when you get the chance. I look
forward to building something real with you.

Conclusion

"Anyone can 'start', but only the thoroughbred will 'finish'!" -Napoleon Hill

Congratulations comrade! You've arrived at the end of this book, but the real journey is just beginning. You have a choice to put this book down and say, "Man I wish I could do what he did." Then go back to a life of having no pen pals. Or you can keep this book handy and begin to implement some of the strategies in this book to start getting all the pen pals you could ever want or need. It's up to you to decide what you're going to do. I know what I hope you do. I want you to be the next Pen Pal Success™. I want you to find your wife (or husband). I want you to get letters everyday like I do. I want you to be able to talk on the phone with your pen pal(s) and go on a visit with them. If things go right, maybe you'll parole out to their house or apartment? Guess what? You'll never make that happen sitting around doing nothing. I can't make it happen for you. Only you can get it done. But I'm living proof that the strategies in this book work. And I will continue to use them for as long as I'm stuck in this cage. I will continue to reach out through my letters and let my heart bleed out on the pages I've put ink on. It's what I do.

There are some prisoners who will be mad that I wrote this book. They will feel that I should not be giving the secrets away. I say forget that. The game is to be sold and told! I wish you all could be successful writers and pen pallers. I can't guarantee you success, but you are now in a better position to get some results. The next time the guy next door starts talking about his pen pal exploits, you'll be able to tell if he's for real or not. Be sure to tell him about this book when you show him that he's full of crap. Then help him do it the right way. Spread your new found pen pal knowledge wide and far. Just be sure to tell them where you got it from. I wish you luck in all your pen pal endeavors! Amor De La Lucha!

The End

Freebird Publishers
Post-Conviction Relief Series

Post-Conviction Relief Books

⇒ Secrets Exposed

⇒ The Appeal

⇒ Advancing Your Claim

⇒ Winning Claims

⇒ C.O.A. in the Supreme Court

⇒ Post-Conviction Relief Second Last Chance

JUST ARRIVED

Post-Conviction Relief: The Advocate

Each Only $28.99
Includes S/H with tracking

Post-Conviction Relief is a subject most often pursued only by prisoners, the people who are most deprived of the necessary information. What is offered in most law libraries, is in inadequate, because what is needed is watered down by piles of useless and confusing information. That's why the Post-Conviction Relief series was written. It is a no-nonsense guide, to legal research, that is written in a language that anyone can understand. Most importantly, each book has been written to serve a specific purpose, as instructions for a specific step in the Post-Conviction process. With this collection of books, the average person can quickly become a more powerful advocate than they have ever been before, even if only on their own case. Within this set of books, the reader will find that there is something for all prisoners, whether it's their first day in prison or their first day of supervised release.

★ The best instruction one can receive is the words of experience. The Post-Conviction Relief series is written by a real advocate who has actually been there and prevailed in many cases.

★ In most cases prisoners have only one year to make their claims, the Post-Conviction Relief series is the no-nonsense path to understanding the process.

★ The Post-Conviction Relief series provides its readers with the court rules that pertain to Post Conviction Relief. A great resource for prisoners who are often locked down.

★ Post-Conviction Relief: you want to succeed, follow my lead.

★ All books are not created equal. Get only what you need with the Post-Conviction Relief series.

All Books Softcover, 8x10", B&W, 190+ pages EACH $28.99 includes s/h with tracking

Written in simple terms for everyone to understand, it's not just for lawyers anymore.

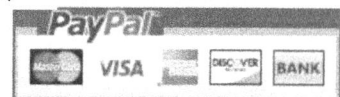

Appendix

Abbreviations

This list is not all-inclusive. But you'll find a lot of these in your correspondence. Some of these below come from text-messaging, and you may come across them in any emails or letters that you get from the younger generation of people who are more comfortable with texting. You may want to use some of these in your letters, emails, cards or notes. These abbreviations are different than those included in the "Speaking the Lingo" chapter. Some of those, and the ones included here, may show up in both ads and letters, but I didn't want to duplicate that list again.

Days of the Week

Su, Sun = Sunday	Th, Thu, Thrus. = Thursday
Mo, Mon = Monday	Fr, Fri = Friday
Tu, Tue, Tues. = Tuesday	Sa, Sat = Saturday
We, Wed = Wednesday	

Months of the Year

Jan = January	Jul = July
Feb = February	Aug = August
Mar = March	Sep, Sept. = September
Apr = April	Oct = October
May = May	Nov = November
Jun = June	Dec = December

Postal Abbreviations

You May Find These on Envelopes?		
AL or Ala = Alabama	Gp = Group	OR or Ore = Oregon
Acad. = Academy	Hgwy or Hwy = Highway	PA or Penn = Pennsylvania
AK = Alaska	HI = Hawaii	Pk = Park
AFB = Air Force Base	Hosp. = Hospital	Pky = Parkway
APO = Army Post Office	Hts. = Heights	Plms = Palms
AR or Ark = Arkansas	IA = Iowa	Plz = Plaza
AZ or Ariz. = Arizona	ID or Ida = Idaho	PMB = Personal Mail Box
ASSN or Assoc. = Association	IL or Ill. = Illinois	PO = Post Office
AS = American Samoa	IN or Ind = Indiana	POB = Post Office Box
ATTN: = Attention	Inst. = Institute	Rd = Road
Ave = Avenue	Inc. = Incorporated	Rdg = Ridge
Bldg. = building	Jct = Junction	RI = Rhode Island
Blvd = Boulevard	KS or Kan or Kans. = Kansas	Rm = Room
Bsmt = Basement	LA = Louisiana	RV = River
Btwy = Beltway	Lk = Lake	RR = Rural Route
Bur = Bureau	LLC = Limited Liability Corporation	Rte. = Route
Bus = Business	Ln = Lane	S = South
bx = box	Ltd = Limited	SC or S. Car. = South Carolina
CA or Cal or Calif. = California	MA or Mass = Massachusetts	SD or S. Dak. = South Dakota
Capt. = Captain	MD = Maryland	Sh = Shore

Canc = Cancelled
c/o = in care of
Co. = Company
CO or Colo = Colorado
Corp = Corporation
Corr. = Correctional
CT or Conn = Connecticut
Ctr = Center
DE or Del = Delaware
Dept. = Department
E = East
Esq. = Esquire
Expy = Expressway
FL or Fla or Flor. = Florida
Fl = Floor
Frwy = Freeway
GA or Geo = Georgia
Govt. = Government

Mdws = Meadows
ME = Maine
MI or Mich.= Michigan
MN or Minn. = Minnesota
MO = Missouri
MT or Mont = Montana
N = North
NC or N. Car = North Carolina
ND or N. Dak = North Dakota
NE or Neb or Nebr. = Nebraska
NH = New Hampshire
NJ = New Jersey
NM or N. Mex. = New Mexico
NV or Nev. = Nevada
NY = New York
NYC = New York City
OH = Ohio
OK or Okla. = Oklahoma

So = South or Southern
Sq. = Square
Srv = Services
Sta. = Station
Ste. = Suite
Ter = Terrace
TN or Tenn = Tennessee
Tpke = Turnpike
TX or Tex. = Texas
Un = Union
UT = Utah
VT = Vermont
W = West
WA or Wash = Washington
WI or Wisc. = Wisconsin
WV or W. Virg. = West Virginia
WY or Wyo. = Wyoming

Additional Abbreviations & Emoticons

AAMOF = As a Matter of Fact
abbr = abbreviation
ack = acknowledge/ment
acpt = accept/ance
actg = acting
addn = addition
adm = administration/ive
advt = advertisement
af = affix
AFAIK = As Far as I Know
AFK = Away From Keyboard
agcy = Agency
agt = agent
aka = also known as
ald = alderman
amb = ambassador
amt = amount
anon = anonymous
ans = answer
approx = approximately
appt = appointment
apptd = appointed
apt = apartment
ASAP As Soon as Possible
ASL = Age/Sex/Location
asst = assistant/assorted
att = attorney

est = established
et. al. = and others
etc. = et cetra
et seq = and the follwing
eval = evaluation
FAQ = Frequently Asked Questions
FCS = First Class Stamp
fn = footnote
fo = folio
FOTCL = Falling Off the Chair Laughing
freq = frequency
ft. = feet or foot
ft. = feet or foot
FTF = Face to Face
FYI = For Your Information
GFAK = Go Fly a Kite
GIGO = Garbage In Garbage Out
GL = Good Luck
GMAB = Give Me a Book
GOI = Get Over It
GP = General Practice
grad = graduate
gtd = guaranteed
GTG = Got to Go
GTSY = Glad To See You
H&K = Hug(s) and Kiss(es)

opp = opposite/opposing
p = page
PDA = Public Display of Affection
PDQ = Pretty Darn Quick
para = paragraph
pb = paperback
pd = paid
PITA = Pain In The Ass
PMP = Peeing My Pants
pp = pages
ppd = prepaid or postponed
pr = pair
rec'd/rcvd = received
RUOK = Are You Okay?
S/H = Shipping & Handling
SFLA = Stupid Four Letter Acronym
Sgd = Signed
std = standard
SYT = See You Tonight
TBA = To Be Announced
TBD = To Be Determined
TBDL = To Be Discussed Later
TNTC = Too Numerous To Count
TYVM = Thank You Very Much
tx = Thanks
w/ = with
w/in = within

avg = average	HAK = Hug(s) and Kiss(es)	wi = when issued
AWYR = Awaiting Your Reply	hgt or ht = height	WGTG = Well, Got To Go
AYOR = At Your Own Risk	HHOK = Ha Ha, Only Kidding	w/o = without
AYPI = And Your Point Is	HHO½K = Ha Ha, Only ½ Kidding	wk = week
BAK = Back at Keyboard	HIG = How's It Going?	WRU = Who Are You
BCNU = Be Seeing You	HIH = Hope It Helps	yo = Year Old
BEG = Big Evil Grin	hv = have	YOB = Year of Birth
BFFL = Best Friends For Life	hvy = heavy	yr. = year
bks = barracks	hw = how	YW = You're Welcome
B4N = Bye for Now	ICBW = I Could Be Wrong	+ly = positivly
BSOD = Blue Screen of Death	i.e. = that is to say	2moro = Tomorrow
BTAIM = Be That As It May	IGP = I Gotta Pee	2nite = tonight
BTU = Back To You	IGTP = I Get The Point	3sum = threesome
BTW = By The Way	illus = illustrated	6y = sexy
BTWBO = Be There Will Bells On	IMO = In My Opinion	(:-p = oops
BWK = Big Wet Kiss	ital. = italics	:-)) = very happy
chap = chapter	J/K = Just Kidding	:-D = laughter
C4N = Ciao for Now	JAM = Just a Minute	:-* = kiss
COD = Cash on Delivery	JAS = Just a Second	{u} = kissing
Cont. = Continued	KISS = Keep It Simple Stupid	{ } = hug
cp = compare	KIT = Keep In Touch	@}-)-,- = a rose
ctf = certificate	L8R = Later	:-< = broken heart
CU = See You	lb(s). = pound(s)	:'c = cry
CUL = Catch You Later	Lg = Large	:(= frown
CUL8R = See You Later	LOLA = Laughing Out Loud Again	:-) = happy
CYA = Cover Your Ass	LTIP = Laughing 'Til I Puke	:x = not saying anything
d/b/a = doing business as	mgt = management	:[= pouting
DLN = Don't Leave Now	mth = month	:-O = scream
DLTBBB = Don't Let The Bed Bugs Bite	neg = negative	;O = shocked
	NIMBY = Not In My Backyard	;O = shocked
DOB = Date of Birth	N1 = Nice One	:P = stuck out tongue
dol = dollar	No. or No.'s = Number(s)	;) = wink
ea. = each	NRN = No Reply Necessary	:O = yell
EG = Evil Grin	N2S = Needless 2 Say	
e.g. = for example	NTTAWWT = Not That There's Any-thing Wrong With That	
encl. = enclosures/enclosed		
env = envelope	OATUS = On a Totally Unrelated Subject	
esp. = especially		

Year	Traditional Anniversary Gifts	Modern Anniversary Gifts	Anniversary Flowers
1	Paper	Clocks	Orange Blossom
2	Cotton	China	Daisy
3	Leather	Crystal, Glass	Carnation
4	Silk & Linen	Appliances	Violet
5	Wood	Silverware	Pansies
6	Iron	Wood	Tulip
7	Copper, Wool	Desk sets	Camellia
8	Bronze,	Lace, Linen	Cat's Tail
9	Pottery,	Leather	Hollyhock
10	Aluminum, Tin	Diamond jewelry	Sweet Pea
11	Steel	Fashion jewelry	Lilac
12	Linen & Silk	Pearls	Lily
13	Lace	Textiles, Fur	Hydrangea
14	Ivory (endangered)	Gold jewelry	Daffodil
15	Crystal	Watches	Calla Lily
20	China	Platinum	Iris
25	Silver	Silver	Yellow Rose
30	Pearl	Diamond	Amaryllis
35	Coral	Jade	Poppy
40	Ruby	Ruby	Peony
45	Sapphire	Sapphire	Mum
50	Gold	Gold	Red Rose
55	Emerald	Emerald	Jasmine
60	Diamond	Diamond	White Rose

Modern Birthstones and Birthflowers

Month	Birthstone		Birthflower	
January	Garnet		Carnation	
February	Amethyst		Violet	
March	Aquamarine		Daffodil	
April	Diamond		Daisy, Sweet Pea	
May	Emerald		Sunflower, Lily of the Valley	
June	Pearl, Moonstone		Rose, Honeysuckle	
July	Ruby		Larkspur	
August	Peridot		Lily, Gladiolus	
September	Sapphire		Forget-Me-Not, Morning Glory	
October	Opal		Calendula (Marigold), Camellia	
November	Yellow Topaz		Chrysanthemum	
December	Turquoise		Holly, Narcissus	

Alstroemeria
Aspiring

Amaryillis
Dramatic

Anemone
Fragile

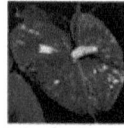

Anthurium
Hospitality

Asiatic Lily
Majesty

Aster
Contentment

Bird of Paradise
Joyfulness

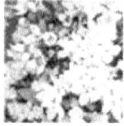

Bouvardia
Enthusiasm

Carnation
Pride and Beauty

Chrysanthemum
Fidelity

Daffodil
Chivalry

Daisy
Innocence

Delphinium
Boldness

Freesia
Spirited

Gladiolus
Strength

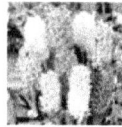

Hyacinth
Sincerity

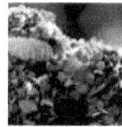

Hydrangea
Heartfelt

Iris
Inspiration

Larkspur
Levity

Lilac
First Love

Lisianthus
Calming

Peony
Bashful

Proteas
Daring

Queen Anne's Lace
Delicate Femininity

Ranunculus
Radiant

Rose – Pink
Thank You

Rose – Red
True Love

Rose – White
Purity

Rose – Yellow
Friendship

Snapdragon
Desire

Statice
Success

Stock
Lasting Beauty

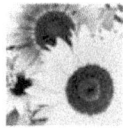

Sunflower
Adoration

Sweet Pea
Shyness

Tulip
Love and Caring

Recommended Reading

Here are some books that could help you step up your game, and give you tons of examples to steal from (excuse me, "borrow" from.☺).

The Art of Love by Ovid
Women Who Love Men Who Kill by Sheila Isenberg
The Female Brain by Louann Brizendine
Everyone Communicates, Few Connect by John Maxwell
The Copywriter's Handbook, 3rd Edition by Robert W. Bly
Love Bytes: The Online Dating Handbook by David Fox
How to Make Anyone Fall in Love with You by Leil Lowndes
Finding the Love of Your Life by Dr. Neil Clark Warren
Plain Fat Chick Seeks Guy Who Likes Broccoli by Kathy Hinckley & Peter Hesse
2002 Ways to Attract and Keep a Mate by Cyndi Haynes & Dale Edwards
Words That Sell by Richard Bayan
Social Media 101 by Chris Brogran
Rainmaking Conversations by Mike Schultz & John E. Doerr
Microstyle: The Art of Writing Little by Christopher Johnson
The Greatest Direct Mail Sales Letters of All-Time by Richard S. Hodgson
The Game by Neil Strauss
Rules of the Game by Neil Strauss
The Pick-up Artist: The New and Improved Art of Seduction by Mystery & C. Odom
Real Men Don't Text by Ruthie Dean
The Perils of Cyber-Dating by Julie Spira
Emily Post's Manners in a Digital World by Daniel Post Senning
Swoon: Great Seducers and Why Women Love Them by Betsy Prioleau
A Million First Dates by Dan Slater
The Improbability Principle by David Hand
The Art of Dealing with People by Les Giblin
Cold Calling Techniques (That Really Work) by Steve Schiffman
The Art of Seduction by Robert Greene
How to Talk to Anybody about Anything by Leil Lowndes
How to Be OUTRAGEOUSLY Successful with the Opposite Sex by Paul Hartunian
Love by Mail by Richard N. Coté
Dot.com Dating by Dr.'s Les & Leslie Parrott
25 Words or Less: How to Write Like a Pro to Find That Special Someone Through Personal Ads by Emily Thornton Calvo & Laurence Minsky
Dig Your Well Before You're Thirsty by Harvey Mackay
Flirting 101: How to Charm Your Way to Love, Friendship and Success by Michelle Lia Lewis & Andrew Bryant
Put Your Heart on Paper by Henriette Anne Klauser
The Pleasure of Staying in Touch: Writing Memorable Letters by Jennifer Williams
Kind Regards: The Lost Art of Letter-Writing by Liz Williams
Personal Notes: How to Write from the Heart for Any Occasion by Sandra E. Lamb

Index

WE NEED YOUR REVIEWS ON amazon

Rate Us & Win!

We do monthly drawings for a FREE copy of one of our publications. Just have your loved one rate any Freebird Publishers book on Amazon and then send us a quick e-mail with your name, inmate number, and institution address and you could win a FREE book.

FREEBIRD PUBLISHERS
221 Pearl St., Ste. 541
North Dighton, MA 02764

www.freebirdpublishers.com
Diane@FreebirdPublishers.com

Thanks for your interest in Freebird Publishers!

We value our customers and would love to hear from you! Reviews are an important part in bringing you quality publications. We love hearing from our readers-rather it's good or bad (though we strive for the best)!

If you could take the time to review/rate any publication you've purchased with Freebird Publishers we would appreciate it!

If your loved one uses Amazon, have them post your review on the books you've read. This will help us tremendously, in providing future publications that are even more useful to our readers and growing our business.

Amazon works off of a 5 star rating system. When having your loved one rate us be sure to give them your chosen star number as well as a written review. Though written reviews aren't required, we truly appreciate hearing from you.

☆☆☆☆☆ **Everything a prisoner needs is available in this book.**

January 30, 201 June 7, 2018

Format: Paperback

A necessary reference book for anyone in prison today. This book has everything an inmate needs to keep in touch with the outside world on their own from inside their prison cell. Inmate Shopper's business directory provides complete contact information on hundreds of resources for inmate services and rates the companies listed too! The book has even more to offer, contains numerous sections that have everything from educational, criminal justice, reentry, LGBT, entertainment, sports schedules and more. The best thing is each issue has all new content and updates to keep the inmate informed on todays changes. We recommend everybody that knows anyone in prison to send them a copy, they will thank you.

FREEBIRD PUBLISHERS

The Millionaire Prisoner's Collection

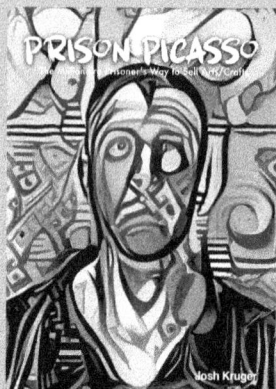

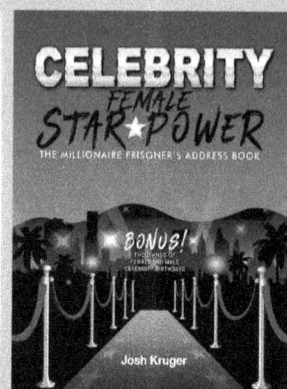

The Millionaire Prisoner and Freebird Publishers bring you Josh Kruger's latest books from earning money from your cell to connecting with pen pals and celebrities.

Cellpreneur: The Millionaire Prisoner's Guidebook **$31.99**
This book is only for those prisoners who want to achieve their business dreams! ... Every word is designed so that prisoners can succeed now!

Prison Picasso: The Millionaire Prisoner's Way to Sell Arts/Crafts **$35.99**
Wish you could sell art patterns to greeting card companies for $400? Want to know the magazine that pays over $4,000 for artwork they like? Are you tired of trading your art/crafts for just typical commissary scraps? Want to know where to go online to find 130,000+ people who like prison arts and crafts? Then this book was written for you!

Pen Pal Success: The Ultimate Guide to Getting and Keeping Pen Pals **$31.99**
You have never seen a pen pal resource this detail on what it takes to succeed in the pen pal game today! Written by lifer, Josh Kruger author of The Millionaire Prisoner. Pen Pal Success contains "insider's" wisdom especially for prisoners.

Celebrity Female Star Power: The Millionaire Prisoner's Address Book **$36.99**
Want to contact your favorite female celebrity? Ever wished you could write for a free photo, get an autograph, or letter back? But you didn't know how or where to send your letter? Well, now you can because this book shows you how!

We accept all forms of payment!

Prices above Include Shipping & Handling.

PayPal
MasterCard VISA DISCOVER BANK
venmo @FreebirdPublishers
Cash App $FreebirdPublishers

For more info on each book, order our catalog!

CATALOG ONLY $5 - SHIPS BY FIRST CLASS MAIL
We have created four different versions of our new catalog A: Complete B:No Pen Pal Content C:No Sexy Photo Content D:No Pen Pal and Sexy Content. Available in full Color or B&W (please specify) please make sure you order the correct catalog based on your prison mail room regulations. We are not responsible for rejected or lost in the mail catalogs. Send SASE for payment by stamp options.
ADDITIONAL OPTION: add $5 for Shipping with Tracking

NO ORDER FORM NEEDED CLEARLY WRITE ON PAPER & SEND PAYMENT TO:
FREEBIRD PUBLSIHERS 221 Pearl St., Ste. 541, North Dighton, MA 02764
www.Freebird Publishers.com Diane@FreebirdPublishers.com Text/Phone: 774-406-8682

FREEBIRD PUBLISHERS
Cook Books

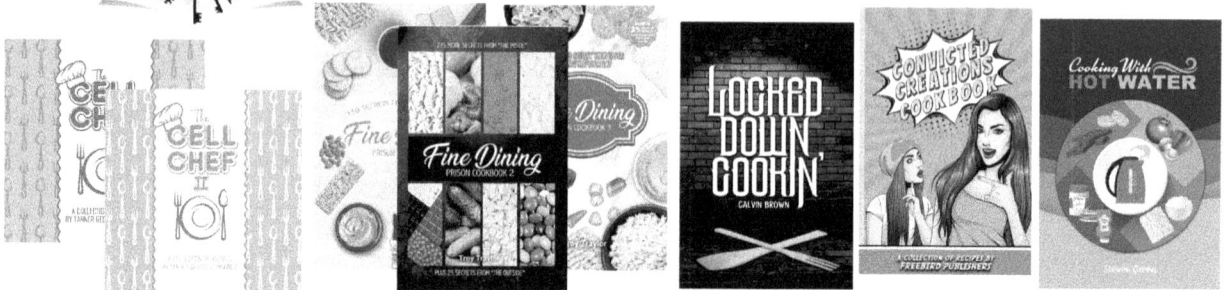

Cell Chef I: Eating the same thing day in and out? Tired of the same boring, bland tasting food? Cell Chef is filled with hundreds of fantastic recipes, simply made with everyday common comissary/store foods. - Meals, Snacks, Sauces, Spreads, Dips, Drinks, Sweet Desserts **$20.99**
Cell Chef II: Completely different and yummier than the past - all new recipes in the Cell Chef's second book. Includes Meals, spreads, sandwiches, sauces, dips, drinks and sweets. **$20.99**
Cell Chef Bundle: Get Cell Chef I and Cell Chef II for the great deal of **$36.99**

Fine Dining 1: Developed by prisoners for prisoners. Cook a delicous, tasty meal with ordinary low-cost ingredients. Tasty drinks, condiments, dips, side dishes, snacks, gumbos, chowders, meals, pizzas, mexican delights, cakes and pies, cheesecakes, and sweets of all kinds. **$22.99**
Fine Dining 2: Ready to be the talk of your unit and discover your creative side at the same time. Over 250 exciting and fun ways to create whatever you're craving in Fine Dining's second book. Including Drinks, dips, soups, beef, chicken, fish, mexican, pizzas, breakfast, pies, cakes, treats, fudge, cookies, pudding and so much more. Bonus content included. **$27.99**
Fine Dining 3: The 3rd and final book in the Fine Dining Prison Cookbook series. Eating healthy in prison can be a challenge. Prison foods are full of starch and many other things. However many comissaries are now beginning to offer healthier choices. The Fine Dining Prison Cookbook 3 has all you need to prepare the healthiest options available to you. Only **$27.99**
Fine Dining Bundle: Fine Dining 1 and 2. Two great books at a great cost. Only **$41.98**

Locked Down Cookin': A culinary touch on prison commissary and prison meal trays. Culinary touch, "The Big Cal Way." **$22.99**

Convicted Creations Cook Book: Just because you're behind bars, doesn't mean your cravings for home-cooked foods are any less real. With these recipes you'll be able to enjoy the flavors of a good meal. Includes: Drinks, Dips, Sauces, Main Dishes, Sweets and Treats! **$21.99**

Cooking With Hot Water: Tired of prison cookbooks that require a microwave, stinger, hotplate, or any other cooking device? The only thing needed for the recipes in this book is hot (190°) water. Recipe categories include: Drinks, sauces, dips, rice dishes, ramon dishes, bagels, snacks, pizza, mexican food, asian dishes, desserts, frostings, and so much more! **$27.99**

No Order Form Needed: Clearly write on paper & send book name with payment to:

Freebird Publishers 221 Pearl St., Ste. 541, North Dighton, MA 02764
Diane@FreebirdPublishers.com   www.Freebirdpublishers.com

We accept all forms of payment. Plus Venmo & CashApp!
Venmo: @FreebirdPublishers   CashApp: $FreebirdPublishers

PayPal
MasterCard VISA DISCOVER BANK

PENACON

Penacon.com dedicated to assisting the imprisoned community find connections of friendship and romance around the world. Your profile will be listed on our user-friendly website. We make sure your profile is seen at the highest visibility rate available by driving traffic to our site by consistent advertising and networking. We know how important it is to have your ad seen by as many people as possible in order to bring you the best service possible. Pen pals can send their first message through penacon.com! We print and send these messages with return addresses if you get one. We value your business and process profiles promptly.

To receive your informational package and application send SASE with two stamps to:

PENACON

221 Pearl St., Ste 533
North Dighton, MA 02764

EMAIL US:
Penacon@freebirdpublishers.com

Penacon is owned and operated by Freebird Publishers, your trusted inmate service provider.

2 MUST HAVE
BOOKS FOR PRISONERS

About The Author

In 1999, Josh Kruger was arrested for felony murder, home invasion, and robbery. At the subsequent bench trial in 2000, he received a direct verdict of acquittal, when the state refused to participate over an evidence dispute. Kruger was released, but eventually rearrested and convicted in a 2003 jury trial and sentenced to life in prison.

After reading several of Zig Ziglar's books, Kruger reached out to the late, great motivational speaker and began corresponding with Ziglar. He adopted Zig's philosophy that you can have everything you want in life if you just help enough people get what they want.

Tired of depending on friends and family for support, the graduate of Crown Financial Ministries decided to leverage his extensive juvenile and adult prison experiences into a freelance writing career. In 2011, Kruger launched his micropublishing empire from his maximum-security prison cell by self-publishing two booklets, *How to Get FREE Pen Pals and How to Win Your Football Pool*. Prison authorities seized his property and threw him in segregation by alleging that he was violating prison rules. Not to be dismayed, Kruger kept going and published his first book, *The Millionaire Prisoner* to help prisoners find their cellpreneurial calling and to look for the opportunities in life instead of the obstacles. This is his second book and is based on his own personal experiences from behind the iron veil of prison. His mission is to change lives, one prisoner at a time. His team can be reached at freejoshkruger@gmail.com. Sorry, he's not allowed to write prisoners directly.

Josh Kruger

www.ingramcontent.com/pod-product-compliance
Lightning Source LLC
Chambersburg PA
CBHW080607270326
41928CB00016B/2961